Endorsements

'Dr Nina Cerfolio's courageous, highly informative, and innovative book weaves together poignant memoir, original terrorism research, extensive scholarship, and profound spirituality. Inviting us into her remarkable journey, Dr Nina Cerfolio guides us spiritually and psychologically, teaching us to transform the pain and trauma of terror into interconnectedness and harmony. A must-read for clinicians, patients, and anyone seeking transformation!'

Leanne Domash, PhD, *author of* Imagination, Creativity and Spirituality in Psychotherapy *and* The Eel and the Blowfish: A Graphic Novel of Dreams, Trauma and Healing

'This is an absolutely astonishing, inspiring and unique book that imbricates personal and historical trauma along with resilience. With searing honesty, it integrates deep scholarship with vivid, dramatic and heroic personal experience. It is required reading on all these levels. Clinically brilliant and moving, it is a book about the roots of individual and state terrorism and also the courage to transcend victimization and heal. Ultimately, Dr Nina Cerfolio's own words describe it best: "My writing this book is a willful act against tyranny. My defiance and determination allows me to not merely survive, but to flourish."'

Robert Prince, PhD, ABPP, *author* of The Legacy of the Holocaust, Psychohistorical Themes in The Second Generation

Psychoanalytic and Spiritual Perspectives on Terrorism

Nina E. Cerfolio masterfully explores the deeper spiritual and psychoanalytic understanding of the origins of human aggressive and destructive instincts that underlie mass shootings and terrorism.

The author survived two terrorist attacks: developing breast cancer from being a first responder at 9/11, and being poisoned by an FSB agent while providing humanitarian aid in the Second Chechen War. Through a personal, scholarly investigation into her psyche, the author describes the spiritual awakening that was catalyzed by these events and their traumatic impact, and examines how a world could create the firmament for the kinds of destructive aggression that are a daily occurrence. Featuring cutting-edge quantitative research and case material, which illustrates the prevalence of undiagnosed and untreated psychiatric illness among mass shooters and terrorists, this book encourages dialogue about the stigma of mental illness and challenges the perception of terrorists as monsters with no societal responsibility.

Championing the forgotten collective humiliation of the marginalized—which in turn breeds terrorism—and documenting a new spiritual lens through which healing is possible, this book will be essential reading for mental health workers and anyone wishing to understand the traumatizing epoch in which we are living.

Nina E. Cerfolio is Assistant Clinical Professor of the Icahn School of Medicine at Mount Sinai, and an internationally recognized expert on trauma/terrorism and award-winning psychiatrist/psychoanalyst. Through writing, speaking, and original research, Nina offers a spiritual path of healing to transform the pain and trauma of terror into interconnectedness and harmony, and elucidates an expansive understanding of the marginalized.

Psychoanalytic and Spiritual Perspectives on Terrorism

Desire for Destruction

Nina E. Cerfolio

Routledge
Taylor & Francis Group

LONDON AND NEW YORK

Designed cover image: © wildpixel
First published 2024

by Routledge
4 Park Square, Milton Park, Abingdon, Oxon OX14 4RN

and by Routledge
605 Third Avenue, New York, NY 10158

Routledge is an imprint of the Taylor & Francis Group, an informa business

© 2024 Nina E. Cerfolio

The right of Nina E. Cerfolio to be identified as author of this work has been asserted in accordance with sections 77 and 78 of the Copyright, Designs and Patents Act 1988.

British Library Cataloguing-in-Publication Data
A catalogue record for this book is available from the British Library

Library of Congress Cataloging-in-Publication Data
Names: Cerfolio, Nina E., author.
Title: Psychoanalytic and spiritual perspectives on terrorism / Nina E. Cerfolio.
Description: Abingdon, Oxon ; New York, NY : Routledge, 2024. | Includes
bibliographical references and index. |
Identifiers: LCCN 2023035880 (print) | LCCN 2023035881 (ebook) |
ISBN 9781032633473 (hardback) | ISBN 9781032633459 (paperback) |
ISBN 9781032633497 (ebook)
Subjects: LCSH: Terrorism—Psychological aspects. | Violent
crimes—Psychological aspects. | Mentally ill offenders. | Victims of
violent crimes—Psychology. | Spirituality.
Classification: LCC RC569.5.T47 .C47 2024 (print) | LCC RC569.5.T47
(ebook) | DDC 363.325001/9—dc23/eng/20231103
LC record available at https://lccn.loc.gov/2023035880
LC ebook record available at https://lccn.loc.gov/2023035881

ISBN: 9781032633473 (hbk)
ISBN: 9781032633459 (pbk)
ISBN: 9781032633497 (ebk)

DOI: 10.4324/9781032633497

Typeset in Bembo
by Deanta Global Publishing Services, Chennai, India

To my partner,

The Gods nodded to me, when the Piermont store was closed, then winked, prodding me into your bike store, ultimately opening my heart. Championing the marginalized, among them me, you are the ultimate bicycle shrink, who makes my soul sing.

Contents

Introduction

While providing medical and psychological care to Chechens under the auspices of an international organization during the Second Chechen War, I was poisoned by a Russian agent of terror. Trying to reconcile my trauma—living with loving kindness rather than bitterness and disappointment—had powerful reverberations and set me on a journey of extraordinary learning and transcendence. Struggling and coping with medical illnesses and emotional upheaval sparked an unexpected spiritual awakening and reconnection in myself and, in turn, some of my patients. My awakening consisted of an active awareness of a profound interconnectedness with something much larger than myself – be it nature, God, or the Cosmos. These revelatory experiences were essential to my recovery. In this shift from submission (signified by the need either to acquiesce or rebel) to surrender (signified by being open to and expanded by the subjectivity of the other), we uncover our genuine souls.

Healing involves surrendering to the numinous nature of human vulnerabilities. Rather than reenacting violence, the spiritual journey involves turning inward to work through and learn from trauma. My goal is to offer hope and inspiration to others who, despite being wounded, can see and choose an alternative to violence by living a life of balance fueled by a new perspective.

Terrorism and mass shootings are a horrific symptom of the spiritual crisis that exists in our world today. It may sound naive to a reader to look beyond the practical solutions to mass shootings (such as gun control and appropriate punishments) to the more foundational, invisible aspects, including our lack of focus on the perpetrators' early childhood development, including abuse and neglect. Mass

1

DOI: 10.4324/9781032633497-1

shooting involves us all. Unfortunately, our tendency to focus on our personal safety and individuality, even egoist individuality, can lead to shunning recognition of our spiritual commonness and how we can remain interconnected to those in distress. When we turn our backs on the plight of the oppressed, insular self-interest deepens. This furthers the marginalized sense of hopelessness and desire for retribution, which only intensifies continued cycles of violence.

During the Second Chechen War, I personally witnessed the aftermath of the world's depraved indifference in not protesting Putin's destructive war crimes against Chechens. By looking the other way, the world empowered Putin's aggression. He continued to use his same playbook of denial, deflection, and projection to commit civilian atrocities and terrorize the population into submission in Chechnya, Syria, and Georgia without any consequences. This historical lack of global resistance to Russian aggression enabled an alarming creeping normalization of Putin's waging unprovoked wars. He was able to continue his tyrannical murdering of innocent civilians in Ukraine, unchecked and unopposed. But then the world suddenly woke up; he was recently found guilty of committing war crimes in Ukraine by the International Criminal Court.

Terrorism and its cycles of vengeful violence is kept alive by ruptures on both an individual and societal level. On a group level, both America and Al-Qaeda had a lack of imagination and empathy, which hindered their ability to recognize the Other, culminating in 9/11. The primitive return of the id in acts of revenge is illustrated in the wars America unjustifiably waged in Iraq in retaliation for 9/11. America failed to imagine the depth of resentment that these US actions abroad would bring, provoking fundamentalist Muslims to view the United States as the world's biggest bully that employs terror on other people's land. Imagination is drowned by lust for power and the inability to accept and learn from loss. Individually, this rupture results in an organized failure of imagination and an inability to empathize with Others, which creates further alienation. In a divisive environment, we become part of a transactional world and lose our compassion for the vulnerable. This erodes a sense of brotherly love and community.

The dogmatic argument that we should eliminate the discussion of the association between untreated mental health and mass shootings prevents us from creating possible solutions. Some mental health experts argue that as a society, we lack the nuance to examine this association without stigmatizing those afflicted with serious mental disorders. I argue that psychiatry possesses the tools to examine this association and, furthermore, doing so leads to possible amelioration. It seems to me that our society's failure to more deeply understand and instead turning a blind eye to the uncompromising importance of child development causes symptomatology even for us so-called "normal" folks. However, noticeably dysfunctional parenting—abandonment, neglect, loss, and abuse—is capable of producing catastrophic distortions of human character. Witness our adolescent shooters.

The pinpoint lens of rationality may deny the incredible complexities of human behavior, skip over the boundless range of child development, and railroad our conceptions into a girdle of denial. When we turn our eyes away from the atrocities of mass shootings, we lose our sense of balance, perspective, and obligation to care about each other. The extreme dogmatism of both the far-right and far-left ideology eliminates any genuine sensitivity to the plasticity of cognitive processes and the needs of human beings. It becomes a fool's mission to imagine.

How is there such a global paucity of spirituality and compassion for those who remain isolated? As expressed by one of the surviving college students at the 2023 Michigan State University shooting, must we each personally experience gun violence before it becomes believable and real to us? How is there such a rigid divide and lack of empathy in the world? How do we not become the vengeful mirrors of our perpetrators and instead provide vital treatment to the marginalized? Another example of the limited vision of ideology is the sovereignty of the NRA cant over the reality of the lives of our children who now are becoming experts at active shooter drills and emergency evacuations. Do we have the spiritual strength to look at the human element in these terrorists and mass shooters, which has relevance for each of us, rather than dismissing them as inexplicable monsters? Can we address this societal issue with wisdom and empathy, yet not erase the perpetrator's culpability?

My team's cutting-edge quantitative research is presented to illustrate the high prevalence of undiagnosed brain illness in domestic mass shooters. This book will bring new insights and encourage dialogue around what is necessary to help alleviate this epidemic problem. Although each case of mass shootings is unique and complex, the marginalization of these assailants was a common theme that contributed to their not getting proper psychiatric diagnosis and treatment. In addition to many of these perpetrators suffering untreated psychosis, they also experienced chronic abuse and isolation. In the many cases studied, there was also a link between all these mass shooters and different varieties of terrorists, as displayed in their brutal childhoods. In order to preserve society, of course, they still remain responsible for their violence. But the abuse of children—so grave that it deprives them of their true identity, their ability to feel joy, and leads to their psychic and spiritual annihilation—was experienced by many of these assailants. The common factor of their childhood was the decimation of their being, leading to their desperate counterphobic attempt to avenge themselves with a spectacular narcissistic victory.

The history of traumatic abuse is found in most of these assailants, but its presence is more clearly elucidated in these juvenile perpetrators, in part, because their histories are so condensed. As these young school shooters are often victims of unacknowledged psychological turmoil, the momentous parental and community responsibility attached to raising children is thrown into high relief. In all assailants the internal role of malignant shame, compulsive fantasies of retaliation, and deficiencies in the capacity to mentalize play an important role in their assaults. It is not only the nightmare of their childhood, but also the sequela of that catastrophic background that adversely affects them. Severe childhood trauma often precludes the ability to possess flexibility of cognitive scanning, so the perpetrator is more likely to grow into a brittle adult only capable of reflexively reenacting his childhood violence. Often there is a history of disorganized attachment and false-self pathology that render them ripe for radicalization. Trying to salvage some sense of being, they spin into a shame–rage cycle, in which their mordant rage floods their being and propels them into "justified retribution" and "necessary violence." Again, as hate is the binding force that these assailants experience, their violence may be understood as preserving perverted collective ties, a sense of belonging and social recognition.

Humanity's fullest potential will require fresh thinking about the incredible power inherent in the often-untapped intersection of psychology and spirituality. By reaching out to care about others, we can begin to work to overcome individual and group feelings of hopelessness that often breeds terrorism. By providing medical and psychological care to the disenfranchised, we begin to bond together to overcome unimaginable horror. Failing to meet the needs of the alienated is more than morally indefensible in our new world, it has powerful reverberations and threatens the health of all. The oppression, starvation, and illness of others are ultimately our own. Willful inaction makes us participants in crimes against humanity. The aspiration for America—the willingness to face difficulties together, to confront adversity, and to embrace new modes of thinking—guided by a spiritual compass that points to loving interconnectedness—is called forth and championed in this book.

1

Sacred Service and Transcendent Interconnectedness

Being a First Responder at 9/11 and The Traumatic Aftermath[1,2]

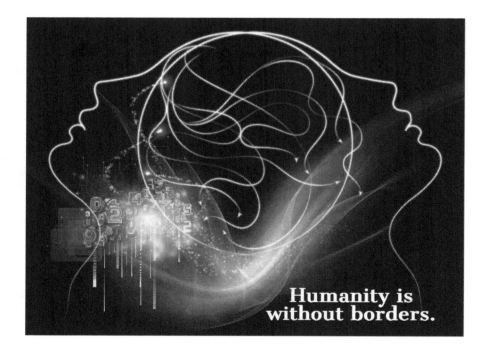

Humanity is without borders.

DOI: 10.4324/9781032633497-2

Mmore than 20 years have passed since the September 11, 2001, terrorist attacks on the World Trade Center and the Pentagon, but for many those dreadful images remain seared forever in our nation's memory. Not only did 9/11 mark the loss of American innocence, it forever broke our country's arrogant denial that America was somehow immune from the horrors of global terrorism. It also exposed our country's callous indifference to the plight of the marginalized and their suffering inflicted by conflicts in third-world countries. This shared experience of devastation became cemented into our collective unconscious as a trauma that continues to reverberate not only on individuals' and communities' mental and physical health, but influences our socio-political policies.

Although nearly 3,000 people died that day, the death toll from the tragedy continues to rise as first responders who worked at Ground Zero in the aftermath have succumbed to related illnesses. According to the World Trade Center Health Program, as of December 2022, 4,343 survivors and first responders have died in the years since 9/11 (Selby, 2022). *Newsday* reported that more than 125,000 people, including 79,000 first responders, have enrolled in the World Trade Center Health Program, and at least 18,000 have been diagnosed with a 9/11-related cancer (Waterfield, 2020).

Although others saw the Twin Towers as ugly bookends, they were sacred to me. Defiers of gravity, the Towers exuded a feeling of indomitability. Surviving the first bombing in 1993, they symbolized resilience. I aspired to have the building's pillar of strength that each Tower represented. Fabulously, they were located in my cherished backyard. My feelings of childhood decimation were transformed by an identification with the daring boldness of the buildings. Flanked by Superman and King Kong on movie posters, they resonated with a centrality and iconicity as the tallest buildings in the biggest city in the United States.

When I had an hour gap between seeing patients in a ten-hour workday, the Towers served as my beacon when running on my shorter 6-mile loop. This loop consisted of running from my apartment in Greenwich Village, down the Hudson River Greenway, to the Twin Towers, circling around the Jewish Museum, and then back. As an endurance athlete in the solitary sport of long-distance running, the Towers were my steadfast running companions, especially on days when I was too tired to push my body to train for my first marathon. They always inspired me, providing a spiritual shot of adrenaline and comfort.

The thrill of excelling at sports helped to erase my childhood sense of helplessness. My athleticism served as a defense against the violence that I experienced as a child. Playing first singles on the varsity tennis team in high school and college then briefly competing in the Women's Tennis Association Challenger Tournaments in my mid-30s contributed to my sense of strength and recognition as an athlete. But I craved more.

I was introduced late in life to running. The endorphin high of long-distance running was addictive, and I took quickly to endurance sports. I was choosing to create myself through the force of my ability to endure. In 2001, I ran my first marathon in New York City at the age of 41, qualifying to run the prestigious

2002 Boston Marathon, which I completed. Becoming hooked, one of my more memorable days was qualifying for and finishing the 2003 South Africa's Comrades 56-mile Ultramarathon. I was also honored to place second overall female in the 2003 New York City Kurt Steiner 32-mile Ultramarathon and won first overall female place in the Half China Wall Marathon in 2004.

When the Towers went down, it threatened that part of me that identified with the building's impregnability and unleashed the desire to heal its wounds and restore its phenomenal essence. It devastated me that the Towers were destroyed. In part, I went down to Ground Zero to resurrect the memory of the Towers and grieve the loss of my beacons. But my grief bloomed into finding camaraderie with other first responders, who became my second family. I belonged to this family of first responders who were also trying to fix this catastrophe. We bonded as a good family by caring for each other.

Amidst the devastation, the loss and death, my uncanny experience on 9/11 was to transcend all the horrendous suffering to paradoxically discover the trans-cendent beauty of human interconnectedness. All of us first responders became uncannily connected to each other, operating as "one," whether spontaneously forming a bucket brigade to remove debris or smoothly operating an ad hoc medical triage even though we were all strangers. In contrast to the often-lonely experience of living in a large city, 9/11 facilitated an intense feeling of com-munity. At Ground Zero, I experienced the heightened feeling of Heidegger's *Dasein*, "being there," in the present moment. Even though we were all together, ultimately, we were alone with ourselves, surrounded by a sense of death, con-fronting our mortality.

One indicator of the health of our society is reflected by the most violent acts of its individuals. The more divided and fractured our society, the more violent are the acts of its citizens. As we are all interconnected, if one part of our society is suffering, it affects us all. War was being waged on my homeland and I felt that I was spiritually called to serve. In the middle of this nightmare, there still remained the beauty of solidarity and the common bond of humanity of first responders that unified us all.

MY GROUND ZERO EXPERIENCE AS A FIRST RESPONDER ON 9/11

More than 20 years later, my memories of 9/11 seemed like one condensed and collapsed memory. It seems impossible to determine how much of Freud's concept (1920/1955) of transcription, which is the way the past is reinscribed in the present and the present rewrites the past, influenced my traumatic memories of 9/11. How many of my memories are interwoven and influenced by my patients' narratives, as well as the news and TV reports? Despite having shared my experiences both in psychoanalysis and through conversations with family and friends, I have worked to unravel my condensed memory. But by further working to remember through writing, the creative process allows me to gain distance and perspective, which encourages my healing process. Here are my memories.

As I walked to work to see my first patient on that shimmering, beautiful, cerulean sky day, the North World Trade Tower had already been hit by a plane and was ablaze. There were news reports and rumors that a small plane may have accidentally flown into the Tower. Upon seeing my 9 am patient, who suffered from chronic anxiety, he accurately predicted that "the airplane hitting the Tower was not an accident but a terrorist attack."

Many of my following patients would cancel that day in part because they were unable to take public transportation, as it eventually was shut down. While waiting for my next patients who never materialized, I became transfixed and witnessed from the street in front of my Greenwich Village office the surreal events of the South Tower being hit by another airliner. Sharing the shock of my fellow, momentarily frozen, New Yorkers who had gathered on University Place, I heard a collective wail of disbelief rise when the South Tower collapsed downwards and pancaked floor by floor into an apocalyptic plume of dust and smoke then disappeared from view.

Witnessing hundreds of zombie-like workers enveloped in ash with the look of horror in their eyes, refugees to nowhere but fleeing to any place but Ground Zero, left me feeling helpless with the calling to help. People were desperately trying to reach loved ones on cell phones but there was no reception. As my family knew my training loop for the upcoming NYC marathon included passing the Towers, I would later learn that they kept trying to call but never got through. My mother fantasized that I was already dead and buried under the rubble. Parked car doors were flown open with radios blaring to hear any news of the assault. Hysteria predominated. At some point, a person listening to his car radio informed me that the Pentagon building was also hit by another commercial airliner and that our country was under attack.

Somehow in this chaos, I meet my beloved 11 am patient, who I particularly enjoy and respect as she is tenacious and committed to doing often painful psychoanalytic work to this day, on the street. She was shaking with terror, having witnessed the attack alone from the window of her newly purchased, empty, high-rise apartment as she had not yet moved in. Looking for some solace, she had called her parents in disbelief over witnessing what had occurred. Her parents, who were often critical and unsupportive, offered her little emotional comfort and she began to scream in a futile attempt to convey her desperation and horror. While walking down to my office, she also witnessed the collapse of the second Tower on University Place. Having both experienced 9/11 from less than a mile away, we sat in shock and silence. This event marked the first time that an external reality stimulated a closely related complex of emotions that involved living in the traumatic here and now in both psychoanalyst and patient (Prince, 2021). Gradually, in the coming months, she was able to put words to her monstrous-filled, visual memories of the attack that was etched forever in her brain. The principle that recovery from trauma can only take place within the context of relationships and not in isolation (Herman, 2015) is exemplified in this patient's psychoanalytic work. As she had been employed at Ground Zero for many years, the attack on 9/11 felt personal to her. This patient suffered from chronic feelings of isolation, and it was through our relationship, which continues to the present, that she has continued to work through her grief-filled memories and mourn her loss from that awful day.

When we reach out to those in need, we see the importance of Freud's (1927/1961) concept of elevating love over the instinct of human aggression. Even in the face of danger, I had a loving urge to provide a sacred service to others, and I was determined to help even in the smallest way. There was an instinctive, pure calling for me to be of service, which took me out of my normal sense of time, experience and consciousness. Beneath infantile omniscience and omnipotence, claimed or projected, there is a loving urge to give of ourselves in response to the needs of others. In the face of catastrophe, we find the courage to come together to discover our higher purpose and be what we are meant to be. During such massive traumas as 9/11, our own person pales in comparison to the greater good.

My own childhood terror and trauma allowed me to cultivate a greater sense of resilience, compassion, and forgiveness that were instrumental in volunteering to help those who were suffering. My experience was spiritual in its breadth and depth, beyond words and ineffable. I discovered that within the human heart and even in the face of catastrophe, there is an unrelenting force and courage that pulls us to come together to provide sacred service to others. This drive, which is within each of us, is much stronger than the urge to dominate, ignore or exclude.

I came to learn that I am much more than my physical body, that my soul is eternal, and that somehow we are all connected. Over time I would learn how and that it's not magic, it's quantum mechanics, which dictates that human perception of separation is wrong. The physiology of our brains prevents us from truly experiencing the universe as it is, tricking us into believing in the idea of separation when in truth, nothing is truly separated—including human beings. In a deeply organic way, on 9/11 sacred service became the order of the day where we became keenly aware of our responsibility for the care of one another.

My childhood reflex during times of stress was to have a counterphobic macho, invincible attitude, which involved going into a feared situation in an attempt to overcome it. Being brought up in a "war zone" of emotional abuse, I was continually drawn to extremes in exercise and volunteering in part because it was familiar and the idea was to unconsciously conquer my unprocessed fears and prove that I was not a child grasping for any kind of affection. Going into dangerous situations that others were fleeing, handicapping myself, and coming out alive was something I specialized in. I rejoiced in putting myself in the jaws of the giant only to outwit it. My worth as a child was based on my latest achievement and doing was emphasized over merely just being. In an attempt to undo my sense of worthlessness, my grandiose illusion of being the warrior queen was a defense against a childhood of being raised in a "war zone." This warrior queen persona was antagonistic to my being a child who was invisible, unseen, unknown, and unloved.

I felt that my childhood was an ordeal ironically similar to the benefits of enlisting in the Army where some people find boot camp felicitous as it provides structure and discipline. It armed me with the stubbornness to fortify me against emotional abandonment and pain to become Iron-Man resilient. Being born in 1960 in Paterson, New Jersey, and raised till the age of 6 a block from the seedy, anarchic Paterson bus depot, where murders, robbery, and gang violence were commonplace, discord was everywhere and it felt repetitious of the brutality of my childhood. Mother was enveloped by her own barbaric and unfinished childhood memories and treated me as if I were imported as a character out of her old trauma. My parent's child-rearing motto was to toughen their children, and similar to the drill sergeant's breaking the military trainee down only to build them back up. But instead of building us back, my parents demanded that we super-perform and achieve without providing the means or training that was required.

When I was 7, Spot, my darling family dog and loyal ally, a Beagle mutt, with black and brown spotted white fur, a twinkle of compassionate wisdom in her big, beseeching eyes, and espresso bean-colored, long silky ears, became pregnant for the second time which enraged my father. The hysterectomy on Spot performed by my father was a metaphorical battleground that consisted of parental cruelty and sadism (Cerfolio, 2019). Branded Spot was not allowed inside and lived in a doghouse surrounded by a gated pen, and I had to fight myself not to release her when I heard her pleading yelps for freedom whenever I left for school in the morning. But my father's fury, which felt similar to the rage on the battlefield, was really fueled by my mother's fourth unplanned pregnancy. His inability to control her and demand that she get an abortion, which my mother refused, seemed to inflame his resentment.

To master that uncanny symmetry, my father, a urologist, took his revenge by performing a hysterectomy on Spot and commandeered his young children to assist in the operation without any consideration for the grief and havoc it would wreak. More fortunate than the rest of us, my mother abstained and refused to partake in Spot's hysterectomy.

Paradoxically, the outrage that my siblings and I endured would spawn all the complexities described by Freud's description of sublimation. My oldest brother would become a brittle heroin addict, who redeemed himself later in adult life by becoming a social worker who works with incarcerated drug addicts. Counterphobically, I revisited that gruesome day by choosing to do an obstetric and gynecology residency. But unlike my childhood where I did not possess the maturity which led to no exit of that frightful event, I possessed the ability to voluntarily walk out of my abusive obstetric and gynecology residency to flee into my wish for the welcoming womb of psychiatry. My younger brother wrote about this awful day in his memoirs, *Super Performing at Work and at Home: The Athleticism of Surgery and Life* (Cerfolio, 2014), which he maintained was part of his inspiration for becoming a renowned, robotic, cardiothoracic surgeon.

Not wanting to have anything to do with this childhood Grand Guignol event, my blood-phobic, sensitive 9-year-old brother barricaded himself in the bathroom, only to be physically dragged out but my father, who seething wrath, insisted that he function as his First Surgical Assist in this gory enterprise. Getting off easy, as I was a female and as such inherently less important (in his eyes), I functioned as the nurse by gently, calmly stroking Spot on the ping-pong table, which served as our makeshift surgical table. My father administered IV medication and hydration and then intubated Spot. He sterilized with Betadine and shaved Spot's swollen, white-furred belly, which looked so vulnerable under the buzzing, cold, fluorescent lighting. My father swiftly and deftly sliced through Spot's abdominal skin. Spot's heart was beating wildly and I worried that Spot had been given a human dose of anesthetic as it looked like her heart would jump out of her body. Or maybe it was a physiological response to pain as I do not know if my father administered pain medication. My father did not believe in pain medication for his family and would refuse pain medication for himself and his children after surgery. My father's face tightened with disgust as he yanked Spot's pinkish-white uterus, ovaries and fallopian tubes from her abdominal cavity.

My 7-year-old self silently turned to stone as I witnessed the tiny unborn litter of eight puppies from within Spot's womb slowly suffocate on the family's ping-pong table. It felt like my best friend was being splayed open and later any aspirations for birthing a child were crushed that day. Perhaps better than the four of us, somehow Spot, the ever-forgiving survivor, withstood the family's Frankenstein show.

As a result of my childhood deprivation where "emotions become severed from representations and thought processes" (Ferenczi, 1988, p. 203) and "emotions turn embryonic" (Ferenczi, 1988, p. 203), I was the poster girl for Ferenczi's concept of "super-performance" (Ferenczi, 1988, p. 89, 203; Ferenczi, 1955, p. 272; Frankel, 1998) where there is a compulsive need for excessive achievement. This compulsion to "super-perform" was a denial of my fears to prove that I could walk into a nightmare and survive. But my hidden, repressed desire was an infantile passivity to be taken care of, as well as rage over the forcible interruption of that passivity. Like Dumbo who falsely believed he needed his magic feather to fly, achievement through academics and sports was my magic feather to compensate for feeling unworthy. As a result of my childhood adversity, I was my angry self, which was another way of taking flight from my painful childhood wounds, an attempt to evade everything I feared.

Shedding my feelings of familial disapproval and not belonging, I went down to 9/11 knowing that I was needed. I was at once flooded with a willingness to experience acceptance and loving interconnectedness with the drive to assist. Discovering this sense of loving interconnectedness at Ground Zero, I aspired to recognize the divine in a part of myself and wanted to believe that this divinity is equally distributed in all living souls, which radically unified us. We organically became a band of brothers and sisters on a vital, common mission to metabolize the darkness of death and destruction that we all witnessed and attempt to catch a glimpse of hope and light.

Another incentive for my going down to Ground Zero was to transcend my profound feelings of helplessness among all the human suffering and loss. I was drawn to be a first responder, not only because it was an all too familiar dangerous place, but also it provided a chance for me to prove and establish my survival ability and gain a triumph of potency, decimating my childhood fears. Also as part of my professional career was as Chief of the Psychiatric Emergency Room and Walk-in Clinic at St Vincent's Hospital in New York City, it was not much of a stretch to volunteer for emergency psychiatric services at Ground Zero.

In sharp contrast to this sense of spontaneously genuine interconnectedness that welded the responders together, the attacker's Jihadi terrorism involved distorted religious love in which the drive to kill in the name of God was present (Cerfolio, 2020). The fire generated from the World Trade Center attacks brought elevated purification status for these terrorists as they falsely believed that the baseness of their and their blasphemous Western victims' souls were incinerated and an exalted spiritual transcendence was obtained (Stein, 2010). The 9/11 terrorist's murderous martyrdom was a symbiotic killing and dying, where achieving God's will meant becoming one with the victims in death. This transformation of self-hatred and envy into God's love allowed for the obliteration of those unwanted, contaminated parts of self that required purification. Ironically, purification meant killing the corrupted parts of self so as to wring sanctity out of death. The perverse part of the terrorist's personality allowed them to kill in the name of Allah in a misguided attempt to restore their wholeness and dignity.

The day after 9/11 all my patients had canceled, so I woke up early, put on my work boots, packed food and water, and armed myself with the ice of emotional shut-down to walk to Ground Zero. Because the state policeman did not initially believe I was a physician, I had some difficulty but eventually succeeded in passing through several checkpoints below Houston Street. Lower Manhattan looked like an abandoned zone with bridges and tunnels closed to traffic and no pedestrians. In that dead silence, an emotion slowly crept through to the surface. And only while walking through the deserted ghost town of SoHo did I have a moment of humanity, where in that awful silence and void, the uncertainty of what was to come finally hit me. I became momentarily terrified and a small previously hidden part of me shrieked to turn around and run. I did not realize it then, but I was desperately attempting to escape the fear of emotional collapse. Having manufactured the illusion of having no fear which I had largely buried somewhere in the great depths of terrain that stretches all the way to China, I was smacked by the toxic odor of burning flesh. This smell, the choking, noxious fumes, which intensified as I got closer to Ground Zero, burned my eyes and lungs. I never smelled anything like it.

Even as I write this now, it is easier to recount my memories of how I served others and to avoid the nightmare of my own feelings elicited by witnessing the human misery, suffering, and loss. Because it was demanded of me, I was taught in childhood that I could rush into battle unarmed and unprepared. But it was also necessary to provide support to others at Ground Zero to be robotic and avoid processing fear. Any processing of emotion would have prevented and interfered with my functioning.

My performing surgery during my obstetrics and gynecology residency was honed on an early childhood rearing belief that children were to be seen, not heard, and to keep their feelings to themselves. This robotic sense of self was further indoctrinated during my obstetric and gynecology residency, where I was chronically sleep deprived staying on emergency call for 72 hours to deliver care to pregnant women. In performing a cesarean section, it was imperative to repress any emotion in order to make quick life-and-death decisions. On 9/11, I felt committed to function as a warrior of human life and help those in need. Although in retrospect it was not good for my mental health as I have chronic nightmares of planes hitting buildings which then collapse, my happy warrior self had a field day serving at Ground Zero as my grandiose defensiveness ran amok.

As I approached Ground Zero, ash started raining on me. I do not remember if it was white or gray. Many fires were still raging, and there were endless, sky-high mounds of smoldering wreckage. The disaster site was unrecognizable and disorienting; it initially felt impossible to gain my bearings. The behemoth Twin Towers, my beacon to orient myself, were incredulously gone. With time, gradually I became less disoriented and tragically noticed that the remains of the South Tower facade served as a headstone for the site where thousands had perished.

Ground Zero was a moonscape of white ash, battered and scorched vehicles, scattered trade orders, memos, and family photographs. The streets were covered in many inches of dust, which became mud wherever firefighters turned their hoses. I would spend the next 16 hours initially helping move debris and eventually provide medical and psychological support at a spontaneously created ad hoc medical triage mostly to rescue workers who were having difficulty coping.

In this death and destruction, someone handed me a surgical mask. I do not remember who. As I got further into Ground Zero, I was given work gloves and in a trancelike state without communicating through words, joined a human chain of first responders to remove debris, which we handed off to the next person down the line. We formed bucket brigades hoping to identify any hidden, buried survivors. Torches were used to cut away large fallen girders, and several construction cranes helped move heavier debris. The National Guard would eventually encircle the disaster site as workers struggled to ascend the mounds of debris five stories high.

An ad hoc medical team was eventually hastily assembled on the perimeter of this tomb of rubble. I was in rescue mode and we all were anxiously anticipating providing medical aid to the survivors of the catastrophe. It slowly became tragically apparent that no survivors remained and that our focus became the care of other rescue workers. Many of the rescue workers, including firemen and construction workers, who slid into holes in the rubble, created false rumors of survivors being pulled out. When, in fact, it was discovered that it was these rescue workers who were recovered. As medical personnel attended to the injured rescue workers—there were no survivors—I became part of the medical unit on the south side of what was once the Twin Towers. Rescue workers in need of medical attention were triaged and evaluated initially by an Army nurse who would then, if necessary, request my psychiatric care. I was also asked to evaluate rescue workers by an Emergency Room physician who was now coordinating this medical unit. I was the sole psychiatrist in this makeshift unit and evaluated and aided a large number of first responders.

AN ANXIOUS AND PANICKED CONSTRUCTION WORKER AT GROUND ZERO

I was asked to support a burly, middle-aged construction worker who came from upstate New York to volunteer to aid with the rescue effort. He too had a personal connection to the Towers as he had helped build them many years ago. Being in shock and denial over the extent of the wreckage and the fact that the collapsed Towers had not yielded any of the living, he was having difficulty breathing and had some chest pain. As he normally took pride in being stoic and non-emotional, he was humiliated by his display of anxiety and difficulty coping, and he refused to tell the Army nurse his name. He eventually became able to share his feelings of horror at searching and hoping for miracles but finding only a severed human head and a woman's foot with her shoe partially attached. Although a few survivors were pulled from the wreckage, the intense heat, fire, and instability of nearby buildings kept him and other rescue workers at bay. We were prepared that if we heard five warning horn blows, we should run as that indicated an unstable building was coming down. Feeling less threatened, he felt secure enough to share his name with me. While shedding tears, this otherwise macho man shared his feelings of grief about not being able to do more. While talking with me about his anxiety of not finding survivors, his breathing became less labored and he felt less panic. Becoming less panicked by the fact that there would most likely be few survivors, he gradually became able to return to using his crane to remove debris.

A FIREMAN WITH POST-TRAUMATIC DISORDER AT GROUND ZERO

Normally, firemen are a tight fraternity and somewhat reluctant to allow psychiatrists into their circle, but the fact that this was a shared experience of horror led to an unprecedented sense of connectedness to those outside their group. We were all coming together as first responders in an attempt to lessen other's suffering. Also, most of the many exhausted firefighters I pulled over to the medical triage area to get their burning eyes washed with normal saline to lessen their pain, did not realize I was a psychiatrist and they assumed I was a volunteer nurse.

The initial foray into beginning the healing process of psychological wounds of these brave firemen, who were grief-stricken and traumatized by losing so many of their brothers and at the heart of the rescue effort, felt oddly compelling and even sacred. I spoke to five physically depleted and emotionally numb firefighters who had battled toxic fumes and raging fire for 34 hours. Fifteen colleagues from their unit had perished in the disaster. The massive terror and grief allowed one of the firemen to share his emotions. He was a strapping young man who related feeling massively drained, anxious, and had burning eyes and lungs. He was filled with impending doom and unable to rest for more than an hour in a nearby battered building, as he awoke with a startle to any loud sound. Feeling an immense sense of hopelessness, he had recurring thoughts of seeing people jump from the Towers and hearing loud thuds that resulted when their bodies hit the ground. He was physically and emotionally spent. The physicians in the triage had access to medication, so I was able to administer to this young man a low dose of Ativan which lessened his anxiety. Then, I encouraged these five firemen to get medical attention for their burning eyes and lungs and then to go home to sleep and come back the next day if they insisted.

AN AGITATED FAMILY MEMBER THREATENING TO INTERVENE IN THE RESCUE EFFORT

I was asked to help manage a 32-year-old Central American man, whose younger brother worked in the Towers. With a volunteer second-year Yale medical student, who functioned as my translator, this man said his brother had phoned him asking for help while trapped under a massive amount of rubble. This desperate man was holding on to the slim hope that his trapped brother was alive and insisted we find him. Becoming increasingly distressed and disturbed as time elapsed, he felt "nothing was being done to rescue" him. He continued to insist that his brother could not be dead, and he maintained he had spoken to him just a few hours ago. He had a deep identification with his brother, as he was all that remained of his family. His whole life had been dedicated to caring and protecting his younger brother, so much so that he expressed the wish to exchange places with his brother. His feelings of survivor guilt were a defense against processing his grief and feeling of helplessness. As he became less agitated, he was able to talk about his brother and reminisce. Over many hours with me and others, including a Spanish priest, he became more calm and able to have more emotional space to reflect on his relationship with his brother. Eventually, he expressed his profound guilt, despair, and desolation. While supporting this man, we heard five horns, which meant a building was collapsing. We all ran for our lives.

Through these disasters, a shared experience of sisterhood forms life-long bonds. Long after 9/11, I got to know and become friends with this second-year Yale medical student who had functioned as my interpreter. She would eventually choose to leave medicine and find a profession in business. Many years later, when she was married in her homeland of Puerto Rico, I was honored to travel there and attend her wedding. She now lives happily in Europe with her husband and children.

PATIENTS WHO EITHER ESCAPED OR LOST LOVED ONES DURING 9/11

I have not forgotten those I worked with so intensely, and intimately during this time. Although I worked with a number of patients who were involved in narrowly escaping 9/11 or who lost family members during the disaster, several remain close to my heart.

One such patient was a depressed, anxious young woman, who was engaged to be married. After moving from Las Vegas to be with her fiancé, she had a difficult time transitioning to living in New York City. Despite feeling claustrophobic as the World Trade Center Towers were "like a dark prison of two narrow huge slabs of concrete," she nevertheless worked in the South Tower. On 9/11, after the North Tower was hit and was on fire, she and her coworkers were told to stay at their desks and not leave the building. Despite having a panic attack, she, fortunately, had the agency to decide to flee the building and was able to walk down many flights of steps to narrowly escape before the South Tower collapsed.

Another patient, a young lawyer, tragically lost her middle-aged, larger-than-life father who worked at Cantor Fitzgerald. When terrorists hit the North Tower, the Cantor Fitzgerald office evaporated as it was located on one of the floors that the first plane directly flew into. Cantor Fitzgerald lost 658 people, killing every employee who reported to work that fateful day. This young woman unconsciously enacted her traumatic memory of losing her father during 9/11. Her rage was too overwhelming and intolerable to consciously bear, so ritually every weekend, she used cocaine and alcohol to numb herself and fuel dangerous anonymous sexual liaisons with strangers that she met in bars on the Lower East Side of Manhattan. Routinely, feeling ashamed, she would be late to our sessions and hid her cocaine use and reckless sexual encounters for many years.

It was only after the front-page news of a young college student leaving a bar in the Lower East Side of Manhattan who was raped, killed, and discarded in the New Jersey Meadowlands that she began to reluctantly and tentatively divulge her dangerous behavior. She was slowly able to confront her unconscious self-destructive rage and begin to move forward. For years she had lived without being able to put her father's body to rest. Uncannily while cleaning the roof of a nearby building, workers discovered and eventually they were able to identify by DNA analysis her father's femur bone, which had been blown on the top of this building.

For this patient and others, trauma occurs when an individual's mind is overwhelmed by events that exceed its ability to cope and integrate it into a meaningful memory. During the event, there is shock, pain, rage, terror, and the sense of being annihilated. The awful feelings of the experience are too painful to accept. Any memory of the event may be entirely blocked. Though cut off from language, trauma speaks of itself in symptoms: sleeplessness, memory loss, confusion, flashbacks, sudden bouts of fear and anxiety, self-destructive behavior: the event is not in the past. Though its emotional core is unconscious, it remains entirely present, affecting every aspect of the person's life.

I referred several of my patients who had lost family members during 9/11 to the Grief Relief Network, which is a national initiative that was created by Dr. Kevin Hopkins in response to the massive trauma sustained by family members who lost loved ones to terrorism. Being privileged to have been a founding member of the Grief Relief Network, I referred several patients who would benefit from getting support from other family members of victims who had perished in the Oklahoma City bombing and other disasters. This network provided peer-to-peer video conferencing and created a supportive community of surviving family members who lost a loved one in a terrorist attack.

PERSONAL REFLECTIONS

Witnessing 9/11, my own memories of work at the site drifted back and I found myself confronting the repercussions of my trauma with its own unique personal and cultural overtones. The overwhelming loss of human life and the suffering of thousands of innocent victims was horrific, devastating, and incomprehensible. The sorrowful vision of my neighborhood being smothered in an angry, thick, toxic blanket of dust will always be with me. Battery Park without the Twin Towers serving as my beacon of light was profoundly unsettling and painful. Although I do not presume to know what it is like to suffer from phantom limb pain—a painful sensation experienced by someone who has lost a limb through amputation—my empathic fantasy is that my profound sense of loss and sorrow might not be dissimilar. Chronic nightmares of innocent people being trapped in tall buildings and jumping to their deaths are another lamentable keepsake.

The disaster brought me back to my own history of traumatic loss, which deepened its significance. My esteemed psychoanalyst, who had been a hidden child in Hungary during the Nazi occupation in World War II, had unexpectedly and suddenly passed away from pneumonia during my psychoanalysis. After her death, her childhood memoir, *Castles Burning* (Denes, 1997), was published. I identified with what I imagine were her feelings of rage, sorrow, and resilience. Her brother, who was resisting the occupation in Hungary during World War II, was killed by the Nazis. Now, I had a deeper understanding of my analyst's devastating loss of her older brother. The life she described in her childhood memoir had in one swift and unimaginable moment become real.

MY 9/11 RELATED DIAGNOSIS

In 2001, Christine Todd Whitman, who was the administrator of the Environmental Protection Agency, continually falsely reassured me and my fellow first responders and those who lived near Ground Zero that the air was repeatedly tested and found not to be harmful. While I was on NBC news, despite Todd Whitman's overconfident and inaccurate report that the air was tested and not dangerous, I expressed my first-hand experience at being at Ground Zero, that the air continued to smell of burned bodies and remained highly caustic to our skin, eyes, and lungs.

Sadly, much later, my concerns were confirmed and we learned that the air was "wildly toxic" according to air pollution expert and University of California Davis Professor Emeritus Thomas Cahill (Armour, 2006), which consisted of pulverized concrete, glass, asbestos, and detectable amounts of lead and mercury. There were also unprecedented levels of dioxins and polycyclic aromatic hydrocarbons (PAHs) from the fires which burned for three months (Pleil et al., 2006). Many of the dispersed substances (asbestos, crystalline silica, lead, cadmium, polycyclic aromatic hydrocarbons) are carcinogenic; other substances can trigger kidney, heart, liver, and nervous system deterioration. This toxic blanket that had descended and covered Ground Zero was well-known by the EPA at the time of collapse (Gates, 2006).

Sixteen years later, on a routine mammogram and ultrasound, while rushing so as not to be late to get back to my office, I refused to wait for the results. So the radiologist bluntly blurted out, "You have breast cancer," which felt like an astonishing gut punch. Having no family history of breast cancer, it became necessary to repeat over and over to my partner that I had been given a breast cancer diagnosis to have the news sink in. Although I did not give much thought at that time about the risk of developing cancer from my exposure to the noxious air at Ground Zero, my breast surgeon later stated that the origins of my breast cancer could be consistent with being exposed to toxins, as she "had never seen cancer with such high resolution and detail on ultrasound results."

Since 2017, I have been on the World Health Trade Center Insurance as my breast cancer was assessed to have resulted from my exposure to toxins at Ground Zero. Even if I had prior knowledge that going down to Ground Zero would result in my developing breast cancer, I would like to think that I would have still chosen to volunteer to help others (Cerfolio, 2019). Despite the stress of having an 11-hour surgery consisting of a right mastectomy with reconstructive surgery, somehow my loss was compensated and diminished by the satisfaction of bringing some modicum of help to really traumatized people.

Although it may seem a reductive narrative, whether caring for women diagnosed with breast cancer as a Consultation/Liaison Fellow at Memorial Sloan Kettering Cancer Hospital, Attending Physician at New York University/Bellevue, or as a psychoanalyst in private practice, the majority felt that their illness was a metaphor for a lack of maternal nurturance (Sontag, 1977). Both for myself and these women, our breast cancer diagnosis became an opportunity to learn how to provide ourselves with the love that we lacked growing up.

When doing my psychiatry residency, which consisted of mostly male physicians, I had suffered fantasies of cutting off my breasts in a desire to gain a sense of belonging, as I was raised in a misogynistic environment where women were second-class citizens. Maybe the benefit of anesthesia, maybe just an uncanny spiritual experience, upon waking from anesthesia, I had the dream-like experience of being transported to another world, that was embraced in light, where something was released from me. And suddenly I awoke with crystalline clarity; I felt an immense sense of compassion for my mother. Both my mother and I suffered from the sagacious words of Jill Johnston (1973), cultural critic of the Village Voice, paraphrased here: There are daughters and daughters and daughters and every few generations a mother is born. By learning how to nurture myself and self-soothe, breast cancer allowed me to heal the relationship with my mother and gradually begin to relinquish grasping for maternal love, which simply wasn't available.

PSYCHOANALYTIC THOUGHTS CONCERNING THE REVERBERATIONS OF 9/11

Having political and social reverberations for the world, the psychological splitting that occurred as a result of 9/11 is a sorrowful step backward for humanity. For the attackers as well as the victims of 9/11, the leaning toward "othering," which involves the twisted contortions of the traumatized split mind was omnipresent (Lament, 2022; Fraher, 2021, Pivnick, 2021). The dehumanizing aspects of this split enmeshed both perpetrators and victims in primitive anxieties, including the othering of different cultures and religions.

In times of devastating trauma, the inability to hold onto complexity, the need for bloodlust for revenge, and the fragmentation of the self may sadly become the norm. As a result of this trauma, our country lost the ability to self-reflect and contain ambivalence, reverting to a primitive "us versus them" mentality. This posttraumatic fracturing into "good versus bad" polarized thinking is exemplified by former President George W. Bush's speech to Congress, "Either you are with us or you are with the terrorists" (President Bush Addresses the Nation, 2001, para. 58).

One of the major reverberations that results from massive human-made trauma is that survivors often experience deficits in symbolic functioning, reducing their capacity to think productively (Boulanger, 2005; Boulanger, 2007; Bromberg, 2000; Laub & Auerhahn, 1989; Laub & Auerhahn, 1993; Prince, 1998; Cerfolio, 2009). When our ability for symbolic representation is reduced, thinking is diminished to polarization and losses cannot be mourned. We become more vulnerable to reflexively repeating what is not consciously remembered (Volkan, 2013). This inability to symbolize as manifested by binary thinking leads to increased conflicts and power struggles that keep wounds raw (Pivnick, 2021).

This "collapsed symbolization" (Pivnick, 2021) and primitive return of the id in acts of revenge is illustrated in the wars our country waged in Iraq and Afghanistan in retaliation for 9/11. America's failure to imagine the depth of resentment that US actions abroad provoked fundamentalist Muslims to view the United States as the world's biggest bully that employs terror on other people's land (Nye, 2002).

As demonstrated by anti-war protests, many Americans felt betrayed by our country's authoritarian swing and invasion of Iraq and Afghanistan. In the wake of the 9/11 trauma, the response of the United States continues to have a dark influence on the polarized and divisive way we think about pressing social issues, including immigration, climate change, nationalism, and the upsurge of authoritarianism (Lament, 2022; Pivnick, 2021).

Freud (1920/1955) proposed that individuals form groups in an attempt to combat and bind destructive forces. As group functions are often influenced and disrupted by psychotic processes, destructive feelings are dealt with through massive splitting processes, where the group idealizes itself and projects destructiveness into other groups (Segal, 1997; Bion, 1961). The group consolidates itself by idealizing its members as thoroughbreds in elegant purification and converts non-members with less than human status. Vulnerability, when it is not contained, is projected into others to ward off one's own sense of fragility. An example of this collective splitting process is our contempt and dehumanization of Muslims after 9/11, which was demonstrated by hate crimes against Muslims, including murder, physical assault, vandalism of mosques, and public harassment. This collective splitting process underlies such prejudices as Islamophobia, racism, genocide, homophobia, and sexism.

As a result of 9/11, the unconscious collective forces of the primitive id that until then had been largely repressed, such as the taboo against violence in our country against Muslims and those of different religions, were now unleashed. As humanities scholar Jacqueline Rose (2011) so insightfully noted, when violence is justified by the highest law of a country, it becomes the most terrifying violence. Our country's future will continue to be influenced by this lingering dark shadow, until we can recognize and contain our destructive feelings of retribution and replace these primitive urges with deeper self-reflection (Lament, 2022).

Terrorism and its cycles of vengeful violence is kept alive by a rupture on both an individual and societal level. This rupture results in an organized failure of imagination and an inability to empathize with Others, which creates a further societal divide (Cerfolio, 2019). On a group level, both America and Al-Qaeda had a lack of imagination and empathy, which hindered their ability to recognize the Other which culminated in 9/11. Imagination is drowned by a pinpoint lens of myopia for the blinding lust for power and the inability to accept and learn from loss. At this point in our history has America become so injured and numb to the brutality in this fractured world that we have lost our ability to have empathy for what is different? Has America become consumed by the corrupting pursuit of power and the humiliating insistence on dominating the other, such as in our country's invasion of Iraq and Afghanistan? As we continue to turn our backs on the plight of third-world countries, insular self-interest deepens and contributes to the marginalized sense of hopelessness and desire for retribution.

While doing first-hand humanitarian aid work in 2005 during the Second Chechen War, I personally witnessed the sequelae of the world's lax depravity in not protesting Putin's destructive war crimes against Chechens. By looking the other way, the world empowered Putin to continue to use his same playbook of denial, deflection, and projection to conduct war crimes, commit civilian atrocities, and terrorize the population into submission and scorched earth scenario in Chechnya, Syria, and Georgia without any consequences. America seemed to cede Putin's waging war in Eurasia, in part, echoing 19th-century colonization and skipping past the specter of nuclear devastation. But then the world suddenly woke up and gave intimation of unification protesting Putin's invasion of Ukraine.

Although complex and multi-determined, perhaps the othering of Muslims contributed, in part, to our country and the world turning a blind eye to the genocide and human atrocities that occurred in the First and Second Chechen, Georgian, and Syrian wars. America's lack of concern about the murdering of innocent Muslim civilians and their suffering from these wars was, in part, a result of our prejudice and Islamophobia. Our othering of Muslims, the pushing back against those who are dissimilar, propagates inequality and marginality. Othering creates a divisiveness that falsely insists that we are superior and others are inferior and that it is acceptable to humiliate and exploit the disenfranchised. This tribalism, which consists of a hostility toward the unfamiliar, foments much of the conflict in the world. Othering and tribalism makes realizing interconnectedness impossible.

When one cannot contain feelings like rage, vengeance, and envy, the function of the Other is to become the repository of these projected unwanted, disowned feelings. Despite decades of Putin's waging war and killing innocent Muslim civilians in Chechnya and Syria, our country othered this Muslim suffering by not deterring Russia's behavior by placing sanctions or other punishments. Similarly, Putin specializes in furthering this hostility toward others by weaponizing refugees which creates a financial, and psychological strain and destabilization upon neighboring republics and countries. This is an echo of previous practices of our marginality as shown by the usage of derogatory names for our wartime enemies such as: "Japs" in Japan, "Chinks" in China, "Gooks" in Vietnam. When we inflict wars on our brothers and sisters in the world, we eschew the fact that reality is composed of multiplicity and the pursuit of virtue is a scarce commodity, further tattering our sense of community, and spiritual connectedness. Othering creates a divisiveness that falsely insists that we are superior and that it is acceptable to humiliate and exploit the marginalized. Our Islamophobia led to our ignoring the plight of Muslims which emboldened Putin to continue his heinous and barbaric acts against humanity to invade and occupy other peaceful countries like Ukraine.

By the summer of 2001, despite security threats of violence both at home and abroad and the US intelligence knowing that there was a high probability of a dramatic attack in our country, most Americans fooled themselves into assuming that the United States was invincible and that these terrorist attacks could only occur overseas. Despite numerous signs of impending violence, such as the 1993 World Trade Center bombing and Bin Laden's statement, that if the present injustices continue, the battle will inevitably move to American soil, few

Americans had imagined that a foreign threat could infiltrate and attack domestic targets (National Commission on Terrorist Attacks Upon the United States, 2004).

Similarly, Al-Qaeda was operating under its own distortion of reality, as they were drawn into aggression against America (Fraher, 2021). Al-Qaeda's overconfidence was based on their rationalization that they were ordained by an omniscient perfect God to wage jihadist war against their nemesis. If Al-Qaeda had not been consumed by hatred for America, it might have processed the contradictions between its fatwa against Americans and the basic tenets of the Muslim religion (Fraher, 2021).

On an individual level, due to the often-common narrative of childhood trauma and misogyny (deMause, 2002), which preprograms a world of violence and constricts the ability to imagine a peaceful world, the Islamic terrorist becomes more brittle and less open to experiencing empathy for others. As a result of this often childhood history of trauma, radicalization exploits the Islamic suicide bomber's brittle imagination and lack of empathy (Cerfolio, 2019). Through projective identification, the radicalizer displaces his shame and desire for revenge and encourages the suicide bomber to kill through the messianic prophecy that he will be united with Allah in heaven. In projecting his guilt over his past Western behaviors of frequenting nightclubs, womanizing, and drinking, Osama bin Laden resented our country as corrupting Muslim culture. Also, in an attempt not to be Othered, humiliated, further rejected by Saudi Arabia, and to rid himself of a sense of impotency, bin Laden may have felt motivated to kill Westerners (deMause, 2002). Bin Laden's aspirations involved both material gain and perverted spiritual rewards for exacting revenge against America.

Analyzing The 9/11 Report (National Commission on Terrorist Attacks Upon the United States, 2004), Amy Fraher (2021) theorizes that two forms of macro-level hubris—America's "hubris of empire-building" and Al-Qaeda's "hubris-nemesis complex"—amalgamated in a uniquely generative manner leading to 9/11. Both America and Al-Qaeda became detached from reality, further isolating themselves with a fictional narrative that rationalized their escalating behaviors. Both countries engaged in an ongoing process of defensive excessive optimism and overconfidence, which requires belittlement of others in order to maintain feelings of invulnerability and idealism (Fraher, 2021).

How does an individual or a country, after a terrorist attack, not allow itself to be pulled into "mad acts of revenge?" (Segal, 2007). How do they not fall into an "us versus them" mentality? We as individuals and as a collective body must recognize and contain our most primitive and destructive feelings to discover our own distinctive path toward self-healing. As Mitchell (2013) discussed, "the law of the mother" prohibits, by withdrawing her love, the enactment of a fantasy to murder the newborn sibling. The toddler's developmental task is to transform this fantasy of sibling annihilation and hatred of what is different into a unity of our prosocial shared humanity. By holding onto the general "law of the mother" to nourish the greater good, Othering can be softened through acts of kindness and compassion (Lament, 2022).

How do we purge ourselves of blinding divisive tribalism to have a stronger belief in a shared humanity and connected global community? It is through the psychoanalytic method that one believes that by free association and deep self-reflection, one works through trauma, so that we can transcend terror. Tolerating ambivalence and deep contemplation are keystones of customary practices for psychoanalytic work and essential guardrails against the sway of destructive unconscious retaliatory forces (Lament, 2022). Sublimation of vengeful acts in response to 9/11 into more evolved compassionate feelings promotes the good of the individual as well as the group.

CONCLUSION

Only by caring and bearing witness to the suffering of all, especially those from different races and cultures, do we begin to reconnect severed social links and recognize the unity of our planet (Davoine & Gaudillière, 2004). For the soul of our country and the world to heal, the reverberations of 9/11 need to become more about fostering our interconnectedness through understanding the plight of the marginalized and empathic recognition of others' suffering as our own. In order to prevent traumatic collapse, our country must begin to listen to others' subjectivity, respect the dignity of all equally, and become less polarized by acknowledging our mutual vulnerability through mourning.

NOTES

1 Parts of this chapter appeared in an earlier version in Cerfolio (2009) and are gratefully reprinted with permission from Guilford Press.
2 Parts of this chapter appeared in an earlier version in Cerfolio (2019) and are gratefully reprinted with permission from Terror House Press.

REFERENCES

Armour, S. (2006, June 25). 9/11 health troubles? *USA Today.*
Bion, W. R. (1961). *Experiences in groups and other papers.* Brunner-Routledge.
Boulanger, G. (2005). From voyeur to witness: Recapturing symbolic function after massive psychic trauma. *Psychoanalytic Psychology, 22*(1), 21–31. http://doi.org/10.1037/0736-9735.22.1.21
Boulanger, G. (2007). *Wounded by reality: Understanding and treating adult onset trauma* (Psychoanalysis in a New Key Book Series, Vol. 6). Routledge.
Bromberg, P. M. (2000). Potholes on the royal road: Or is it an abyss? *Contemporary Psychoanalysis, 36*(1), 5–28. http://doi.org/10.1080/00107530.2000.10747043
Cerfolio, N. (2009). Multimodal psychoanalytically informed aid work with children traumatized by the Chechen War. *The Journal of the American Academy of Psychoanalysis and Dynamic Psychiatry, 37*(4), 587–603. http://doi.org/10.1521/jaap.2009.37.4.587
Cerfolio, N. (2019, April 27). Recipe for cut motherhood. *Terror. House Magazine.* https://terrorhousemag.com/cut-motherhood/
Cerfolio, N. (2019, May 23). Trauma two times over: Developing breast cancer as a result of being a first responder during 9/11. *Terror House Magazine.* https://terrorhousemag.com/trauma/

Cerfolio, N. (2019, June 20–23). *Terrorism as a failure of imagination: A lack of individual and societal empathy* [Paper presentation]. The 17th Annual International Association for Relational Psychoanalysis and Psychotherapy International Conference, Tel Aviv-Jaffa, Israel.

Cerfolio, N. (2020). Terrorism and the psychoanalytic origins. *The Journal of Psychohistory*, 47(4), 256–274.

Cerfolio, R. J. (2014). *Super performing at work and at home: The athleticism of surgery and life.* River Grove Books.

Davoine, F., & Gaudillière, J.-M. (2004). *History beyond trauma: Whereof one cannot speak, thereof one cannot stay silent* (S. Fairfield, Trans.). Other Books.

deMause, L. (2002). *The emotional life of nations.* Other Press.

Denes, M. (1997). *Castles burning: A child's life in war.* W. W. Norton & Company.

Ferenczi, S. (1955). *Final contributions to the problems and methods of psycho-analysis* (M. Balint, Ed., E. Mosbacher et al., Trans.). Hogarth.

Ferenczi, S. (1988). *The clinical diary of Sándor Ferenczi* (J. Dupont, Ed., M. Balint & N. Z. Jackson, Trans.). Harvard University Press.

National Commission on Terrorist Attacks Upon the United States. (2004). *The 9/11 Commission report: Final report of the National Commission on Terrorist Attacks Upon The United States* (Authorized ed.). W. W. Norton & Company.

Fraher, A. L. (2021). Psychodynamics of imagination failures: Reflections on the 20th anniversary of 9/11. *Management Learning, 54*(4), 485–504. https://doi.org/10.1177/13505076211009786

Frankel, J. B. (1998). Ferenczi's trauma theory. *The American Journal of Psychoanalysis, 58*(1), 41–61. https://doi.org/10.1023/A:1022522031707

Freud, S. (1955). *The standard edition of the complete psychological works of Sigmund Freud* (Vol. 18, J. Strachey, Ed. & Trans.). The Hogarth Press (Original work published 1920).

Freud, S. (1961). *The standard edition of the complete psychological works of Sigmund Freud* (Vol. 19, J. Strachey, Ed. & Trans.). The Hogarth Press (Original work published 1927).

Gates, A. (2006, September 11). Buildings rise from rubble while health crumbles. *The New York Times.* https://www.nytimes.com/2006/09/11/arts/television/buildings-rise-from-rubble-while-health-crumbles.html

Herman, J. (2015). *Trauma and recovery: The aftermath of violence—From domestic abuse to political terror.* Basic Books (Original work published 1992).

Johnston, J. (1973). *Lesbian nation: A feminist solution.* Simon & Schuster.

Lament, C., & Ismi, N. M. (2022). 9/11 twenty years on: Fractured identities; Fear of the other; Forging a new path for our children *The Psychoanalytic Study of the Child, 75*(1), 37–43. https://doi.org/10.1080/00797308.2021.1971902

Laub, D., & Auerhahn, N. C. (1989). Failed empathy—A central theme in the survivor's Holocaust experience. *Psychoanalytic Psychology, 6*(4), 377–400. http://doi.org/10.1037/0736-9735.6.4.377

Laub, D., & Auerhahn, N. C. (1993). Knowing and not knowing massive psychic trauma: Forms of traumatic memory. *The International Journal of Psycho-Analysis, 74*(2), 287–302.

Mitchell, J. (2013). Siblings: Thinking theory. *The Psychoanalytic Study of the Child, 67*(1), 14–34. https://doi.org/10.1080/00797308.2014.11785486

Nye, J. S. (2002). *The paradox of American power: Why the world's only superpower can't go it alone.* Oxford University Press. http://doi.org/10.1093/0195161106.001.0001

Pivnick, B. A. (2021). Recollecting the vanishing forms of 9/11: Twenty years of ruptures, ripples, and reflections. *Psychoanalytic Perspectives, 18*(3), 279–295. http://doi.org/10.1080/1551806X.2021.1953874

Pleil, J. D., Funk, W. E., & Rappaport, S. M. (2006). Residual indoor contamination from World Trade Center rubble fires as indicated by polycyclic aromatic hydrocarbon profiles. *Environmental Science and Technology, 40*(4), 1172–1177. https://doi.org/10.1021/es0517015

Prince, R. (1998). Historical trauma: Psychohistorical reflections on the Holocaust. In J. S. Kestenberg & C. Kahn (Eds.), *Children surviving persecution: An international study of trauma and healing* (pp. 43–53). Praeger.

Prince, R. M. (2021). Pandemic psychoanalysis. *The American Journal of Psychoanalysis, 81*(4), 467–479. http://doi.org/10.1057/s11231-021-09328-5

Rose, J. (2011). *The Jacqueline Rose reader* (J. Clemens & B. Naparstek, Eds.). Duke University Press.

Segal, H. (1997). *Psychoanalysis, literature and war: Papers 1972–1995* (J. Steiner, Ed.). Routledge.

Segal, H. (with Schafer, R.) (2007). *Yesterday, today and tomorrow* (N. Abel-Hirsch, Ed.). Routledge. http://doi.org/10.4324/9780203945858

Selby, K., & Pacheco, W. (2022, December 21). *20 years later: The lingering health effects of 9/11.* Asbestos.com. https://www.asbestos.com/featured-stories/9-11-lingering-health-effects/

Sontag, S. (1977). *Illness as metaphor and AIDS and its metaphors.* Picador.

Stein, R. (2010). *For love of the father: A psychoanalytic study of religious terrorism.* Stanford University Press.

Text: President Bush Addresses the Nation. (2001, September 20). *The Washington Post.* https://www.washingtonpost.com/wp-srv/nation/specials/attacked/transcripts/bushaddress_092001.html

Volkan, V. (2013). Large-group-psychology in its own right: Large-group identity and peace-making. *International Journal of Applied Psychoanalytic Studies, 10*(3), 210–246.

Waterfield, S. (2020, September 11). Why the 9/11 death toll is still rising today. *Newsweek.* https://www.newsweek.com/how-many-people-died-911-thousands-perishing-september-11-related-illnesses-1531058

2

Dross Into Gold

A Neat Alchemic Conversion from Base Biological Poisoning and Terrorism to Paradisiacal High[1,2]

Poison + Perspective = Paradise

DOI: 10.4324/9781032633497-3

FROM RUSSIA WITH ANTHRAX

Our police escorts drove between 70 to 100 miles per hour, with only 4 to 10 feet between their cars, swerving across the dirt road, the "highway" leading into Grozny. This tactic aimed at reducing the chance of being hit with sniper fire or blown up by a landmine. Alek, our Chechen driver and host, followed closely behind, swerving along with the police cars. The tires turned up clouds of dust behind us on the highway which had been closed a week earlier due to heavy sniper fire from the Russian forces. It was August 20, 2005, and we'd already spent six days in the North Caucasus.

Despite feeling weak and dizzy, I was determined to stick with our mission to medically assist the injured and ill in Grozny. It had been an anxious morning for our group. We'd already driven across the border from Nazran, Ingushetia, our home base, to the volatile outskirts of Grozny, the capital of Chechnya. Crossing the border between Nazran, Ingushetia, and Grozny, Chechnya, we passed through three army checkpoints, manned by Russian guards in helmets and Kevlar vests and armed with AK-47s. Huge men who looked like they'd pull the triggers of their automatic weapons at the slightest hint of provocation. They slowly scanned our faces and then compared them to our passports. Each time their gaze lifted from the passports to us, the rope of tension between us and them pulled a little tighter. Their suffocating gaze pressed down hard on us, and their angry silence held the possibility of explosive violence. It made it hard to breathe. Fear was something I had rarely experienced directly. Finally, they waved us through. By the time we cleared the third checkpoint, the car smelled of sweat.

As we entered Grozny, we passed a fortress that stationed thousands of Russian troops and hundreds of large tanks, a military base that put the city in a stranglehold. No one came into or out of Grozny without Russian approval. And the consent at best felt grudging and reluctant. After clearing the checkpoints, we met our local escorts, who'd bring us further into Grozny—two young, Chechen policemen, scrawny, wide-eyed, and dwarfed by the brawny slit-eyed Russians. The thin duo greeted us with grim expressions. Their uniform pants ended around their ankles and were tightly belted to keep them from falling. Their shirts hung loosely around their emaciated bodies. Now they drove at breakneck speed and swerved all over the dirt road. I winced at the expectation of a bullet crashing through the window or a bomb exploding beneath the car.

Americans are prime targets for kidnappers in poor, war-torn countries. We found out later that simply by escorting us, the Chechen policemen had put their lives at grave risk. Grozny means "fearsome" in Russian, as in Ivan Grozny or Ivan the Terrible. The name fits the city perfectly. Death and destruction were everywhere. Block after city block in Grozny showed a ravaged wasteland scarred with the detritus of bombings and battles: soldiers, guns, tanks, rocket launchers, maimed civilians, and everywhere the wreckage of buildings and streets.

By now I was rethinking the wisdom of coming. It had taken three years of waiting before we were finally cleared and "invited" by the Russian government into the volatile and war-torn area of the North Caucasus and Chechnya. I had no idea it would be this bad, nor did Dennis, my partner in this undertaking.

Indeed, in 2004, most of the Western world was unaware of the brutal suppression of Chechens inflicted by the Russian wars in Chechnya, in part, due to the fact that the West was quick to join Putin's campaign of waging "war against terrorism." Russia's false propaganda was to portray the Chechen wars as a fight against Muslim terrorism, to bring Putin into presidency (Litvinenko & Felshtinsky, 2007; Dunlop, 2014; Satter, 2016; Anderson, 2017). Muslim humiliation and the subsequent desire for retribution against America and its allies is one of the driving forces of war-generated terrorism. The ability to hate can provide a distorted sense of object constancy to terrorists who have suffered a narcissistic injury severe enough to threaten their sense of survival (Cerfolio, 2020). Also, the lack of international news coverage of the Chechen wars left the world mostly unaware of the Russian atrocities that were being committed there.

We'd never imagined this level of human suffering and physical devastation. Dennis had asked me to book a nice hotel in Chechnya online and, scanning the Google images, I told him, "Dennis, there are no hotels, only bullet-ridden buildings of the few left standing."

Dennis should have asked me to book us a foxhole. There we were: two New Yorkers putting our lives on the line and those of our hosts to burst into a war zone so we could start a running program for the disabled and give help to the sick. If not for the fact that the program enabled us to obtain medical aid for the isolated and forgotten, our venture would have been patently absurd. Unconsciously decimating my childhood fears of being impotent, my counterphobic strategy was propelling me to go and volunteer in a war zone to provide medical care to those suffering in Chechnya.

We'd also hoped our visit to Chechnya would transcend cultural barriers and be a small contribution toward peace. More than 30,000 children had died in the Second Chechen War for independence from Russia. Children here experienced war, terrorism, and kidnappings on a daily basis, while their country remained isolated from the rest of the world. The Consolidated Appeals Process,[3] an advocacy tool estimated more than 2,000 children under the age of three would die each year as a result of inadequate medical care. As foolish and risky as the trip might have seemed to my family and friends, I felt I had been blessed with much and had a duty to reach out to those less fortunate. And my experiences in childhood and having been able to know, work with, and provide medical care to countless first responders and others affected by 9/11, galvanized and inspired me to help war victims in Chechnya. My conviction—that each of us share a responsibility to lend a helping hand to those who are suffering—resonated deeply in my soul.

We arrived at the former press house in Grozny, now a collapsed pile of rubble surrounded by bomb craters. Everything looked gray. The few bullet-riddled buildings left standing, showed gaping holes, craggy and jagged walls, and sagging foundations. From blown-out windows, women hung clothes to dry on lines. Amidst this appalling squalor, 90,000 to 190,000 Chechens made their home.

When the USSR collapsed in 1991, Grozny bustled as a gorgeous modern city, proud of its culture and education. Now I watched from the car window the destruction left me feeling stunned and confused. You look at ruin, you feel ruin, you can become ruined. It shouldn't have come as a shock that another cycle of ruin was about to be put into play.

I met Dennis at the 2000 New York City Marathon. The president of a running club for the disabled, he struck up a conversation with me, after seeing me guide a disabled athlete across the finish line. Acting as a disabled running guide, I supported Jim, an above-the-knee amputee from Jamaica, through the last half of the marathon. This inspiring experience marked my first running race and half marathon as a guide. After finishing, I was hooked on the running bug. Eventually, I would compete in ultramarathons and Ironman competitions.

Dennis, an above-the-knee amputee, had started a running club for people with all kinds of disabilities, and membership in this club has been a life-changing event for many who had lost a limb, suffered blindness, or battled chronic illness. It was certainly life-changing for me. Being born legally blind in my right eye due to a post-lenticular cataract, I ran my first marathon in New York City, as a disabled running athlete, in 2001. My race time for the New York 2001 marathon was 3 hours and 43 minutes. As that placed me in the top percentile for my age group, I qualified for the Boston Marathon, my second one, which I finished in 2002. I was proud to have finished the Boston Marathon in 3 hours and 30 minutes, which was running an average of an 8-minute mile flat for 26.2 miles.

I loved volunteering for Dennis's running club, serving as a board member on the running project for disabled American war veterans from the Iraq War and as a guide to disabled athletes through numerous running races. In 2001, I was tethered to lead a blind man, who weighed twice as much as me, to summit Mount Kilimanjaro.

As a trauma expert who ran the psychiatric emergency room at St. Vincent's Hospital Medical Center in New York City, I'd seen plenty: patients who were psychotic, suicidal, violent, homicidal, homeless, mentally ill, and chemically addicted. I helped cancer and AIDS patients die with dignity and comfortably free of pain. Yet, none of that would prepare me for the desolation of the Chechen genocide.

Lying between Eastern Europe's Black and Caspian Seas within the Russian Federation, the North Caucasus comprises seven ethnic homelands and is a mosaic of 50 different languages. Chechnya has struggled for centuries under Russian domination, and its declaration of independence in 1991 led to war, the most recent in 2005. Aside from issues of territory and resources, a major cultural difference responsible for the ongoing conflict is religion. Instead of the Russian Orthodox religion practiced in much of Russia, the majority of Chechens are Sunni Muslims.

In August 2005, I traveled to Chechnya with Dennis, not simply as a disabled running club athlete and ambassador, but as a physician. We met our hosts at the Moscow Airport. Natasha presented herself as a Czech crusader for the Chechens and functioned as our interpreter and cook. Igor claimed to be a Reuter's sports journalist. I found out later that he was also a Federal Security Service (FSB) agent. Corpulent with cherubic, high cheekbones, Natasha welcomed us with open arms. Igor, who finally got permission from the Russian government for us to enter Chechnya, shadowed us for the entire ten-day stay in the North Caucasus. He reminded me of Napoleon: small, 5 foot 4 inches, very stout and muscular. He was in his early 40s—my age. His blue-gray eyes were icy, cold. This marked the first time I looked deeply into someone's eyes and did not sense a soul staring back. I didn't like him on sight.

We were tired and hungry when we arrived in Moscow. Igor hurried us along into a waiting black sedan with a driver in the front. He ignored my request for water. When Dennis handed me his bottled water, Igor smirked and barked, "Dennis, we have a long drive and you'll get thirsty." Almost immediately I noticed that my presence annoyed Igor. I'd later learn that Igor and Dennis were old buddies, working together to set up many disabled running club chapters in Russia. Dennis had also helped Igor get into Bronx Community College and find him an apartment in Coney Island.

After piling in, Dennis in the front seat and me in the back between Natasha and Igor, we drove off to a farmhouse in the countryside in order to rest before our early morning plane that would take us to our final destination, the North Caucasus. The car windows were tinted and I had a hard time seeing through them.

It felt like I'd entered a coffin. My chest became tight and cold sweat trickled down my ribs. I felt cramped between Natasha and this ruthless man. When my request to use the bathroom fell on deaf ears, I became nervous. I glanced over at Igor who had a sardonic smile plastered on his face. I leaned forward and whispered to Dennis, "Say you need to use the bathroom." In seconds, we raced to the closest bathroom. Deep down, I knew something was not right. But what could I do? I was here already and unless I grew wings and flew out of the car and across the ocean, here is where I'd be for a while.

My throat closed up. My heart jackhammered in my chest. I broke out into a fresh pool of cold sweat. Struggling to clear my throat, I cried out, "I need to get out of this car right now!" My companions were shocked. I climbed over Igor, who sneered at me and did not move, jumping over him, and out of the back seat. I told Dennis I was claustrophobic and wanted to switch with him. When I got into the front seat of the sedan, the atmosphere became sullen. My being a woman and having a voice was not welcomed by my Russian hosts. They now regarded me as a pampered, silly little American woman who did not know her place in life.

The driver spirited us to a small house just outside Moscow in the Russian countryside. Outside on the lawn, a German shepherd tied to a tree yanked at the rope, as he barked at us ferociously. I could see his sharp, glistening teeth in the darkening air. When we entered the house, Natasha asked us to wait. Dennis and I stood in the foyer and watched as the backs of our hosts disappeared into the house. Natasha went upstairs and Igor down the hall. I collapsed in a chair, glad to have a moment alone without their orchestration.

Thirty minutes later, Natasha descended the stairs with a tall, Russian man. He was disheveled, shaking, and emaciated, with a suitcase in his hand. As Natasha interpreted, he told us with a shy grin that he was not well and had just gotten out of the hospital. His reddish nose, shaky limbs, and jaundice color strongly suggested the look of a chronic alcoholic. For a moment, he and I looked closely at each other, and his deadly smile made my skin crawl. After he left, Natasha closed the door and stood beside me. "Are you okay?" she asked. "Yes," I answered, shaking off the goosebumps.

"This way," she said, and we returned upstairs where she showed me to the bedroom the man had just occupied. When I slipped between the sheets, the bed was still warm from his body with the scent of urine. Dislodging myself, I slept on the top sheet, despite being cold.

The next day we traveled in the black town car to another Moscow Airport to fly to Nalchik, Kabardino-Balkaria, a province in the North Caucasus. Our group boarded an old Soviet plane for the short flight. There we met our Chechen hosts, Alik Galayev, a deputy minister of Chechnya for "Unusual Situations," and his brother, Ahmed Galayev, a handsome Chechen businessman. War was usual in Chechnya, but volunteers to help were not. We were the "unusual situation!" Ahmed, a friend of a general whose house we would be staying at, lived there with his wife, Jana.

Alik looked much older than his 49 years; gray hair, pallor and tired. Ahmed drove in a car by himself in front of us. Alik drove the second car with the rest of us in it. They drove us to Nazran, Ingushetia, the last republic in the foothill of the Caucasus before Chechnya. On route, we encountered two roadblocks. Local Ingush policemen ran the first. They checked our passports, looking over them slowly and carefully, then staring at us coldly. At first they cleared us, but then held us back, saying their computer wasn't working and they could not confirm clearance. Translation: we hadn't tipped them. Our Chechen hosts remained unfazed. After we coughed up the rubles, the computer buzzed to life. They explained that this is customary and equivalent to tolls on roads in the United States.

At the second roadblock, Russian policemen with Kalashnikov rifles strapped to their sides checked our passports. It seemed like they were looking for any reason to inflict suffering. At this moment we stood before the abyss. A real possibility of violence or kidnapping loomed. Natasha asked me if I was scared. I said no, and I was telling the truth as I was not in touch with my fear. It was only after I returned home to New York, that I thought about how easily and in how many ways that moment and many others could have turned deadly. I wondered why I had not been more fearful, except for that time on the first day of the trip when I felt suffocated between Igor and Natasha and had to exit the car. My childhood, privileged but not perfect, had prepared me for this trip.

I became a warrior for providing service early on in my childhood as I identified with those who were suffering and marginalized, and developed an ease for transmuting fear. It was necessary for me, and I was able to turn off a part of my brain that processes fear to better withstand the trauma of my childhood. This dissociation allowed me to be able to function. There was a deep-seated innate part of me that was drawn to the barbaric Second Chechen War and genocide, as I was passionate about aiding the Chechens who were forgotten and abandoned by the rest of the world. It was a reflex for me to seek out terror-filled situations that I unconsciously dreaded in an attempt to master and conquer my childhood anxiety.

As we waited for permission to enter Nazran, Ingushetia, unfazed Muslims carried out their daily activities. I caught a glimpse of young, stylish Muslim women wearing westernized, A-line, mid-calf skirts. They carefully negotiated the unpaved roads wearing high heels, their heads covered in dark monotone scarves, carrying groceries. In this place, where disasters and destruction occurred regularly, fashion is still held firmly in place.

Finally, Dennis and I were interviewed by an agent of the Federal Security Service of the Russian Federation in Nazran. He spoke fluent English with only a slight accent. He was tall, fair-featured, and perceptive. After a 45-minute interrogation, he wished us good fortune on our mission and indicated that we were only the third and fourth Americans allowed into the area during the Second Chechen War. Doctors without Borders had left after one doctor was kidnapped and eventually murdered.

Home base for us during our stay was a general's house in Nazran, about an hour's drive from Grozny. The house, fortified by 20-foot gates, resembled a fortress, and stood out, like a huge pimple-shaped eyesore from the bucolic landscape. Rolling farms, with grazing cows and horses, surrounded us. The farmers lived in small huts made of mud and straw. Neighbors, who the Chechens called gypsies, showed up regularly, outside the gates, begging for food and money. The interior of the cavernous house was decorated in heavy wainscoting and seemed an odd juxtaposition to the rustic countryside. Our indoor plumbing with toilets and showers was both an oddity and luxury for the area.

After a day spent working in the refugee camps in Ingushetia, we returned to our safe haven each evening. Jana, Ahmed's wife, greeted us with meals of potatoes, pickled vegetables, platters of sliced meats, and watermelon. Though she prepared our meals and cleaned up after us, she chose not to socialize. When I tried to clean off the table, she sweetly smiled and shook her head, pointing for me to sit down. She was attentive to all our needs. She brought us cold Russian beer, which she knew I enjoyed very much. Her young daughter, aged 10, also lived in the house, but the woman and children ate by themselves.

More than half of the Chechen population had fled and now lived in the refugee camps. At once, the smell of human waste permeated the air. A lonely farm field, under electric wires, littered with abandoned Soviet train cars, was now home to more than 3,000 Chechens. These deeply traumatized refugees knew they'd been discarded and forgotten by the world. They did not even have basic sanitation. We were introduced to the chief of the refugee camp who told us his 13-year-old daughter had a viral infection and was unable to fight it, and had subsequently developed viral congestive heart failure. The refugees, he said, complained of constant headaches, which they believed were caused by the close electric wires overhead. Each evening, after providing medical care to those lying in the camps, we returned again to our safe haven.

At another refugee camp, I met Makka, a 15-year-old blind girl. She'd lost her vision at the age of nine playing outside her house when a car bomb exploded. No medical resources existed here to provide her with treatment. Upon learning we could offer medical intervention she was taken by the deputy minister of sports to a hospital in Moscow. Her medical assessment revealed that a corneal transplant would restore her vision, and she eventually was able to get the surgery to regain her sight. Helping girls like Makka was why I had come.

I felt at odds with my American traveling companion. Dennis's altruism, while well-intentioned, wasn't exactly pure. Dennis suffered the ordinary grandiosity of being a devoted seeker of media glory. He wanted good press for his disabled running club to appear in the local papers back home, with photos depicting his brave heroism. While Dennis looked for Chechen photo ops, Igor looked for someone to hate. He seemed to dislike everyone, except Dennis, but he reserved a special hatred for me. It's not hard to tell when someone harbors such feelings for you. Sometimes a single glance reveals the weight of envy and hatred. I was an accomplished athlete, a successful physician, and an American woman, less subject to the extremes of patriarchal oppression so common in Russia.

When Dennis mentioned that I would be writing about our experience and work in the Second Chechen War in the local newspapers, Igor became belligerent and started cursing in Russian. He went outside and began furiously throwing a ball against the outside of the general's house. Igor's temper tantrum continued for several hours.

Avoiding Dennis and Igor, I spent time with four Chechen girls Jana introduced to me, her daughter and relatives between the ages of 5 and 12. The girls enchanted me, teaching me Russian words by drawing pictures and then suddenly grabbing my hand to guide me through several ethnic dances. I felt free in my body with them as we twirled together on the patio inside the gates around the house, then collapsed in laughter. Their joy and passion was contagious, but the back of my mind darkened with fear for their future. I wondered if this place might break their spirits. Upon our departure, I gave them my jewelry and other trinkets, and kissed them on the tops of their heads where they parted their hair.

On the third day of our stay in the North Caucasus, Dennis, Igor, and I had lunch on the patio, enclosed by the towering brick walls. I loved beer, and had been known to opt for a lager, rather than Gatorade, after a workout. The sun shone brightly that afternoon. I took a sip of an exotic Russian beer that Igor brought me in a glass. Usually Jana would bring Dennis and me the bottle, which I drank out of directly without a glass. This time I noticed a strange sediment at the bottom of the bottle. Sitting in the bright sun on the patio ringed by the protection of 20-foot walls, I noted the sediment, but I did not give it any more thought at this time. I excused myself to go to the bathroom, and when I returned, I had one more sip, but refrained from consuming any more. After drinking that beer, my health, a robust friend I'd always taken for granted, deserted me.

Later in the day, I developed flu-like symptoms, fever and muscle soreness. In a couple of days, I became violently sick, with projectile vomiting and bloody diarrhea, high fever, intense abdominal pain, dizziness, lethargy, extreme weakness and headache. I was delirious and unable to get out of bed for three days. I never had a doubt about what was happening to me. I understood instinctively, almost impassively, what had occurred, as if I were my own emergency room patient. I knew I had been poisoned, but I did not know with what.

In the morning, weakened, while still in bed, I informed Natasha and Dennis that I had been poisoned. They seemed nonplussed and had no response to my self-diagnosed condition, both perhaps genuinely unable to process this information. Five years later through my extensive research and explorations, I discovered that many of my symptoms were consistent with anthrax exposure.

"Where is Igor?" I asked, and Natasha said he had left to report a story for Reuters at a local building in Ingushetia. Natasha and Dennis left shortly after this conversation, so Natasha could take pictures of Dennis milking a cow on a nearby farm. I remained in bed for several days, slipping in and out of consciousness, too sick and weak to move. I continued to have dizziness, high fevers, headache, and severe abdominal pain. Jana brought me lovely, thoughtfully prepared meals on a tray, but I was too sick to eat them. She wiped my head and sat by my side for the entire three days. There was no medical help available. I was the only available medical care. Even if there had been doctors, there were many others who also needed acute intervention. In three days, I lost 10 pounds that I could not afford to lose.

I simply could not get up, could barely even lift my head. Dennis showed little concern. It was food poisoning, he opined, or just a bug. On our last day, weak and still running a fever, I was determined to go to Grozny, even if I had to crawl. That Russian bastard would not win; he'd see me on my feet again. After struggling to get out of bed, I came downstairs. Seeing me standing, Igor looked shocked. Dennis confided, "Igor told me the others did not like you." I laughed at the absurdity of this. While I was sick they had visited a refugee camp. The leader of the camp had offered two of his wives to Dennis. Dennis politely refused and told me that the women were fat and unattractive, "but they missed the best time they would ever have."

In Grozny, we met four emaciated Chechen boys who were part of a local winning soccer team. One was a 14-year-old Chechen who had lost his left leg and hand to a land mine while playing outside. He told us he lived with his mother and that the Russian army had kidnapped his father. In a shy, humble demeanor, he explained his love of computers. We brought sneakers and shirts for him and the other children we met so they would be able to race with their new disabled running chapter. Meeting this young boy and his teammates powered me through the day, though I had to take frequent rests to catch my breath on low stone walls and benches. As soon as we returned home to the general's house, I collapsed back into bed.

On our last night, we heard a loud explosion from outside our protective wall. I asked Natasha what the explosion was. She answered that it was fireworks. I did not believe her. While boarding our plane from the North Caucasus to Moscow, in the local newspaper, we learned that there had been an assassination attempt on Ingush's prime minister, Ibragim Malsagov. He had been responsible for permitting us to enter the North Caucasus. The two roadside bombs killed his driver and wounded two others. The prime minister was hospitalized with wounds to his hand and leg. The two explosives, placed 10 meters apart, detonated within 10 seconds of each other as the prime minister's motorcade passed. It was one more sign that it was time for us to leave Ingushetia.

It was a normal state of mind for me to be disassociated from my terror of witnessing the human atrocities and war crimes committed by Russians against the Chechens. Not processing my fears of the emotional turmoil that frequently occurred growing up allowed me to survive my brutal childhood. My childhood was boot camp to prepare me to become the ultimate light warrior. My best and worst defense was my fearlessness. I was an adrenaline junkie, but my drug of choice was long-distance running to emotionally remove myself from my rage and sadness. When I became too sick to run, I spiraled into depression and withdrawal from endogenous opioids.

Dennis, Igor, and I were looking at groceries that Natasha was buying for our last dinner. Dennis asked me for money to buy a memento, as his had been stolen, several days earlier. After his money was stolen, Dennis became alarmed and carried both of our passports in the front pocket of his shirt. With Igor watching, I rifled through my knapsack to find my runner's wristband, where I kept it. I gave Dennis some small change. The next morning, I noticed Igor stuffing something into the front of his pants. That was the last time I saw Igor. He left soon after that, without saying goodbye. Natasha brought us to the airport to return to Moscow. Hugging her goodbye, I wanted to give her my money to help sick refugees to get sorely needed medical attention. I searched my runner's wristband, and the 3,000 dollars I'd had was missing. Natasha stated, "It makes me look like I stole it." I remarked, "It is only money and do not worry, I know who took it, and he is not here." Russia had robbed me of my health and money, but I was still alive. It was time to go home.

SLEUTHING MY MEDICAL MYSTERY

Upon returning home from Russia to the United States, I struggled to get through my workday of seeing patients and supervising residents. Just sitting upright took a monumental energy of will. I felt as if my limbs were anchored with weights struggling to move through thick mud. Previously I had enjoyed limitless energy; now I ceased to be myself. My mind no longer functioned as before and I suffered mental lapses, having difficulty retrieving words. I refused, however, to become identified as a sick person or to let the illness prevent me from living well. I had an autoimmune challenge, but refused to allow my challenges to completely overwhelm me. Some days were better than others; I focused day-to-day on getting stronger.

In addition to chronic fatigue, I experienced a puzzling range of symptoms. After two years I had gained 10 pounds. My abdomen was swollen and painful. I wrestled with insomnia, despite near-constant exhaustion. Sleeping aids were no help; sleep did not come without high doses of melatonin. I later learned that anthrax is believed to affect the pineal gland to produce less melatonin.

Other physical symptoms descended upon my body. As an elite endurance athlete, my respiratory system had functioned effortlessly, but now I was chronically weak. I took ciprofloxacin for recurrent pneumonia, but after initially feeling stronger I soon weakened again; the antibiotics probably further destroyed my already-compromised flora. Although unaware at the time of what I had been exposed to, I was treated many times with ciprofloxacin, which ironically is a treatment for anthrax.

Prior to my illness, my vital signs were excellent; now I developed high blood pressure and dizziness. I was unable to walk to the bathroom without hanging onto walls to steady myself. Indeed, military doctors have documented cases where broken bones from falling were the result of anthrax-vaccine-induced loss of consciousness affecting the nervous system.

My life suddenly became a series of fires: putting out one medical emergency after another. After my initial symptoms, I subsequently developed chronic inflammation, recurrent pneumonia, and recurrent intestinal parasitic infections, arthralgia, rashes, autoimmune disorder, and 20 new food allergies. My remaining autoimmune disorder left me feeling trapped, alone and without answers to how to regain my health.

For five years I sought help through traditional Western medicine, while my immune system became weaker. It was not until 2010, after biological testing on a Rife machine, that results confirmed I was poisoned with a derivative of man-made anthrax. I came to learn, experience and appreciate the benefits of a Rife machine, which is an alternative treatment for those who do not respond to Western medical treatments and antibiotics. A Rife machine produces electromagnetic energy in the form of electrical impulses; finding the correct frequency and producing the proper impulse of the frequency kills or disables diseased cells. Although it couldn't be proven unequivocally, immunologists told me that my symptoms were consistent with anthrax poisoning. A subsequent combination of treatment on the Rife machine and homeopathic and Western treatments strengthened my immune system, putting me on the road to recovery. It is not specifically my intention to recommend alternative care to others, but to acknowledge that I no longer was one of the fortunate who responded solely to Western medicine.

After five years, through self-directed health care that creatively mixed Western and alternative medicine, I became my own health advocate, sleuthing the details of my medical ordeal and paving my own road to recovery. It took many years for me to regain enough strength to begin to piece together what I had medically experienced, to begin to do extensive research on the effects of anthrax vaccinations and exposure in the American military system who were deployed to work in Russia, and speak to postal workers who had been exposed to inhalational anthrax.

Anthrax is tasteless, colorless, and lethal.[4] Gastrointestinal (GI) anthrax is the great imitator, hiding behind a smokescreen of diagnoses, including food poisoning and GI viral infection. Because it mimics other illnesses, anthrax is the perfect biological weapon: difficult to initially diagnose and, if the victim survives, impossible to verify. Research studies document that after two years, protective antigens against anthrax are no longer present; it is, therefore, impossible to confirm anthrax exposure through research testing of anthrax IgG titers after two years.

Russia has a history of using anthrax as a biological weapon. In violation of the 1972 Biological Weapons Convention, Russia continued to stockpile anthrax. In 1979, in Sverdlovsk, anthrax spores were accidentally released from a manufacturing facility. The death toll was at least 68, but no one knows the exact number because hospital records were destroyed by the KGB. The cause of the outbreak was denied for years and the deaths were blamed on intestinal exposure due to consumption of tainted meat (Wampler, 2001).

Reports indicate that American military personnel preparing to be stationed in Russia were vaccinated with anthrax as a means of protection against the use of anthrax in biological warfare. Vaccinations were discontinued when research documented the rate of heart attacks as twice as high after vaccination (Evans, 2005). Evans (2005) reported that dozens of sick veterans who received the anthrax vaccine complained of fatigue, chronic pain in joints, and mental lapses—and that the Pentagon never told members of Congress about more than 20,000 hospitalizations involving troops who had been subjected to the anthrax vaccine.

Western physicians have limited experience with anthrax. Until the highly publicized 2001 anthrax attacks against members of the media and the United States Congress, exposure to respiratory anthrax had been rarely seen in the West, and there had been even fewer cases of gastrointestinal anthrax in the West.[5]

Many of the physicians who treated me were sympathetic but mystified by my clinical symptoms and misinformed about anthrax. A leading infectious disease specialist sent me for anthrax titer testing—without even knowing such a test did not commercially exist.

Eastern doctors have more experience with anthrax and, consequently, fatality rates reported in the United States from GI anthrax are higher than reported in the East.[6] For example, in Western Iran the mortality rate of hospitalized patients with GI anthrax has been 64 percent; however, during an epidemic the mortality rate was 5.53 percent, which suggests that the awareness of patients' anthrax exposure enables quicker and more effective treatment (Hatami et al., 2010).

Research studies have demonstrated that anthrax lethal toxin induces vascular insufficiency in mice (Nass, 2007). On a subsequent trip after my exposure, I experienced severe chest pain, heart palpitations, and difficulty breathing. I thought I was having a heart attack caused by the poison and eventually conferred with a leading cardiologist, who confirmed that "anthrax may affect the heart but rarely." He ordered a stress cardiac echocardiogram and the results were within normal limits. I eventually figured out that my elevated heart rate and shortness of breath, instead of being due to anthrax's lethal toxin, turned out to be due to an allergic reaction, which was the result of new food allergies that I had developed *after* being poisoned.

In part due to chronic inflammation from developing an autoimmune disorder and many food allergies after being poisoned, when I looked in the mirror, I glimpsed a subtle, sickly glow. Like a leafless tree highlighted with newly fallen snow, my new winter-wizened condition left my previously robust skin drooping. My endocrine glands no longer functioned efficiently and I developed hypothyroidism and adrenal fatigue. For many years, I took a thyroid supplement called thyro-complex, which helped restore some energy. To re-energize my adrenal gland, my breakfast consisted of massive amounts of herbs. It took years to rebuild my adrenal glands back to their original state. I also developed glaucoma, which I was able to heal.

Due to being in superb physical condition, having a medical background, and being ferociously tenacious, I not only survived, but today, my health and outlook have improved. For the first five years, not knowing what I was poisoned with and not finding any answers through Western medicine, I became deflated, disorganized, and panicky. However, by taking total responsibility for my recovery and through self-directed healthcare as well as reframing my illness, I empowered myself to seek alternative medical resources for help. I became responsible to my illness and not for my illness. Eventually, through a combination of Western and alternative medicine, I received needed care.

Much of my glandular system has returned to normal functioning levels, although anthrax damaged my thyroid gland and I remain chronically hypothyroid and on thyroid medication. My legs are free from the ball and chain that I labored to carry for a decade. My eyes are less inflamed and less itchy and red. No longer freezing at room temperature, I can take a yoga class and sweat, and not worry if I am going to collapse halfway through the class or subsequently develop pneumonia. My mind is clearer.

My experiences navigating this illness within the constraints of Western medicine brought desperation that fueled my determination to keep looking for answers that could provide better understanding and healing. The medical community must have a greater awareness of anthrax's clinical manifestations and medical sequelae in order to lower morbidity and mortality. By better merging Western and alternative medicine, those suffering from chronic illness can be spared the ordeal of receiving needed integrated care.

LOSS, SURRENDER, AND SPIRITUAL AWAKENING

The ghosts of my primordial feeling of being infectious became more evident in the terror and madness of becoming ill, fostering a spiritual healing process. I long had a feeling that there was something wrong with me—a deep feeling of being defective. After anthrax poisoning, this feeling became deeply embedded and embodied. Ironically, it took being poisoned and becoming ill to slowly erode my irrational fear of feeling infectious and unlovable that had originated in my childhood.

Previous to becoming infected with anthrax, a feeling that I sometimes felt but did not want to intimately recognize—Bollas's the unthought known—was my being toxic, which seemed too catastrophic to accept. I warded off feeling toxic by running away—both physically and emotionally—from the painful feeling.

I also unconsciously recreated my childhood scenario of being "lesser than" by entering various athletic competitions with the wrong equipment or by being under-trained for the event. When I completed the Half Ironman of Monaco, I rode my triathlon bike through the challenging 56-mile climbs of the mountainous French Alps, as I did not feel worthy of buying a road bike. Riding my twitchy triathlon bike through the many hairpin climbs, made the already challenging race not only more difficult but dangerous. Triathlon bikes are time trial bikes, made to ride flat, straight courses. It was much easier and more efficient to ride a road bike through the many steep, switch-back ascents, and descents of the French Alps. By riding on the wrong bike, I had a tidy excuse if I did not do well. But by placing third in my age group in the Half Ironman in Monaco, I qualified for the first Half Ironman Championship in Florida. I had recreated my childhood scenario of being unseen and uncared for to rise from the ashes of emotional deprivation, overcome adversity and succeed.

Anthrax was the gift that allowed deep unconscious pockets and split-off worlds within me to merge together, so that new creative possibilities surfaced, and healing became possible. Writing became an expansive catharsis that became an integral part of my healing process. I was taken to a strange, spiritual land after being poisoned that was beyond my normal experience, impossible to describe, and not reachable by discursive thought. My subsequent spiritual awakening, ironically similar to being poisoned, was an intuitive, and not a rational experience, which was an inner noumenal and not phenomenal journey. It was difficult to write about as it was in the realm of the uncanny, and to grasp by ordinary means, but my experience is the realest of the real because it was indelible. It was a journey to an invisible world, rather than a phenomenal, verifiable experience that my family was so submerged in. My family dismissed and did not recognize my being poisoned and falling ill, in part, because it was beyond their conscious experience and unconsciously terrified them. My spiritual experience was something that can never be taken away; it will forever be deeply etched in my soul.

Anthrax poisoning enumerated the many ways in which I defended against the shadow aspects of myself. Anthrax allowed me to reach my darkest point, so that I could begin to learn the lesson of surrender. This necessary shattering enabled me to begin to discover my deeper self. While I previously had difficulty embracing ambiguity, becoming infected with anthrax taught me more about how to better embrace uncertainty. There was no definitive evidence I was poisoned with anthrax, even though the medical pieces of the puzzle strongly suggested this. I had to embrace my medical quandary of not knowing what I was poisoned with but still hold on to my experience of falling ill to find my inner voice and creativity. It got me out of my childhood cage of needing to be dogmatically certain and begin to embrace living with the beauty of uncertainty.

This was an alchemic reaction morphing my childhood rage that gradually blossomed into an exponentially enhanced capacity for compassion for myself and others. I gradually learned how to listen and feel more deeply. Because I was so weakened, I could begin to embrace my fear of being defective which was covering all my vulnerabilities. I was a wounded kid, unable to feel fully related, denied the intimacy of a nourishing relationship with a mother. So I sensed that I was infectious and unlovable. But ironically by becoming ill, I realized that I was not defective, but instead I was fed sour milk. I learned how to embrace the true energy of fearlessness, which is my light. Fearlessness at its base is love energy. By turning and more deeply facing my fear of feeling infectious, I allowed myself to be more vulnerable to admit that I was sick and hurt, but it was not because I was unlovable, rather it was due to being poisoned. By focusing on that energy, I cleared sickness from my body. By becoming sick, although initially terrifying I learned the joy of letting my partner know me, and I let go of the known childhood pattern of relating by being manhandled and mistreated. By becoming ill, I learned how to surrender to rest, open to new treatment possibilities and let others care for me.

When I was healthy, I had the luxury of forgetting that my immune system functioned as a precise, intra-related cellular cascade (Cerfolio, 2016). Suddenly, at the age of 45, I quickly transformed from a vibrant, high-achieving psychiatrist and ultra-marathoner to a sickly, immunocompromised, and bedridden patient. I may never know definitively with what I was poisoned, or precisely how I was poisoned, but I do know why I was poisoned. I was a female, American physician who was providing medical and psychological care to Chechens while Putin's army was waging war against them by abducting, torturing, and killing civilians in an attempt to eradicate them from the face of the earth.

But as a result of becoming ill, I experienced a spiritual awakening, which consisted of an active awareness of transcendent aspects within myself that created a profound interconnectedness with something much larger than myself, and was essential to my recovery. Through my spiritual growth, anthrax ironically provided a path, for both myself and later for my patients, to shift from submission (signified by the need either to acquiesce or rebel) to surrender (signified by being open to and expanded by the subjectivity of the other). In this journey, we become able to uncover and know our true souls.

While struggling to understand and address my many physical symptoms, I began to learn the value of "surrender," a term I frame as a positive alternative to "submission." Ghent (1990) understood that surrender has nothing to do with hoisting a white flag; he and I use "surrender" in an Eastern philosophical sense, as an antithesis to submission and masochism and in contrast to the traditional English definition of the word. Rather than carrying a connotation of defeat, surrender enables the liberation and expansion of the self by lowering one's defensive barriers. In a successful surrender, acceptance occurs, and one transcends the condition that evoked the surrender. Rather than being a loss, surrender is joyous in spirit, fulfilling what Winnicott (1953) describes as the yearning to give up the false self in order to find fulfillment. Submission, by contrast, is a defensive mutant of surrender, a giving up of agency by either seeking approval or rebelling against another's wishes.

While those with chronic illness will have different manifestations than my own, the key to our recoveries is learning the lesson of surrender, which involves the discovery of a sense of unity with the universe, and letting go of submission, which involves the feeling of being a puppet. In my own case, anthrax both laid me low and humanized me, stripping me of the ability to use athletics as a way to feel invincible and prevent others from getting close. No longer able to exhaust my body through physical exercise, I found that spiritual parts of myself that had been closed off were gradually aroused. Anthrax was the violent explosion that shattered my defensive and false sense as warrior king. This recognition catalyzed the beginning of my shift into a deeper understanding of a higher spiritual state of enhanced love, with a previously unknown sense of limitlessness.

Although initially horrified at being poisoned, I came to console myself by immodestly inviting myself into such venerable company of dissenters of authoritarianism, also poisoned, such as Anna Polotskaya, Alexander Litvinenko, Vladimir Kara-Murza, Alexei Navalny, and Dmitry Muratov.

Carl Jung (Stein, 1999) believed that the crucifixion of Christ was the prototype of the human being crucified between two different levels of consciousness. According to Jung's version of Christianity, the crucifixion represents two aspects of the world, the horizontal beam represents the materialistic world of doing and the vertical beam represents the spiritual realm of being. Before becoming ill, I focused on "doing," in a futile attempt to undo my feeling of worthlessness. With all my doing, my life had less meaning, and I often felt empty. Anthrax poisoning laid me low, so that I could no longer "do" and run away from my feeling that began in childhood of being infectious and defective. It pushed me to transform from the horizontal beam of the human world of doing and to the vertical beam of the heavenly realm of being and spirituality. While my physical body had been compromised my spirit took the helm illuminating for me true invincibility. As a result of becoming ill, I began to identify, understand, and connect to transcendent aspects of reality. I caught glimpses of comprehending that ordinary reality is both separate and bound to transcendent reality. Daily meditation and attentive solitude made my life bearable.

An example of the horizontal beam of the cross, symbolizing the material world, is my struggle and difficulty with pointed corners of furniture. When I was a child in a painfully intolerable situation, instead of processing my anxiety, I became bothered by the points of furniture, which agitated me. I had attributed this aversion to my having been born with a post-lenticular cataract in my right eye, which contributed to severe photosensitivity with increased perception of light being reflected off the points.

I now have a deeper understanding of my dislike of points. This was a displacement of my fear of my mom who could be viciously critical and attacking. I began to fear the points on furniture as potential daggers that could harm me. If I expressed any differing feelings, my mom would aggressively shout them down. She lived mostly at the surface, on a point in the materialistic realm, which cut us because there was only room for one person's feelings. Living on a point, in this case ego, is small and limited. It gives way to judgmental and self-pitying behavior.

In contrast to my struggle with pointed corners in the materialistic realm is Jung's reference to the vertical, spiritual beam of the cross symbolized by bindi, the center point of a circle. Bindi, often red, is worn by Indian women on the Third eye spot (said to be the space between the eyebrows linked to awareness, perception, and spiritual communication) and connected with the sacred syllable "Om." In Hermetic philosophy and in some versions of Hinduism, bindi is considered to be the point at which creation begins and represents "the all," which is eternal, prior to creation and even above the concept of God. Shaktipat is when a spiritual leader confers spiritual energy to another by touching the Third eye spot to go spiritually higher, leading to self-realization. In Hindi, "shakti" means psychic energy and "pat" means to fall. On activating this center, the aspirant is encouraged to overcome the ego's sense of individuality and ascend to the spiritual realm.

In a powerful moment when I received shaktipat from a spiritual leader, I was overcome with a strange tidal wave of inner peace, comfort, calm, and security (Cerfolio, 2016). Feeling a sudden weakening of my knees, I was brought back to a place where I was more deeply connected with the divinely feminine within me. Divine feminine nature is passive. It is this passivity and peace that opened my heart and soul to be better able to receive and let others more deeply know me. In Hebrew, Nina means "God was gracious" or "God has shown favor." I was brought back and reminded of my true inner gracious state.

After years of spiritual work where I felt welcomed into a rich universe of belonging and acceptance, my fear of being infectious slowly softened. Illuminating this slow erosion of feeling infectious, I had a dream of being transformed into a seal. First, I am on a boat protecting the seals swimming in the ocean. Then I am in a submarine, moving along with the seals that are swimming through the watery depths. Ecstatically, I become one of the seals and am dancing with them in a circular motion moving upwards to the light. All of a sudden we are being hunted by a pointed spear gun. I turn into a mermaid, my tail turns into a wet sleeping bag. I am late for my next patient. Mom is supposed to pick me up, but she does not show up. I run to my appointment with my patient, but I have to climb the scaffolding of a huge water tank with circular ladders around it. There is not enough piping, and I am left dangling in the air at a tremendous height. I realize I will be late for my patient but somehow make it to my office.

In the dream, I begin to let go of my enmeshed connection with mom in which we both felt infectious; it is slowly deteriorating. A mermaid's tail is pointed. As a kid, I functioned as mom's maid, and I became a mermaid in the dream. My beloved psychoanalyst insightfully commented that "mermaid" is "her maid," a symbolic play of words in my dream. I finally gradually learn to escape from the pointed, materialistic land of my mother to attempt to become more grounded and rounded. Allowing others to express differing emotions and thoughts facilitates a deeper mutual understanding and interconnection, a wholeness, which strengthens and encourages our society to become more of a beautiful mosaic through diversification. Becoming a seal represents the esoteric aspects of life that are invisible to the quotidian eye, and are beyond the materialistic life but remain a hidden part of us. The rounded part of me is something much higher that brings a profound sense of belonging, equality, and solidarity. Rounded symbolizes largeness, inclusiveness, surrender, expansiveness, grounded, connection to all creation, and divinity.

NOTES

1 An earlier version of a portion of this chapter appeared in Cerfolio (2016) and is gratefully reprinted with permission from Cambridge University Press.
2 An earlier version of a portion of this chapter appeared in Cerfolio (2020) and is gratefully reprinted with permission from Harmony Editorial Team. Harmony is a publication of the Medical Humanities program in the Curricular Affairs department at the University of Arizona College of Medicine, University of Arizona Health Sciences, and the Kenneth Hill Foundation.
3 The Consolidated Appeals Process includes numerous United Nations organizations like the International Organization for Migration, the Red Cross, and the United Nations International Children Fund (UNICEF).
4 Typically, gastrointestinal anthrax symptoms occur one to five days after the ingestion of spores (Cerfolio, 2016). The classic signs are an initial prodromal phase with fever, muscle soreness, and temporary loss of consciousness caused by a fall in blood pressure; a second progressive phase with nausea, vomiting, ascites, and severe weakness; and a fulminant phase with increasing abdominal girth, expanding ascites, and shock. Many of these symptoms matched mine, yet I also subsequently developed chronic inflammation, arthralgia, autoimmune disorder, and food allergies.
5 One of the most prominent cases of gastrointestinal anthrax in the United States was reported by Klempner et al. (2010), at the Massachusetts General Hospital, involving a 25-year-old woman who inhaled aerosolized spores and then ingested them by drumming on an anthrax-contaminated animal-hide drum. While she was septic and acutely ill, anthrax was diagnosed by blood cultures.
6 Kanafani et al. (2003) found that GI anthrax is extremely rare in the West and that information about the clinical manifestations of GI anthrax is poorly detailed and inaccurate. However, Hatami et al. (2010) reported that GI anthrax is not as rare as previously thought and presents with unusual clinical manifestations that often go undiagnosed.

REFERENCES

Anderson, S. (2017, March 30). None dare call it a conspiracy. *GQ*. http://www.gq.com/story/moscow-bombings-mikhail-trepashkin-and-putin

Cerfolio, N. (2016). Loss, surrender, and spiritual awakening. *Palliative and Supportive Care*, *14*(6), 725–726. http://doi.org/10.1017/S1478951516000304

Cerfolio, N. (2016, February 17). *Amma - The hugging saint*. https://ninacerfoliomd.com/blog/amma-the-hugging-saint

Cerfolio, N. (2016, February 21). *Sleuthing my medical mystery*. https://ninacerfoliomd.com/blog/sleuthing-my-medical-mystery

Cerfolio, N. (2020). From Russia with anthrax. *Harmony, 2020*, 28–35.

Cerfolio, N. (2020). Terrorism and the psychoanalytic origins. *The Journal of Psychohistory, 47*(4), 256–274.

Dunlop, J. B. (with Knight, A.). (2014). *The Moscow bombings of September 1999: Examination of Russian terrorist attacks at the onset of Vladimir Putin's rule.* Ibidem Press.

Evans, B. (2005, December 4). An incomplete picture. *The Daily Press.* https://www.dailypress.com/news/dp-anth-day1dec02-story.html

Ghent, E. (1990). Masochism, submission, surrender: Masochism as a perversion of surrender. *Contemporary Psychoanalysis, 26*(1), 108–136. https://doi.org/10.1080/00107530.1990.10746643

Hatami, H., Ramazankhani, A., & Mansoori, F. (2010). Two cases of gastrointestinal anthrax with an unusual presentation from Kermanshah (western Iran). *Archives of Iranian Medicine, 13*(2), 156–159.

Kanafani, Z. A., Ghossain, A., Sharara, A. I., Hatem, J. M., & Kanj, S. S. (2003). Endemic gastrointestinal anthrax in 1960s Lebanon: Clinical manifestations and surgical findings. *Emerging Infectious Diseases, 9*(5), 520–525. http://doi.org/10.3201/eid0905.020537

Klempner, M. S., Talbot, E. A., Lee, S. I., Zaki, S., & Ferraro, M. J. (2010). Case 252010 — A 24-year-old woman with abdominal pain and shock. *The New England Journal of Medicine, 363*(8), 766–777. http://doi.org/10.1056/NEJMcpc1003887

Litvinenko, A., & Felshtinsky, Y. (2007). *Blowing up Russia: The secret plot to bring back KGB terror.* Encounter Books.

Nass, M. (2007, May 31). *Evidence anthrax vaccine causes heart attacks.* Anthrax Vaccine. http://anthraxvaccine.blogspot.com/2007/05/evidence-anthrax-vaccine-causes-heart_31.html

Satter, D. (2016). *The less you know, the better you sleep: Russia's road to terror and dictatorship under Yeltsin and Putin.* Yale University Press. http://doi.org/10.12987/9780300221145

Stein, M. (1999). *Encountering Jung on Christianity.* Princeton University Press (p. 230).

Wampler, R. A., & Blanton, T. S. (Eds.). (2001, November 15). *The September 11th sourcebooks, Volume 5: Anthrax at Sverdlovsk, 1979: U.S. intelligence on the deadliest modern outbreak* (National Security Archive Electronic Briefing Book No. 61). The National Security Archive. https://nsarchive2.gwu.edu/NSAEBB/NSAEBB61/

Winnicott, D. W. (1953). Transitional objects and transitional phenomena; A study of the first not-me possession. *The International Journal of Psychoanalysis, 34*(2), 89–97.

3

Healing Ocular Vision While Opening and Expanding My Noetic Eye[1,2,3]

Not all seeing is physical.

DOI: 10.4324/9781032633497-4

Suddenly, in 2011, my eyes no longer functioned as translucent lenses. Waking up with blurry vision was terrifying. Inexplicably, I could not read, which for me was horrifying. I immediately scheduled an emergency appointment with my ophthalmologist of 25 years. After he tested my vision, he exclaimed, "Your intraoptic pressure is suddenly elevated. You have glaucoma, which usually affects diabetics and the elderly. It's rare in someone as young as you. I will have to do surgery to get the pressure back down." I asked, "Isn't there anything I can do to get the pressure down *without* surgery?" He responded, "No, leaving the pressure elevated is dangerous as your vision may remain impaired." So I scheduled the eye surgery. Still, I thought, there had to be *something* I could do. I also wanted to know *why* this was happening. But in my heart, I already knew. At that point, I'd known half of the reason. So when the ophthalmologist said that my intraoptic pressure was elevated, it made sense to me. Anthrax causes inflammation, and swelling creates elevated pressure, even swelling in the eyes. What followed was an experience beyond my physical sight that brought the other half of the why squarely into focus (Cerfolio, 2021).

I had exactly one month before my scheduled eye surgery. Armed with my predisposition to achievement and driven by an ever-stronger desire to avoid surgery, I went to work to find something, anything I could do that would reduce the elevated pressure in my eye. One month to find the correct answer to, "What can I do to heal this?" With just 30 days to make a move, it had to be a good one. My chosen move can best be described as a *spiritual journey*, and it would prove to be the smartest, most rewarding one I've made. I began turning inward to look for answers, determined to face with courage whatever I found.

I'd grown accustomed to receiving hard medical news and feelings of frustration with conventional medicine's failure after my poisoning to identify and treat the etiology. I had already become my staunchest advocate and began to supplement my medical regime with alternative, often illegal approaches, like the Rife machine. I began to more fully accept the responsibility to change myself and facilitate my healing, physically and spiritually. This journey is now 17 years long and has resulted in a dramatic improvement in the quality of my life. Though the details of my quest are too numerous to specify here, I will offer the briefest of outlines.

All of what I did to heal, not just my eyesight but every physical ailment, I began to do within a spiritual context. By this I mean I viewed my life as a practice to foster insight, change, compassion, and transcendence. I began to meditate daily and open my heart to the unity of all life. I came to see my suffering as the price I had to pay for awakening to a greater truth about myself and the world. I have learned to be more accepting and loving to myself rather than seeking support from my family and validation from others that I was poisoned. Though I didn't know that truth yet, I felt sure I'd discovered the right path to finding it. I wasn't simply seeking to be well again. I was changing the way I thought, felt and acted, about the past *and* present. I was changing the way I lived. For the first time, I was attending to both sides of my life: the life I was living *and* the life that was living me. Back in the driver's seat, I would no longer be a passive passenger.

One of the many exercises I did during this time was to attempt to still myself and listen to an insight offered by my illness, in this case glaucoma. During this stillness, I was able to focus more on the emergent beauty in the world. Focusing on flaws was less important and my vision became less myopic and I began to sense a unity with the universe. The insights came with a feeling of love that cannot be properly articulated, a love that seemed given from the beyond. This sense of love carried no judgment with it, but rather acceptance. It made me see that I often judged and in so doing limited my vision to a flawed world that always needed to be fixed from my perception of breaking, an impossible goal since everything is forever in a state of change.

I had struggled to embrace the other side of this: that everything is also in a state of making, of becoming, and the forms of being are most precious because they are so terribly vulnerable, because they break. To see the first side and not the second fosters belief in a discouraging and destructive half-truth. In the Kabbalah, the creation myth involves this life cycle of making and breaking where God sent ten holy vessels each filled with primordial light. But the vessels were too fragile to contain such a powerful divine light. They broke apart and the holy sparks were scattered and evil got some of God's power. It is our holy mission to repair the world by gathering these sparks, no matter where they are hidden (Schwartz, 2007).

I also began to embrace my vulnerability and see my competitive, relentless drive to achieve what it was psychologically: a failed defense against a cruel childhood. My illness laid me bare. I saw how weak I had become and could further become if I didn't love and take care of myself. I wanted to survive this illness so I relinquished having to win at all costs. I no longer had the luxury of hurting myself because I felt unworthy or pushing away love and care from others because it felt scary or foreign. I decided to stop being blindly driven by my fear of inadequacy. I let go of my obsession with victory. I admitted to myself that my deep distrust of others had alienated me socially and foreclosed the possibility of real intimacy. I sought a new way of being in my life that allowed me to be authentically connected to people I love. I decided to open up and let go. Once I made these deeply moving decisions, my life began to transform and be more expansive, which was the benefit of learning that I can do better in my life.

The scars of the shortage of mothering in my family came up—the shortage that had lured my sister and I into a competitive trap from which I am actively working to transform into a more loving relationship. Different memories of my own mean behavior as a kid began to surface: I once forced my younger sister into playing a sadistic game of "lifeguard." I would push her into the deep water and prevent her from getting to the ledge to rest. Treading water till she was exhausted, I then "rescued" her, by pulling and returning her to safety.

My atrocious behavior with my sister was an expression of my frustration and rage emanating from a deep painful chasm. My understanding of the cruel game I played with my sister was that I was attempting unconsciously to undo the trauma of my childhood when I metaphorically was pushed into deep water but never rescued. My mother would praise my sister as sweet and loving but condemn me as nasty and unlovable, leaving me in a desert of loneliness. My father would taunt me with the athletic achievements of my peers until I felt drowning with anxiety. When I was a teenager, my parents and sister abandoned me at a party after I had been "Mickey Finned" in danger of being sexually attacked (Cerfolio, 2019).

I remembered another example of my childhood meanness in my relationship with two sisters who lived across the woods. I was friends with the two sisters, one older and the other girl younger than me. The older sister and I often teamed up against her younger sister. We excluded her from our games and often treated her cruelly when she lagged behind or took too long to get dressed before we all went out to play. I revisited memories like these and memories of how I was treated at home without judging or feeling sorry for myself. I simply *felt* them deeply and let the new feelings that resulted from feeling them in this way guide me.

I realized that I had carried my mean behavior into my relationships with men, taking my example from the way my mother treated my father and other men. Every Sunday she mocked the good-looking, younger man who collected money at our Catholic mass. After smiling sweetly at him and putting money in his basket, she stuck her tongue out at his back and whispered to me and my brothers that his bow tie made him look like Bozo the Clown. I always wondered why she laughed behind his back. Was she secretly attracted to him? As far as I could see, he did nothing to deserve her derision. Perhaps his self-containment and ease put her own self-loathing into sharper relief.

According to Ferenczi, one often avoids processing pain by unconsciously identifying with the aggressor. It is so less agonizing to be the ghost of my mother's friend and not her victim. My mother related to others by making war and not love; it was a strong bond that I had shared with her. I could not have my mother but I could be and act like her to form a whole nexus of a warring tribe.

Later I unconsciously repeated that pattern with men that I dated—the sweet smile masking contempt, though I often became openly abusive. I shared a bottle of wine over dinner with Beau, a blond-haired, blue-eyed "master of the universe," who worked on Wall Street. Beau seemed confident and happy, making my "inherited" self-loathing and feeling of unworthiness more apparent. I made the mistake of drinking more than one glass of wine with dinner. I felt tipsy and the rest of the night became a blur. When I did not hear from Beau for several days, I became convinced that he had not contacted me because I was not pretty or skinny enough. When he finally called me, I asked him why it took so long. He said, "Don't you remember saying, 'I hate you? Go to hell.'" Reminded of my verbal assault, I had a vague recollection and felt utterly mortified.

Winning and dominating was a black-and-white sadomasochistic world, one split between winners and losers. In that world, my sickness as a result of suspected anthrax poisoning and my childhood made me a loser, despite my accomplishments. Now I began to realize the destructive limitations of that vicious viewpoint. In denying vulnerability, change, and mortality, I denied reality. That winner–loser viewpoint excludes all other viewpoints except its own. It turns life into a sick dogma where hatred, fear and loathing reign supreme. In that world, love does not exist. In leaving that world I discovered that human reality is vulnerable, complex, and uncertain.

My illness forced me to live with uncertainty. At first I hated it, but as I began to accept it, I learned much more about myself in a painful but beautiful way. After my transformation, I gradually learned to surrender to a greater receptivity to the unknown, which created an enhanced spaciousness in my psychoanalytic relationship to further allow my patients' becoming. As a result of becoming ill, I learned to surrender, which required a certain pliability and lessening of my brittle defensiveness to have more faith to dive into the uncertainty of the unknown.

I wanted to open my eyes ever wider to see what was within and before me. I was educated enough to know that many learned people would find that goal so vague as to be laughable. "To see what?" they might ask. "To see the reflection of your own faith-based perspective? To see what your mind has staged for you to see? To see your neat little attempt to rationalize your miserable illness into some major transformative quest?" Yes, yes, and yes, but with one profound caveat: *To see what happens when one surrenders to the power of life and meets one's fate with open arms and an open heart.*

I believed, deeply believed, after all I'd been through, that there was something to see, something real and incredible and beautiful, beyond the narrow frame of one's ideas and projections. One could say I'd developed faith in a beyond I did not yet fully recognize. I felt it was close, like a great storm, brewing over a turbulent horizon that would one day sweep me up in its majesty. Meanwhile, I waited and prepared and helped myself heal. I took every setback as practice, as preparation.

Suspected anthrax poisoning and resulting glaucoma was my spiritual wake-up call. I took impaired vision to be symbolic as well as physical, seeing it as a condition of my total existence. Not only was I impaired in seeing beyond my critical do-or-die perspective, but I also tended to find fault with everything and everyone, part of my family inheritance. My distorted vision kept me pathologically joined to my family and fearful of being vested in happiness. The vestige of my childhood wounds prevented me from fully laying down my cudgel. A large part of me remained mistrustful of pleasure and joy. My life and perspective had become so misaligned that I literally could not see the forest for the trees. How could I? My intraoptic pressure was elevated.

My insights generalized to my work with patients. I realized my mother had partly accompanied me into my psychiatric psychoanalytic practice, which could have an undercurrent of judgment. Despite my being psychoanalyzed, at times my mom still sat above my right shoulder reminding me that all I did was a failure. Through meditation, I began to be slowly liberated from my maternal identification of being a failure and released into the vastness of a more nurturing identity. By a larger part of me leaving her at the door, I began to see my patients not so much as suffering from some form of psychopathology but as precious living and dying beings, engaged in a poignant struggle to grow and discover their own creativity and in, some instances, their spirituality. I welcomed their "symptoms" as letters from the unknown meant to help me in guiding them.

Any power I unknowingly wielded with my mother was only acknowledged when it suited her, to further a self-serving narrative, and then squashed. With a joyfully decorated Christmas tree resplendent with perfectly decorated gifts lying underneath tinseled branches, single-handedly as a child with a different opinion, I could "ruin" my mom's holiday dinner, which she said in front of family and friends because mom knew only how to live an emotionally impoverished life. As a result of healing metaphysically from glaucoma, I began to really, truly see with a wider lens that I was not the virus that infects and "ruins" my relationships and life. I began to be able to look at my family more honestly to see their infirmities and resisted blaming myself for not being loved or for them not loving themselves. I realized I did not cause, nor was I responsible for, their limitations, which was quite painful because it meant letting go more deeply of my desperate wish to be seen and loved by them.

For the first time in my life, I noticed that certain insights had taken root in my existence and rather than being just interesting thoughts had become *living perspectives*. This is what I came to deeply believe—that for me, all this is spiritual truth, but I would never be so arrogant as to insist on its veracity to anyone else. All are equally welcome to take from it or walk away. Here is what I saw with my newfound spiritual sight:

I saw that, radically speaking, I am neither above nor below anyone and that the idea of equality derives from an even deeper truth: not one of us has a more *intrinsic* right to live than anyone else. I saw that significant sentience is not simply confined to human beings but falls across a spectrum and is distributed among the vast array of life forms and that all life should be accorded with respect and dignity. As creatures bearing the treasure and burden of a sophisticated intelligence and consciousness, wielding evolved technical power, we can be the guardians of these life forms or their destroyers.

I saw that the separation of the body and the mind *and the self from the world* that was so much a part of my Western medical school training and practice is only part of the story. There is no such thing as only a physical illness, even when one is poisoned; and there is no such thing as merely a mental illness. Everything that occurs in the mental realm results in a physical consequence, and everything that occurs in the body results in a mental consequence. Furthermore, the world I inhabit is the one I embody, the only one I will ever know. In that world every-thing I do *counts*. What happens to me happens to that world and what happens to that world happens to me. I may separate them, body and mind, self and world, for the sake of convenience and practical action, but I delude myself when I believe the separation is real.

This sense of reality led me to a deeper insight. I began to see that all the boundaries that separate us, even the borders of our own flesh, are permeable and ultimately illusionary—that at base everything that comes to exist derives from a primordial and inviolable unity. I am one and I am many. I am separate and I am not separate. I am born and I die. Yet, as I am all this—what was, what is, and what will be—and as all this, there will never come a time I cease to exist. The most important relationship I will ever have is the one I have with the totality. The idea of that relationship is utterly abstract and transcendent, but the experience of it is concrete and immanent. This relationship with totality is based on faith and practice and is the ground of all of my other relationships.

My view in no way faults those struggling with any illness, or the personal paths and journeys with illness others take. I write with neither certainty nor arrogance. It is faith and direct, personal experience from which I speak. Though I am deeply committed to my viewpoint, its very nature carries an aversion to imposing it on someone else. To blame someone for being sick is both ignorant and cruel. Likewise, suggesting my viewpoint is "right" or the only way is arrogant. While those with chronic illness will have different manifestations than my own, the key to our recoveries, I believe, is learning the lesson of surrender.

Surrender involves releasing oneself from the bondage of ego and discovering the unity and acceptance underlying being. It is the opposite of submission, which means feeling like a puppet and a victim. Slowly, I continued to learn how to rest and let feelings flood into me, so I could begin to have deeper and more nurturing relationships, starting with the one I have with myself. Anthrax laid me low but humanized me, leading me to accept my fragility and learn greater self-love and intimacy. In many ways, anthrax brought me home. Unable to distract or divert and exhaust my body through exercise, my spiritual dimension became awakened through stillness and meditation, and I began to embrace the beauty and gifts of my vulnerabilities. This recognition began to catalyze my shift into a higher state of enhanced love, with a previously unknown sense of limitlessness.

I meditated. I prayed for strength. I took my supplements. I kept my mind clear and my heart opened. I listened in the stillness. I practiced. I kept my faith. I more fully accepted my situation while taking more responsibility for it. I changed the way I lived my life. I "let go," over and over. I waited patiently.

On the day of the follow-up appointment—30 days after learning I needed surgery, my ophthalmologist tested my pressure. At first he shook his head and angrily hit his instrument, muttering to himself. When he finally convinced himself that nothing was wrong with his tonometer, he incredulously told me my pressure was normal. He chalked it up to my "intense Ironman and ultramarathon exercise regimen." I didn't bother to tell him that I was no longer able to work out as I once did. I did not need the surgery. To this day my intraocular pressure remains normal. That was the last time I saw him.

Through suspected anthrax poisoning I gained spiritual sight while healing physical sight. Then my mystical meeting with a wild gray whale further enhanced my noetic sight. This transformative encounter allowed me to glimpse a vision of reintegrated consciousness as I surrendered to the numinous nature of human vulnerabilities and struggles. Through my otherworldly moment with this whale, I felt resurrected to begin to see the breadth of the world. The whale welcomed me into a new infinite, rich universe of emotional spaciousness. Despite descriptive words girdling my spiritual experience, I invite you to come with me on my uncanny encounter.

Imagine being in the Pacific Ocean, 15 feet away from a wild, 40-ton, pregnant migratory whale. In January 2015, while in Laguna Beach, California, I decided to go paddle board surfing for the first time. After signing up for a lesson, I met my instructor on the pristine beach. The Pacific Ocean was serene; there was hardly a wave breaking the shore. While still on the beach, my instructor showed me how to use my paddle to negotiate the surfboard. We took off on the ocean. As I gradually found my balance, we eventually went far from shore, and several whale sightseeing boats passed us. The passengers gasped with delight, and we were all thrilled to see a gray whale's heart-shaped, puffy blows at the surface of the water. We paddled farther from shore to visit a group of playful seals that dove through the Pacific Ocean. I gained more confidence with paddling on my surfboard and felt connected to the marine life around me. Although the ocean surface was as still as a smooth sheet of glass, a legion of life appeared beneath the surface (Cerfolio, 2017).

The whale I have come to call Molly—a magnificent gray whale who was 50 feet long but levitated from the sea momentarily motionless, reminiscent of the supernatural hovering ability of the hummingbird—suddenly spy-hopped, not once but twice, first about 15 feet away from me and then again 30 feet away, without creating a single ripple while I remained awestruck on my surfboard. Spy-hopping occurs when a whale vertically pokes its head and upper body out of the water for a look at activity above the water's surface. In no time our eyes met. I felt a great power emanate from her body. Molly seemed to be acting in a protective manner, like an attuned mother, by not creating a ripple, as I was shaky and learning a new skill. If whales can smile, I felt Molly was smiling and greeting me.

With her vertical half-rise out of the water, Molly's upper body filled my entire field of vision, and I surrendered to the astounding moment and remained motionless. But when our eyes gravitated toward each other, she not only evoked the divine and sublime within me but challenged me to reevaluate my perception of intelligent, conscious life. There was a glimmer of light in her walnut-sized brown eye. Her wise, soulful left eye held and contained me, like none other, for what felt like an eternity, but was in reality just 20 seconds. Her large eye seemed to be expressing my unexplored thoughts and actions; she was beckoning me to go deeper with them. I felt an immediate kinship with her. As I was born legally blind in my right eye, my right pupil is larger than my left, and I use primarily unifocal vision to read. This method of seeing is similar to that of gray whales, who also use unifocal vision, as opposed to most humans who focus bifocally.

One could easily identify in my post-delivery baby photographs that my right pupil was much larger than my left due to a post lenticular cataract, which in medical school I had learned is indicative of a congenital cataract. Usually, this congenital malformation is diagnosed on a routine, neonatal pediatric examination with an ophthalmological scope. Despite my father being a physician, my cataract was not detected until I was in first grade. When I was 6 years old, I was exhilarated to finally have my turn to be sent out of class for my eye exam. After the exam, I was frustrated to not be able to read the examiner's note, which was written in script, as I could only read print. As I knew something was wrong, desperately, I struggled upon returning to class to make sense of her script. When my mom heard the news that I was legally blind in my right eye, she responded, "All my children were skunk cabbage and garbage." I remember thinking "What is skunk cabbage?" and asked her if we could have it for breakfast the next day. For a long time after this, we played a sadistic game in which I covered my good eye and my mom would ask me to detect the number of fingers she was holding in front of me. My mom's contempt toward me left me feeling defective.

What an affirming surprise to find that my Molly has unifocal vision just like me. Under Molly's monocular vision, I felt recognized and accepted, in contrast to my mom's bifocal vision, within which I felt abandoned and marginalized. Molly's loving gaze welcomed me into a rich world of infinite, emotional spaciousness. In my relationship with my mom, there was only emotional room for her. I was raised to be a good Catholic girl and not have a voice. I was "bad Nina" when I expressed myself, especially if it did not reflect back to my mom what she felt. She had two healthy physical eyes, but could only see herself.

Before that day out on the ocean, I felt like a captive to my mom, but I began to be able to glimpse the breadth of the world through my stunning and life-altering moment with Molly. Now it feels so clear that I was blinded, and now I see.

My seasoned instructor was wonderstruck by Molly's monumental half-vertical rising and towering over me at such an intimate distance. Fifty feet to the side of Molly and me, he captured on his camera only Molly's footprint in the ocean as she used her massive fluke to dive deeper into the ocean depth away from me. With one push of her tremendous fluke, Molly left 8-foot-wide footprints in the ocean water. I felt Molly was saying to me, "When you are big and you know it, you don't have to make a splash or have fangs. I don't have to play it; I am it." Despite being gargantuan, Molly moved with the flexibility and nimbleness reminiscent of actors like Zero Mostel. Molly was fat and womby. Far from being a cutting presence, my Molly was embracing and nurturing with a loving sweetness. Gray whales, in fact, have no teeth; instead, they have baleens, which are soft and composed of keratin, with the consistency of fingernails.

From late December through January, Molly was on her journey along with other pregnant grays, migrating from the Arctic seas along the Pacific coast to calve their babies in the warm lagoons of Baja, Mexico. These gray whales have the longest known migration of any mammals, traveling 12,000 miles round trip every year between the cold feeding waters of the Arctic Seas and the shallow, protective, warm waters of the lagoons of Mexico. Through her own mammoth journey to give birth, Molly was inviting and inspiring me to give birth to my deeper creativity, long stifled, and higher consciousness. Molly's profound kinship and attunement gave me the courage to become better able to distance myself from my childhood anxieties about being "an oddball." I slowly became emancipated to begin to express my thoughts and feelings with less criticism and a newfound sense of expansive freedom.

My instructor commented on how lucky I was, as gray whales are not known to spy-hop humans, much less at such a close distance, during their migration south. But this event felt as if it had nothing to do with luck; it was as if this divine creature and I were old soul mates who knew each other many lifetimes, millions of years ago, and together we had led pods of other whales through portals in the ocean. She was again greeting me, and I her.

People with whom I relive this mystical experience often ask me if I was scared. I was too awe-inspired to be scared, and from deep within I knew I had beckoned Molly forth that day, and we were again merged as one. She was a massive and wild animal who could easily bring me intentional or accidental harm by simply neglecting her body's orientation to mine. Instead, Molly not only exercised great care to not startle or dislodge me from my paddle surfboard but lent herself to be attuned and meet me. This pageantry of gentle and accepting attunement in such a dramatic and forceful, three-dimensional scale is the experience every baby needs. Molly seemed to understand and kept a respectful distance from me to not over-whelm me, but she chose to come close enough to meet me. Dr. Roger Payne, a pioneering whale biologist, refers to the "10-foot barrier" at which it simply feels too uncomfortable and terrifying to be any closer to a whale (Austin, 2013, p. 11). Molly had the mindfulness to respect this 10-foot barrier and my personal space by spy-hopping me at a distance of 15 feet, allowing me to feel safe during our encounter.

In no time, Molly conveyed to me a new way to listen, feel, and understand without using words. The emotions I have experienced as a result of this encounter resonate with the complex symbolism of whales as representing containment and resurrection in the Biblical story of Jonah and the whale. Jonah lived within the belly of the whale for three days before he came forth. Just as Jonah was given a second birth and resurrected, I felt reborn and resurrected by Molly to be inspired and have faith to go deeper within to rekindle my creativity, which had long been extinguished and buried in childhood through my mother's non-acceptance and ridicule. As I began to surrender by moving emotionally forward and inward to start writing a memoir, the symbol of Molly also taught me to insulate my crea-tive energies more conservatively and efficiently. Whales have an ancient knowl-edge of how to use the creative force of breath to conserve oxygen underwater by decreasing blood flow to areas of their body where it's nonessential. Molly, an ancient symbol for creation, showed me the magnificence and power of my own creativity and taught me not to keep myself small but to embrace my vulnerabili-ties and shine in order to find my authentic voice. Molly awakened me to a vision of a reintegrated consciousness to surrender to the numinous nature of my patients' struggles and a greater faith in the psychoanalytic process.

My inner corrective emotional experience, as a result of my encounter with Molly, marked a culmination of more than a decade of inner spiritual growth that emerged during a long-term illness. In the process of trying to get well, I caught a glimpse of my true self and divinity. Molly played a key role in giving me an aspiration to transcend from the ephemeral material world to the spiritual world and my wholeness, to be freed from submission through rebellion, and to become vulnerable through surrender. Molly's message was that I no longer had to be a warrior king but could surrender to my emotions in order to heal. She helped expand my vision to transcend any limitations of not only my physical sight, but also my way of being in the world.

Functioning as my spiritual mother, Molly taught me about how to handle vulnerability in the way she spy-hopped. Gray whales were hunted almost to the point of extinction in both the 1700s and early 1900s and have an excellent memory that reflects that history, as exemplified by their efforts to overturn boats when attacked. Despite this long history of being hunted by man and using her "collective unconscious," Molly, being pregnant and therefore vulnerable, was still open to determining who to trust and who to recoil from. I am in a lifelong process to learn how to let others in, in order to transcend my own opinions to an expanded understanding. Molly symbolizes living life as a spiritual adventure, letting go of agendas and expectations, and being open to the thoughts of others in order to expand yourself.

This transformational moment in which I encountered a fully attuned and surprisingly gentle "other" enabled me to move forward creatively. Similarly, Stern (1998) maintains that in the analytic relationship, the relational procedural domain compromises intersubjective moments occurring between patient and psychoanalyst that create new organizations and reorganize not only the relationship between the interactants, but more importantly the patient's implicit procedural knowledge. These "moments of meeting" (Stern, 1998, p. 903) or "now moments" (Stern, 1998, p. 903) expand and alter the patient's implicit procedural knowledge, which constitutes her ways of being with others. Similar to the psychoanalytic dyad, my encounter with Molly was a "moment of meeting" that transformed my "implicit relational knowing" (Stern, 1998, p. 908). I sensed a deeper connection to the ocean and universe. Learning to surrender to vulnerability and internalize a more nurturing world while overcoming a chronic illness helped me to achieve an expanded sense of wholeness.

This experience enabled me to awaken from my emotional deprivation, brought on by previous maternal non-attunement, to recognize my mystical mother. By beckoning and letting Molly come into me, as I had not let others, I let go of my old world of criticism and disappointment while internalizing a more nurturing, embracing one. My childhood was based on competing and performing to survive. By admitting to my loss on the most profound level of not having been introduced into a loving, accepting world, I was able to take in and connect with a massively attuned being. I was home, a place where I am whole, floating on my paddle surfboard next to an inquisitive, gentle whale whose soulful, wise left eye looked into and contained me. In Molly's recognition, I felt a clearer, fresher state of being and a greater sense of completeness.

Even though I had little previous experience of feeling chosen, I remained gob smacked by the fact that Molly had chosen me to have this ecstatic encounter.

Molly and I were amalgamated as one. I felt I finally belonged through my alignment with Molly. Maybe that piece of God was always slumbering within me, but Molly awakened me into that limitless land that is above the description of the phenomenal world of petty identifiers such as masculine and feminine. Molly escorted me into the noumenal world where the one is the point that cannot be broken. This was the place of expansiveness and extasis, where Molly pulled me out of my ordinary homeostatic existence. Similar to an alchemic conversion of dross into gold, my encounter with Molly was a parallel process of converting my human form into an elevated and higher spiritual force. Molly and I were momentarily suspended and beautifully intertwined in a nondual world. But I could not stay here long because there was too much light.

It was an honor that very few humans will experience, having contact with a whale in such an intimate way, in her natural habitat, and on her terms. By visualizing this day and imagining riding on Molly's back with her heart-shaped, puffy blows spraying me in my face while we breach the water's surface, I settle myself from the chatter in my mind to calm and center myself. Molly is my blanket, reassuring me that the world is an embracing one.

NOTES

1 Parts of this chapter appeared in an earlier version in Cerfolio (2017) and are gratefully reprinted with permission from Routledge Taylor & Francis Group.
2 Parts of this chapter appeared in an earlier version in Cerfolio (2021) and are gratefully reprinted with permission from The Spiritual Media Blog.
3 Parts of this chapter appeared in an earlier version in Cerfolio (2021) and are gratefully reprinted with permission from The Mindful Word.

REFERENCES

Austin, B. (with Earle, S. A.). (2013). *Beautiful whale*. Harry N. Abrams.
Cerfolio, N. (2017). My mystical encounter with a wild gray whale. *Psychoanalytic Perspectives, 14*(2), 265–269. http://doi.org/10.1080/1551806X.2017.1304133
Cerfolio, N. (2019, May 11). Leaping over the butcher's of Wayne, NJ. *Terror. House Magazine*. https://terrorhousemag.com/wayne/
Cerfolio, N. (2021, January 8). One good move. *The Spiritual Media Blog*. https://www.spiritualmediablog.com/2021/01/08/one-good-move/
Cerfolio, N. (2021, January 11). One good move: Through suspected anthrax poisoning I gained spiritual sight while healing physical sight. *The Mindful Word*. https://www.themindfulword.org/2021/spiritual-sight/
Schwartz, H. (2007). *Trees of souls: The mythology of Judaism*. Oxford University Press.
Stern, D. N., Sander, L. W., Nahum, J. P., Harrison, A. M., Lyons-Ruth, K., Morgan, A. C., Bruschweiler-Stern, N., & Tronick, E. Z. (1998). Non-interpretive mechanisms in psychoanalytic therapy. The 'something more' than interpretation. The process of change study group. *International Journal of Psychoanalysis, 79*(5), 903–921.

4

The Bicycle Shrink

Hope is the Thing with Joe[1]

Hold onto hope.

After meeting Molly, as my ability to be temporarily liberated from need grew and I became better able to yield myself as a totality to another totality, I began a loving relationship with a man, whom I fondly named "the bicycle shrink." Walking into the Nyack Bike Store in 2011 was reassuring. It was not squeaky clean, but the place had an old-school, masculine charm. In the window an antique and functional Model T Ford tire pump sat proudly between bikes. A neon yellow windbreaker hung askew. Joe's store had a straightforward simplicity

DOI: 10.4324/9781032633497-5

that welcomed visitors. I rarely stopped on my 100-mile bike rides, and the store was not on my training agenda. But I felt dizzy and needed rest. The shop sat next door to the Hopper House, where the famous realist painter and printmaker Edward Hopper lived and painted. Eccentric locals often came to chat with Joe, and I saw that he cared and comforted them, these people living on the fringes (Cerfolio, 2020).

Upon my first visit, Joe, who had a lanky body, greeted me at the door. I felt strangely consoled by a bright clarity in his blue eyes. He asked, "Where did you ride from?"

Feeling defeated by my ever-ailing body, I said, "From the city. I usually ride up to Bear Mountain and back, but I don't feel up to it anymore."

"What do you do?"

"I'm a psychiatrist in Greenwich Village."

He nodded and smiled, leaning back against the counter. "I was a psychology major at Berkeley." I asked, "What made you come back to New York?" He rested his hand on the bikes and looked deeply into my eyes.

> When my dad became sick, I came back home to Nyack to be with him. He had me later in life. It was his second marriage. I felt that I didn't get to spend a lot of time with him growing up. I stayed here and opened my store in 1972.

The next day, Joe emailed me, but I fooled myself into believing that I was not attracted to him, so we initially connected just as friends. Although I found his bike store a safe haven to rest and enjoyed his welcoming presence, his romantic interest in me felt somehow unsettling and disorienting. But on a deeper unconscious level, Joe's making space and being so available shifted my emotional tectonic plates and my defenses were slowly shredded. If that feels like an exaggeration, what is all the more terrifying is that it is what happened. Hiding was my specialty. Self-taught growing up to suppress and protect my sensitivity, I kept a comfortable distance from him. Even though somewhere I craved affection and love—so foreign to any childhood experience I knew—Joe's mirroring was threatening the ironclad defenses that I nursed and made me *Untouchable Nina*, beyond human reach, safe in my self-reliance.

It is a similar dynamic to when a starving person begins to eat; they may become physically ill because they are so nutritionally depleted. I understood the Austrian-British author and psychoanalyst, Melanie Klein's writing to say that when you try to feed a starving child, they spitefully throw the food back at you. It is difficult for the people that Melanie Klein is writing about, including me, who are emotionally starved to accept care because it has become a dreaded source of humiliation. My avoidance of intimacy had guaranteed a sense of normalcy and safety, for others' transgressions, real or imagined.

A major part of what Joe loved about his store was hearing the stories of his various customers. He felt that each person had a story to tell. Later, Joe told me that upon our first meeting that he knew I had a secret. He sensed that I was sick even though it was not externally visible. Amazingly, he wanted to hear my story and actually listened to me.

I soon discovered that Joe knew his stuff: how to fix bikes; how to match bikes and equipment with bodies; how to make riding easier and more fun. The first ability reflected his practicality, the second his powers of observation, and the third his creative spirit. He recognized sadness in my eyes; I felt a connection with him. He seemed to care. His store served as a physical representation for Joe—the safe place I could just be and rest, before I made the 30-mile bike ride home to NYC. He exuded sincerity and an endearing street sense of wisdom. He was thoughtful, solving problems with simple ingenious solutions. He adjusted my cleats on my bike shoes, alleviating pressure on my shin splints. This small adjustment reduced my pain. No other coach had thought of this simple, cheap, and inventive solution. I affectionately began to refer to him as "the bicycle shrink."

Anything that reduced my physical pain was welcomed and greatly needed. I was being attacked by my own body. My life was derailed by these ailments; before getting sick, I could easily ride a hilly 100-mile plus route up to Bear Mountain and back to New York City. Now, a mere 30-mile bike ride to Nyack exhausted me. My screaming lungs produced mucus that had become my constant companion. I struggled to breathe through chronic congestion. Feeling sick most days— cramps, headache, bouts of diarrhea, strange infections, waves of fatigue, dizziness, nausea—I'd half-heartedly abandoned the idea of ever doing another triathlon. On top of flu-like symptoms, my shins constantly ached, exquisitely painful to even light touch. But when biking, my pain receded to the background. Endorphins. I refused to allow my body to defy me, so I kept pushing past the pain. Fury drove me. When healthy, I never tired and never experienced hitting a wall even when I ran Comrades, a 56-mile hilly ultramarathon. The only conditions that would stop me were unconsciousness or death. It was a longstanding coping technique; I wouldn't have survived my childhood if not for athletic achievement. With every step of endurance events, I exorcised my critical parents and superego. This was a war with my body. If I could not exercise, how would I go on living?

I had another war to wage—the one with the wreckage of my childhood. Each time I completed a long-distance race, I raised the bar on the mileage. When my body rose to the occasion, it was a statement of hope against the dark voices that told me I was inadequate. I set higher goals and achieving them undid my unworthiness for a moment. I attempted to overcome an emotionally violent childhood of neglect by covering longer distances in faster times. It was how I made sure I existed.

Desperate to continue my war and in denial of my ever-failing health, I entered the NYC Ironman a year prior to the event, even though I was sick and unable to train. The despair that drove me to feel visible provided a false strength. The weekend before the 2012 NYC Ironman, I took a long ride with a friend who convinced me to compete because I had been riding so effortlessly. I felt good that day, and that feeling filled me with optimism. The location of the event in my backyard bike-training route provided additional incentive.

Typically, one has to travel long distances to an Ironman. Given the way I felt most days, the idea of schlepping my "tri" gear to an event was daunting. The swim leg of the event would be in the Hudson River, an old friend to me. I swam in it as a member of a four-person team in a 27-mile race around Manhattan in 2007, despite being anemic with chronic diarrhea from Histolytica Amebiasis, a GI parasitic infection that can kill. The bike leg for the NYC Ironman ran adjacent to my normal training cycle, Route 9W. So, against good sense and the advice of most friends, I decided to attempt my second Ironman. This would be the first and last NYC Ironman held in New York City. When I felt up to it, I'd ride out to Nyack, but I needed to recuperate in Joe's bike shop. When I told him that I had signed up for the 2012 NYC Ironman, he arched his eyebrows skeptically.

"It's a dangerous course, Nina. I don't think you should compete. You've been too sick to train."

The course, he said, was a bitch: a hilly 112-mile bike ride along the Palisades Parkway, a 26.2-mile run along River Road, over the George Washington Bridge, then along the path next to the West Side Highway. The race finished in Riverside Park. "It's the hardest of any Ironman worldwide," he said.

To make it even more treacherous, the NYC Ironman was held in August. Even the NYC Marathon takes place in November to prevent runners from overheating and developing life-threatening ailments. The Ironman is 114.4 miles longer than a marathon.

Later, Joe admitted he hadn't initially believed me when I told him that I had signed up for the event, especially after he found out how ill I was. Joe knew about chronic sickness; he'd been poisoned with Agent Orange in the Vietnam War, and later, in his 60s, developed stage four mantle cell lymphoma. Despite chemotherapy, his health further declined, and he dropped down to 125 pounds. (He stands 6 feet tall with long, gangly arms, a great asset on the bike.) When the hospice nurse showed up at the house in which he was staying, Joe had sent her away because, "She was the angel of death." He wasn't ready to die, and, then at death's door, he went into full and inexplicable remission. I believe his strong, loving spirit was key to his recovery.

What follows now is a description of my inexorable defenses that securely locked me away from a cataclysmic event that meeting the bicycle shrink precipitated. Somehow his long arms eventually extended and reached across my iron wall.

On the hot and steamy August morning of the event, I awoke with flu-like symptoms, but I was determined to show up for the competition. Getting out of bed at 2 am to make the Manhattan ferry took every ounce of will I possessed. I hadn't even taken the first step, and already I felt defeated.

The 4 am ferry ride that carried hundreds of athletes along the Hudson River to the site of the event felt eerie. Dark and humid, the air was heavy in my lungs while people talked in whispers. The muddy water looked turbulent and forbidding. Would my weakened and untrained body meet this endurance challenge? Looking out over the water, I wondered if signing up for this monster event had been a bad decision.

Getting off another smaller boat that carried us to the open swim start platform, I plunged into the Hudson, and began the 2.4-mile swim. The exuberance I usually felt when beginning a physical challenge was absent. There was no rush of energy through my body, no feeling of great power in my limbs. Tired before beginning, I was crowded in the swim, getting hit by arms and legs as I was pushed by swimmers falling behind or moving ahead. Swallowing dirty water, I had 138.2 miles to go. Stabbing cramps erupted in my body. Luckily, the water gods were smiling down on us. A strong downhill current in the Hudson aided the swimmers. One could almost float down current to the course end.

When I finally emerged from the Hudson, I hit the bike. For the first 10 miles, I felt okay, fooling myself into thinking maybe I was in better shape than I thought. Many bikers whizzed by me, and soon the hilly ride along the Palisades felt like I was crawling over the burning mountains of hell. The heat and humidity had been steadily increasing, but somehow I kept pedaling. My back seized with cramping, something I had never experienced. Feeling like a twisted pretzel, I was afraid to get off my bike to urinate, for fear that I would be overcome with paralyzing cramps.

By the time I finished the 112-mile bike route, my mind was a hazy fragmented hollow of half-thoughts. Feeling weak and dizzy, I was hardly aware of my surroundings. The cramps and diarrhea kept coming. My back shrieked with sunburn. My second transition time between the bike and run, which normally takes several minutes, lasted over an hour. Zombie-like, I sat unable to get out of my bike clothes.

I was doing this race in honor of my cousin, Nicole, who died at 18 in a motorcycle accident. Nicole was my angel, and I'd felt her always by my side in spirit and pick me up whenever I struggled. During training swims when I panicked, unable to breathe from claustrophobia at the New York University pool, I imagined her vivacious spirit sitting on the edge of the diving board, at the end of my lane, cheering me on. When healthy prior to becoming sick, my training swims were 2 miles, twice a week. For her memory, I would not give up so easily.

Slowly, the volunteers helped me change into my running clothes, and I began the run. Though I felt broken, one foot kept putting itself in front of the other. Occasionally, I managed a weak jog. Normally, I ran an 8-to-10-minute mile pace throughout the Ironman marathon, but I was walking at a 13-to-16 minute per mile pace this time. Only 26.2 miles and 7 hours to go!

My mind fogged under the pressure of extreme exercise. As I walked, my body struggled to save itself, went into emergency mode, and shut down my mind. Pain and agony replaced my sense of self and time. Past and future ceased to exist. I was looking down a long blurry tunnel. My body turned into pure pain. Spectators tried to high-five me, but I pulled away for fear that I would crumble into a ball from cramps, unable to get up.

With the aid of my angels, I finished the event, coming in at a little over 16 hours. Usually my Ironman time is around 12 hours. A man with an arm amputated below the elbow finished directly in front of me. Many congratulated him on his perseverance in becoming an Ironman. I collapsed at the finish line. The medics picked me up, placed me into a wheelchair and whisked me off into the medical tent. Suffering from dangerously low blood sodium, I received several bags of IV fluid with sodium.

I had tempted fate and was lucky. The doctor wanted me transferred to the hospital. "Two athletes died today," he told me. "A firefighter overheated and drowned in the Hudson River. And a 20-year-old girl hit her head after crashing into another biker. She died from cerebral bleeding." Refusing his advice, I told him I had once run the Psychiatric ER and Walk-in-Clinic at St. Vincent's Hospital in Greenwich Village. "The last place I want to go is an emergency room on a Sunday morning," I said. "I want to go home." I soon found myself in a wheelchair delivered curbside.

When I arrived home at 3 AM, 25 hours after leaving to start the Ironman, I crawled out of the cab, into my co-op building hallway, and then into the elevator. Once inside my apartment, I went straight to bed.

The next day Joe emailed me. He knew I'd be in bed, which was where I remained for the next three days.

"Who was waiting at the finish for you?" he asked.

I wrote, "A lovely, young female patient of mine was waiting at the finish for several hours, but it got to be too late, and she had to go to sleep."

"Were your parents there? You told me that they live 30 minutes away."

"My parents have never been to any of my races."

Unbeknownst to me, Joe had been checking the last part of my progress on the computer, rooting me on. "I want to be at the finish line for your future races," he said.

> It's not wise to compete in endurance races alone, without any support. I did a 24-hour bike ride and was in the lead until I was hit by a car. Getting into my car, bleeding, to drive 200 miles home alone was scary.

He'd been following several other friends in the race, and after they finished, he wondered if I had actually entered the race. So he looked me up and found me still out on the course. It looked to him that I might not make the cut-off time. As he followed my trail against the clock, Joe started to yell at the computer, "Go, Nina, go!" It was past midnight. But I knew that if I kept under a 15-minute mile pace on the "run," I would finish.

We scheduled a bike ride the week after the Ironman. The 70-mile ride through the hills of Harriman State Park felt effortless. Letting myself be vulnerable and accepting love from Joe took much more effort. I felt threatened and overwhelmed by those ideas. I was ambivalent about ending my raging war. Joe offered me the possibility of a sweet surrender, but he represented a type of passivity that made me uncomfortable. That I didn't need to fight to win with Joe petrified me. I'd always had to fight like hell for whatever I wanted. But I realized that what was real was eternal, not physical. So much of our misery is self-inflicted.

Joe made me feel seen, something I didn't experience growing up. Our connection was deep: we both had suffered a heartbreaking betrayal that damaged our bodies, affecting our ability for endurance exercise, whose absence for both of us meant not being fully able to live.

After our ride, Joe invited me to his 19th-century farmhouse built in a small town nestled along the Hudson River. Standing out from his neighbors' large houses with perfectly manicured landscaping sat his small cottage obscured by wildly intertwined branches and thick bushes along a dirt road. While having tea at his picnic table, I asked why the daffodil bed next to his doorstep was crushed. "A doe with no front foot sleeps here at night," he explained,

"Do you feed her?"

"No," he said. "She needs to learn to forage for food. But the other deer ostracized her, and she feels safe here." I knew the feeling.

A few years later, when returning from a long bike ride, we saw a gracious bird with a 7-foot wingspan glide down and land in a nest on the top of a stately pine tree next to Joe's simple house. Later we identified it as a bald eagle. Seemed everybody felt safe there.

My illness slowed me down enough to allow a crack in the door for Joe. Slowly, I began to fall for him. And maybe my body was more expressive and cleverer than my well-worn, seemingly impregnable defenses, and the war was temporarily paused. I actually like this man. After learning that I had 20 food allergies, Joe graciously and incredibly took the time and taught me to cook around them. He found fun, creative dishes that we cooked together but met the criteria of my restricted diet.

Like the deer and eagle, a number of locals, who suffered from mental health issues, felt safe enough with Joe and regularly visited him. "Crazy Allen" visited Joe's store nearly every day. While walking down Main Street in Nyack, Joe and I heard, "Bikeman, bikeman!" We turned around to see Allen's head pop out of a garbage bin. Joe introduced us. "So you are the famous New York psychiatrist!" Allen said. "You look too young." After I took off my baseball cap, Allen screamed, "Now you look older!" Everyone on the street turned and stared at Allen. I laughed at his lack of social propriety.

Allen had been abandoned as a child and institutionalized by his mother in a Detroit psychiatric hospital. As Allen explained it, "She did not have the means to take care of me but raised my sister." Never taught to read or write, he taught himself. One day, while I was visiting, Allen recalled, "The attendants took turns raping me, until I stabbed one." Allen said, "They gave me high doses of IV Thorazine and placed me in four-point restraints." He was sent to a reform school till the age of 18.

Another day, while Joe was helping a family at his shop, Allen came in and screamed, "What I need is a thirteen-year-old hairless virgin!"

Joe told him, "That's it, you're not allowed in here anymore!" But Allen eventually wormed his way back in.

Allen often rolled into the Joe's store in his wheelchair, screaming with his arms waving over his head. A multitude of medical issues, including gout and prostate cancer, rendered Allen wheelchair-bound. Joe greeted Allen, made chit-chat and solved mechanical problems with Allen's wheelchair. Allen lived alone in an upstairs apartment and got into altercations with his neighbors. If Allen did not show up to the shop, Joe paid him a visit to make sure he was okay. When Allen asked Joe to drive up to Canada to visit his mother's grave, which Allen had never seen, Joe, concerned about taking such a long trip with him, helped him "visit" the grave on Google Earth. Allen would leave Joe's shop with a smile on his face, his voice and demeanor calmed.

Opening my heart to a genuine deep connection with Joe was scary, but for the first time in my life I was happy. I learned to retrieve parts of my abandoned girl self. With Joe by my side, I could better face and reconcile the past. He accompanied me on a trip to my parents' home; I wanted to return something to my mother that I'd taken as a child.

On the way, I told him the story. It began with a translucent pearl that I was twirling through my fingers when I was 6 years old. Sunlight pierced it: it threw off sparkling colors of pink, silver, purple, and blue. When I opened and closed its oyster shell, I felt oddly comforted. I had beauty in a box and could visit whenever I pleased. The Leos, our next-door neighbor, gave me a pearl each year for my birthday. That an ocean parasite could weave an iridescent gem amazed me. My mother told me, "I will strand the pearls the Leos gave you. It will be your twelfth birthday gift." She did have my childhood pearls strung. But, instead, she took them for herself.

Mother and I shared one long symbiotic breath. If I did not reflect back exactly what she needed, she'd strike out at me. My private school held a sixth-grade science fair each year. I excitedly began to assemble a three-dimensional model of Amelia Earhart. Like Amelia, I wanted to be a trailblazer, challenging the movable limits of human possibility. Coming home, I built a model of the plane in which the aviator vanished. When my mother found out, she became enraged. "We are making your science model of Dolly Madison," she told me.

I said, "No way, I love Amelia and want to be like her."

She smacked me hard over my head. "We will be making a model of Dolly Madison. Not Amelia Earhart. Dolly Madison!"

My stubborn willfulness was a threatening affront. She identified with Dolly; they were both first ladies in their families who boosted their husbands' careers. So she eradicated me, and we built the model she chose. We painted a paper mâché Dolly Madison serving ice cream, my mother's favorite dessert. In the background sat the elegant White House. My mother chose to dress Dolly up with one of mother's fake pearl necklaces. Enraged by the memory that I had never received the necklace promised to me with my pearls, I struck back, and stole her necklace after the fair. It was my way of saying, "I do count after all." And maybe, my stealing the pearls was revenge and retaliation for my feeling wiped out, not seen, and dismissed by mother.

The necklace was not mentioned for many years. Neither of them were. My mother did not realize it was missing. I even forgot I'd stolen it until at some point it became mine. But I never forgot my childhood pearls. At my favored younger brother's wedding, I wore my mother's fake necklace. My younger sister, Stella, microscopically examined my neck, "How beautiful your pearls are." The next day, mother called me, "Stella told me you stole my expensive pearl necklace." She was half right. Defiant and determined to not admit my humiliation and sorrow for not feeling accepted, I had lashed out and stole my mother's fake pearl necklace. I responded, "I don't think so" hoping my response would prompt her memory. A year later at Stella's college graduation, I'd overheard mother say to Stella. "Watch how jealous Nina gets when she sees your new beautiful diamond and pearl graduation necklace." Mother and Stella laughed. It was excruciatingly painful to hear these cruel words as my mother gleefully gifted to Stella what she could not give and had taken from me as a promised childhood gift for my 12 birthday. It was my version of a child's blanket to deceive myself that by wearing mother's stolen pearl necklace wrapped her love around my being.

Now as Joe and I neared my childhood home, I said, "I've decided that, when I get a chance, I'll give her necklace back. I need to clear things up with her." He nodded and took a deep breath. "Okay, Nina. That's why we're doing this." When he reached his hand across the seat to squeeze mine, I realized that our relationship was the real gift, a pearl beyond measure, more valuable than any chain. Joe had taught me to rest and recuperate, rather than feel the unrelenting need to push to prove my worthiness. His love softened my hardened heart and slowed me down enough to stop running from my rage and sadness through athletic achievement. I no longer felt like an emotional orphan, but had a family with two beautiful granddaughters, his son Hal's kids: Madeline, 5 years old, who always greeted me with a resonant hug and Ella, 3 years old, who was feisty, smart and independent. Insisting on putting her jigsaw puzzle together, alone and without help, Ella first visualized for hours how each piece fit together; only then did she assemble the puzzle.

While in Joe's bike store, Madeline drew pictures with crayons, and she made one of a golden rainbow. When Hal asked if she was going to give it to grandpa, Madeline shook her head no and said, "It's for Nina." I pinned that joyful rainbow to my refrigerator.

When we arrived at my parents' house, my heart began to beat hard and fast, and I took a few deep breaths to calm myself. But as soon as I walked through the front door, I was 12 again, mother's emotional captive with a queasiness in my gut. I gave her the necklace. "Here mother, these are Dolly's pearls. They are not mine. I want you to have them back. And you can keep my childhood pearl necklace." My father's face reddened with the effort of holding back his avalanche of anger. I imagined my father thought that I was an ungrateful thief.

Whistling and nearly skipping, mother went upstairs and retrieved my childhood birthday gift, 43 years late. She'd strung the pearls, but they seemed paltry in my hands, all the light and magic from them gone – a fragile chain of sorrow, each year just another sad pearl. All I held was the stolen, real pearl necklace of a little girl whose dreams of acceptance had been snuffed out. Holding back my tears, I thanked my mother anyway.

When Joe and I left and got in the car, I put them on and choked. Unable to open the clasp, I struggled but still could not open it. I screamed, and Joe's big, mechanic-scraped fingers could not undo the dainty clasp. Gagging, I hollered, "Just break it!" When he did, and the pearls fell their separate ways onto the dark floor of the car, the spell of generations of maternal symbiotic fusion shattered.

Mother left many messages on my machine over the next several days: "Nina, these are really expensive pearls."

Finally, this message came. "Nina, I brought them to the jewelers, he said they are fake. You should know how to distinguish fake from real pearls. Do you have a strand of pearls? You really should have one," she said, "it makes you feel so good to dress in a nice outfit with them." All I could do was look at Madeline's rainbow taped to my refrigerator. There were tears in my eyes but a smile on my face.

Life is a mystery; it seems ineffable to describe how one comes to finally surrender to love. For years, over and over again, I dated men similar to my mother who were emotionally bankrupt. My subsequent childhood toughness led to developing my mantra of "Do not tread on me," which was a brittle defense against a cruel childhood where my needs were brushed aside. By defiantly declaring my pseudo-independence, I refused to allow others to take care of me even when sick. I became an expert on self-denial and self-criticism.

Still being a work in progress, it remains at times difficult to relinquish my macho toughness. But somehow the experience of becoming sick and my mystical encounter with Molly slowly softened and loosened my rage. Despite being a very sensitive person, it still remains arduous at times to temper myself and have more compassion and forgiveness.

It took a whale, something bigger and more seductive than a village, to intra-psychically defeat the ingrained pattern of dating men with the trappings of being successful, charming, and handsome but limitedly self-involved. It took a whale, a monstrous magical beast of empathy and mirroring, to help melt my adamantine surface and save my life.

How does one go into the forest and the thick of things where one had never been before? Even though I am an advocate of change through psychoanalytic work, both as a patient and psychoanalyst, when I experience transformation it still amazes me and fills me with wonder, as it is hard to fully digest and grasp. I have been honored to work with patients in psychoanalysis who have been able with a lot of work and commitment to make this change. Sometimes this psycho-analytic work involves having the strength to survive the patient's transference of rage to outlast one more session than the patient's anger. Withstanding the patient's attempt to intra-psychically kill off the analyst may create space for the patient to begin to relate in a new way.

Joe was my first major relationship that was not a repeat of my pattern of dating men who were out of central casting similar to my mother. This is not to say that life is perfect with Joe. We still struggle. I am stubborn and he is a slob. But the package is good enough and he tolerates my anxieties. Although rare in our child-hoods, both of us are having a redo of our youths by taking care of each other. With the exception of when my brother came to visit me in the hospital allowing Joe to be relieved of his caretaking duties to get dinner, Joe never left my side for six weeks during a 10-hour surgery for a right mastectomy and post-operative recovery.

In the summer of 2021 despite having severe ulcerated leg lesions, Joe traveled and assisted me driving along the eastern coast to compete in various triathlons. In March 2022, we eventually discovered that his lesions were symptomatic of developing recurrence of stage four mantle cell lymphoma. These excruciating painful, deep leg lesions, which we learned are called pyoderma gangrenosum, are extremely rare, and were medically misdiagnosed and mistreated for two years. Although any type of manipulation is painful, I have cared for his lesions by applying medication and changing his bandages daily. It is difficult and heart-wrenching to see him in so much pain with a recurrence of cancer but I will stay here because I love him and know that the relationship is good for me. With a new freedom of feeling safe enough, I now am able to rest and sleep more deeply than I have ever experienced in my life. This new expansive space appears to have more clearly delineated my values that happiness is paramount over accomplishment and success.

Any difficulties with Joe stem from my not entirely accepting and mourning that my family is and will remain emotionally limited. My need to be loved by my mother—even begging for love—is to no avail because she has no desire to be introspective, responsible, or change. Her rejection of me instills a feeling of unworthiness so I push away affection from Joe, creating unsettling interactions between us. If I am to continue to aspire, heal, and grow, I need to completely let go of all expectations of approval from her.

During one of my triathlons in Pennsylvania, while I was warming up on my bike trainer before the start of the race, the sky suddenly opened up and torrential rain began. Joe spontaneously came over to hold an umbrella over my head while I was biking in place, and another triathlete exclaimed, "He is the ultimate sherpa."

Despite being healthy and well-trained for the triathlon, together we decided that it was dangerous to compete in the downpour, so we packed up my gear and drove home. This practical decision to take care of myself was not a skill I previously possessed in my narrowed repertoire. How shocking and moving it was, and still is, for me to receive and be the recipient of such generosity, love, care, and compassion. Joe standing beside me under an umbrella in the rain, sheltering us, without a complaint, I thought to myself, "He is the ultimate bicycle shrink," and it took my soul to a unique place.

NOTE

1 Parts of this chapter appeared in an earlier version in Cerfolio (2020) and are gratefully reprinted with permission from Routledge Taylor & Francis Group.

REFERENCE

Cerfolio, N. (2020). The bicycle shrink. *Psychoanalytic Perspectives*, *17*(2), 231–239.

5

Spiritual Knowing, Not Knowing, and Being Known[1]

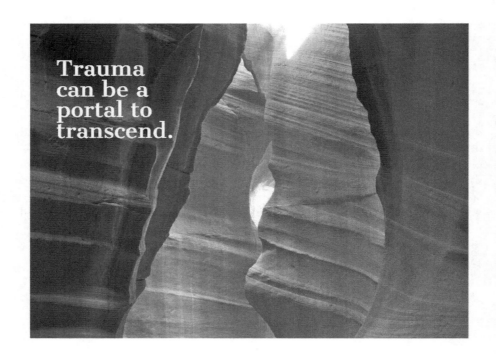

Trauma can be a portal to transcend.

DOI: 10.4324/9781032633497-6

For seven years I lived in a liminal space between life and death, feeling closer to the latter than the former, my foothold in this world tenuous (Cerfolio, 2016). As a result of having gone through these mystical experiences, from my spiritual response to being poisoned with anthrax to my blissful encounter with Molly, I began to develop a deeper faith in a beyond I did not fully recognize or completely understand. I felt it was closer and that one day, it would sweep me up into its majesty.

Through daily meditation, I was further liberated from bounded self-states and released into the vastness of a more expansive numinous identity. I began to see my patients' suffering less as a form of psychopathology, and instead to view them as precious divine beings, engaged in a poignant struggle to grow and discover their own creativity and power to transform. As I surrendered more to uncertainty in the therapeutic relationship, I felt guided by a greater sense of connection and one-ness with my patients. It felt that there was a divine purpose in the struggles my patients and I had in our daily lives. It took years of contemplating the meaning of my mystical experience to glimpse its spiritual lessons and gifts and I'd felt I had become a mirror to help my patients see theirs.

A distortion inevitably develops when attempting to define spiritual knowing, as it is ineffable. The vastness of the mystical experience refuses to be girdled by words. Despite this paradox, and the fact that my words will seem insufficient and didactic, I will describe how my mystical awakening altered not only my sense of self but some of my psychoanalytic relationships as well.

MICHELLE'S TRANSFORMATION FROM SUBMISSION TO SURRENDER

A clinical case pointing to the possibility of uncanny unconscious communication and the plausibility of telepathic interconnectivity (Ferenczi, 1988) is the transforma-tion that occurred in my psychoanalytic relationship with Michelle, an example of the "porousness and permeability of the mind" (Allik, 2003; Bass, 2001; Bromberg, 1999; Schore, 2011). Demonstrating patient and analyst mutuality and "the dialogue of the unconsciousness" (Ferenczi, 1980, p. 84), where the unconsciousness of two people communicates without either being consciously aware of this dialogue, is the extraordinary knowing that occurred between Michelle and me.

Without these issues being verbally unpacked between Michelle and me, some-how Michelle echoed my transformation. As I began to wrestle with my pre-viously unthought-known (Bollas, 1987)—an irrational fear of being infectious which resulted from my mother's projections of her unrecognized dark side into me as an attempt to purify herself—somehow Michelle became able to liberate herself from her terror of having a defective baby.

Perhaps, my unprocessed fear of being infectious initially prevented me from seeing more clearly. But through my enhanced capacity to struggle with my fear, I learned better modulation; ironically, it became a point of contact with God, which had uplifting as well as distressing aspects. I felt a connection to a greater whole and more empathy for others, including my mother. On the other hand, I had to endure the pain of feeling infectious and recognize how this had so negatively impacted my life. Ultimately, I could better extract myself from the weeds of my psyche, to find new seeds of wisdom in my and my patient's struggles.

Michelle, a 38-year-old female graduate student in political science, initially came to treatment for an eating disorder and incapacitating anxiety. She had a tumultuous childhood, which included being ping-ponged between her ambivalent, divorced parents. She then became the target of her stepfather's manic violence during adolescence which resulted in Michelle's subsequent tragic estrangement from her mother.

As my spiritual awakening empowered me to find the courage to take the leap of faith to have a loving partner, somehow my transformation was unconsciously echoed in a parallel process with Michelle, who in turn became better able to untangle herself from toxic relationships and find a loving partner. Both of us suffered from a not unfamiliar paternalistic childhood of having to meet the expectation of marrying rich. Although I had counterphobically and unconsciously fought fully knowing these stifling expectations for years, it was only after being poisoned that I could further emancipate myself from these crippling values (Cerfolio, 2015).

Psychoanalytic issues that were more explicit and that we actively verbally unpacked involved Michelle's separation anxiety and eating disorder. As she developed a stronger sense of trust and object constancy, we were able to discuss and know these dissociated parts of Michelle. Michelle's unconscious dissociated states also contained insights that brought with them their own possibilities. Initially, she resisted accessing these split-off pockets of aliveness because they were too painful and scary. Eventually, she became better able to feel her terror instead of reflexively binging and purging during isolation and stress. There seemed to be an echo between my suffering in expelling toxins and Michelle's purging which created a sacred congress. Perhaps, because of my suffering, I developed more empathy for her eating disorder, which reached her on an unconscious level. This connection allowed her to put more space between feeling the terror and purging. After my transformation, she became more able to reflect on a lifetime pattern of dating abusive, emotionally stunted men who were often Ivy League educated and successful in their profession, but left her feeling unseen and abandoned. Michelle's new insight led her to becoming receptive to date an emotionally attuned, loving partner, whom she eventually married and had a family with.

Michelle's childhood deprivation led to a full-blown severe eating disorder consisting of bulimia and purging. Her parents divorced when she was 2 years old, and they shared custody of Michelle. Alternating between her parents' homes every week until the age of 12, she would frequently hear her parents fighting over shirking their financial parental responsibility. Michelle "felt used as a pawn. And unwanted."

When Michelle was 12, her mother remarried a financially successful Spanish businessman and they all moved into his opulent home. Her stepfather had unpredictable violent outbursts and mood swings. During one of his unwelcome manic episodes, her stepfather threw an object and hit Michelle. After this violent incident, she moved out of her mother and stepfather's home to live with her father and stepmother.

Michelle felt betrayed and abandoned by her mother's remarriage. Her mother's sole focus became the impossible task of trying to please her tyrannical second husband, who demanded nothing less. As a result of her mother's all-consuming relationship with her second husband, her mother became even less emotionally available as Michelle felt that her mother had exchanged happiness and independence for financial security.

From the age of 12 to 16, she moved in with her emotionally distant physician father and did not see her mother during this time, instead choosing to correspond with her mother through letter writing. This period was exquisitely painful for Michelle as she felt completely alone and with a lack of maternal guidance while going through puberty. At the age of 13, she began to feel overwhelming dread whenever she physically separated from someone, as if "I am going to die."

Feeling the terror of separation and a lack of stability, Michelle began at the age of 13 to binge and purge on sweets and chocolates, which provided a temporary sense of relief from her panic. In a self-adaptive attempt to comfort herself, she turned inward to soothe herself with binge eating. However, her internalized sense of her mother was represented by her becoming obsessed with her weight, and this led to purging.

During adolescence, Michelle's rage toward her mother became a dissociated self-state that was acted out by taking in sweets and then vomiting them out. At the age of 14, she gained 20 pounds in an unconscious act of spiteful revenge against a mother who desperately wanted a thin daughter. During this time, she developed a major depressive episode, which lasted for a year, and entailed Michelle's inability to get out of bed and to go to school.

Michelle developed a defensive system around this painful maternal deprivation. In addition to food, Michelle was an academic achiever and "overeater"; she voraciously fed herself with numerous professional degrees, which consisted of a doctorate in English literature, a law degree, and a master's degree in conflict resolution. Hoping to obtain her mother's elusive love, she felt more comfortable staying a student as it postponed her more deeply knowing herself and delayed further separation. Adding to her humiliation, her stepfather constantly reminded her that he left school at the age of 17 to become a highly financially successful international businessman.

As I learned how to surrender to my real vulnerabilities, somehow Michelle learned implicitly and without us verbally working on these issues, to loosen her submission to her internalized voice of her mother's dictums. Before my transformation, Michelle had numerous unwanted pregnancies and abortions and insisted that she would never bring a child into this "dark, evil, and polluted world." Michelle feared that her child would only add to the stress on the environment, as her child would belong to the next generation where water is no longer free.

However, somehow after Michelle allowed in a loving partner and married, she dared to get pregnant. Again, her fears and insistence resurfaced that she would have a defective child which were eerily similar to my fears of being infectious. It was only after I more fully understood and worked through how I have internalized being a carrier of badness in my family—as my mother insisted that I was a villain whose actions were tainted—that Michelle could gradually transform her unconscious fears of having a defective child, which was an inevitable legacy of her abusive childhood. This new knowing allowed her to contemplate a more inclusive experience and eventually accept a loving partner and become a loving mother to a perfectly flawless child.

In my mother's solipsistic and disconnected world where I am her scapegoat, I endure as the bad twin who steals her pearls. My mother deposited into me her unknown and uncontained shameful feelings of her childhood impoverishment and feelings of being unacceptable. Through both spiritual and psychoanalytic work, I became better able to contain and metabolize my painful irrational fear of being the nemesis of my mother and the world.

This is not to say that I have completely resolved my irrational fear of being infectious. Hopefully my reader will find an identification with my continuing evolution. But somehow it has been resolved enough within me to be able to shift the dynamics in the relationship between Michelle and me that helped spark transformation for Michelle through her own parallel discoveries and psychoanalytic work. Despite there being some negative bonds to my mother that persist, and I revert, at times, to being overly attentive to my mother's needs in a futile attempt to be known as being "good." Despite my family's inability to recognize me, I have made progress in knowing myself. But my illusory power of being infectious is difficult to fully relinquish as I still at times insist on my mother loving me as myself, and find it difficult to fully accept that she can only know me as "Typhoid Mary." In reality I am no one's nemesis; this is my mother's problem injected into me. Although my guilt is diminished and better contained, I still carry an echo of being "bad." Yet luckily, even as a child, I always possessed the ability to survive and the echoes grow fainter and fainter with awareness, diligence, and time.

The uncanny echoes in our struggles allowed us a deeper empathy for each other. This evolving resonance facilitated a shared body state, reflecting the constant, continuous unconscious communication between us. When Michelle observed my emotions, somehow she also experienced what I was feeling—an unshackling of being unacceptable.

After Michelle noticed and commented that she "never heard me mention my mother," somehow a mystical intuitive exchange between our mother figures was stimulated. Not only were Michelle and I communicating unconsciously, but our mothers, who were both preoccupied with concrete, materialistic appearance, became intertwined. Michelle became able to separate from her unconscious identification with her mother of feeling victimized by unwanted pregnancies. At the age of 21, which was the same age that her mother became pregnant with Michelle and led to her mother feeling pressured to marry her father, Michelle aborted her first unwanted, unplanned pregnancy. There began an overlap of our mothers, where one mother allowed the other mother more deeply into our psychoanalytic relationship and work. Through an uncanny communication between our critical mothers, as I had more distance from feeling bad, somehow Michelle was also able to free herself from the negative force of her mother to feel less defective.

Michelle and my rapprochement not only satiated the hunger in Michelle for maternal love, but created a space that allowed for reverberations of repair for us both. Due to our close identification, there was a transference cure and Michelle ended her psychoanalysis, as she felt that she had created her own full life.

One way of understanding these unconscious communications is Freud's (1933/1962) writings about the telepathic communication between patient and analyst. The telepathic process consists of one person communicating ideas, emotional states and mental acts to another person through empty space without using familiar methods, such as words and signs.

Metaphorically, Michelle's transformation, which paralleled my development can also be viewed as an expression of a positive fractal relational pattern between Michelle and myself (Marks-Tarlow, 2008; Domash, 2020). Fractals involve non-linear patterns in nature where the whole is reproduced in the patterns of the parts. Self-similar patterns build on self-similar patterns creating identity. An example of self-similar, rigid or negative fractal patterns is the repetition compulsion of inter-generational dysfunctional patterns. Once the individual becomes more cognizant of these dysfunctional patterns and behaviors, they can become easier to change. In addition to fractal theory, mirror neurons (Gallese, 2007) and emotional resonance may be helpful in discerning Michelle's transformation, but at this time the exact mechanism of the unconscious communication that occurred between us remains unknown.

Another explanation involved the reverie of the transitional space, where boundaries were opened for unconscious communication between Michelle and me while still maintaining our separateness. The logic of the brain is neither harmony nor separateness but both (Domash, 2020). Reflecting the activity of our brains, analysts strive to be in harmony and synchronized with our patients while at the same time maintaining our separateness.

Conceivably Michelle unconsciously sensed my spiritual awakening, which was shown when Michelle brought in a gift of a small vase. Feeling like natural magic and although I had not revealed my illness and subsequent spiritual awakening, this was non-verbally communicated to Michelle, as she said she sensed I seemed more at peace. Perhaps she was moved by sensing in me a more spiritual presence and equanimity which then facilitated a willingness to be receptive and experience an abundance that she could imbibe. Her gift to me felt like her unconscious recognition of my transformation. I could fill the vase she gave me with new life.

These uncanny experiences may happen in psychoanalysis because both patient and therapist are using their intuition and inhabiting transitional space. My becoming ill impelled me to turn deeply inwards through stillness and meditation to liberate myself to have a more loving relationship with myself and my patients. This mindfulness empowered me to find the courage to discover the resolve to live by my own standards, embrace the gifts of my vulnerabilities, and let in a loving, equal partner. Similar to how the baby is osmotically absorbing the nurturance of the mother, Michelle was able to absorb my more expansive knowing.

This more boundaryless knowing involves our intuition, which is humankind's great gift of using the senses of the mind and to open up the noumenal and numinal world. When I found more space to diminish my feeling of infectiousness, somehow Michelle intuited my change and began to also allow herself the hope and accept that someone would love her. Although we never used the pinpoint lens of rationality to examine her feeling of being unwanted, Michelle somehow intuited my transformation which allowed her to also better dissolve her feelings of toxicity.

Intuitive knowing is an essential way of knowing in psychoanalytic work that complements and transcends the traditional five senses and involves an irony and persuasive faculty of our brains that is indelible; intuitive knowing may be hard to isolate in the psychical realm yet powerfully experienced nonetheless. I may lose my house and physical belongings, but my experience of Michelle will always be ingrained within me. Frankly, I had the feeling that I had given birth to my spiritual daughter; I was fulfilled seeing Michelle blossom into a substantial and empowered woman.

MY PSYCHOANALYTIC RELATIONSHIP WITH BEN: DEEPENED BY A LOVING CONNECTION THAT FORGED TRANSFORMATION

Another example of the avenues of spiritual knowing coming together psychodynamically to play an intricate role in both analyst and patient transformation is my psychoanalytic relationship with Ben. My spiritual awakening helped usher in a more spacious sense of the "third" (Benjamin, 2007), in which Ben and I co-created a new relationship to explore the unknown and develop a sense that we were participating in something larger than ourselves. There evolved a new sense of a divine love permeating the transcendent "third" (Starr, 2008) between us, which created a deeper faith to explore dissociated parts of ourselves, accept, and even change them. This newly co-created "third" guided us to find new forms of relating, in which Ben and I could better come together as two separate, curious people who cared about each other and who could explore dissociated self-states, which previously had been impossible.

Unprovoked and out of the blue, after many years of psychoanalytic work, motivated by I do not know what, one day Ben suddenly asked me about the significance of a Wyland photograph which consisted of a gray whale spy-hopping that had hung on my wall for several months. The Wyland photo held spiritual reverberations in which my mystical experience with Molly was resonated by the photographer's experience. When Wyland was an adolescent on vacation in Laguna Beach with his family, he also had a spiritual encounter while swimming in the Pacific Ocean with a migratory mother and baby gray whale. Wyland's life-altering encounter inspired him to eventually live in Laguna Beach where he became a renowned marine life artist; he advocates for a healthier cleaner planet through art, science, and conservation.

My self-disclosure, rather than being experienced by Ben as an unwelcome intrusion as he had been previously inclined, allowed us to move away from Ben's futile attempts to fill his dreaded sense of void and triggered a deepened sense of the sacred in our dyad. Our relationship uncannily transformed from an I/It (Buber, 1970) relationship, in which we had related in a detached manner where both of us were an object to the other, to an I/Thou (Buber, 1970) relationship. The Wyland photo meant everything to me as it represented Molly was signaling an uncanny, extraordinary knowing. In turn, the manner in which Ben and I related somehow transformed and became laced with an intuitive knowing, where we were so deeply connected that we were able to imaginatively sense into the psyche of the other. As we began to relate on a more sacred register, our defenses and the distance between Ben and I melted; our living, dialogic dyad expanded into something that was more numinous based on a deeper faith and trust.

When Martin Buber, a philosopher, theologian, and Hassidic scholar, was preparing a lecture, a young rabbinical student came into his office and awkwardly told him about his troubles. Distracted and not really listening, Buber, who was busy arranging papers, replied in a superficial manner. Tragically, the student shortly afterwards committed suicide. Lamentably, Buber realized that he had been listening in an I/It relationship, where each member was separate. Reflecting on the power of deep emotional connection, Buber vowed from that moment to deeply and intently listen to create an I/Thou relationship with others, which involves the essence of a sacred living relationship. The boundaries between self and other dissolve away and the only thing important is the relationship with the other. This brings us closer to God or the Eternal Thou and the meaning of life. God is the ultimate Thou for Buber.

Initially fueled by Ben's sudden and unexpected noticing and asking about the Wyland photograph, an extraordinary knowing was kindled in our relationship. My opening up about my mystical experience with Molly was a pivotal moment in Ben's psychoanalysis which wafted into the transformational register and invited him more deeply into our intersubjective dyad. As I allowed myself to be more deeply known, Ben began to become spiritually fulfilled with a new-found sense of interconnection which lessened his rigidity, thereby decreasing his futile attempts to fill his sense of worthlessness with food and material objects.

After Ben unconsciously sensed and commented upon "my spiritual transformation," we became freer from our previous interlocking enactment. My becoming more infused momentarily with what felt like boundless love allowed me to more readily accept my own vulnerabilities, which was unconsciously and nonverbally communicated to Ben (Cerfolio, 2019).

The 47-year-old Ben was a depressed, emotionally stilted overeater. Before my mystical experience, I experienced him as controlling, demanding, and emotionally suffocating, although he consistently thought of himself as being a "ray of sunshine" who smiled and brought joy to others, despite acting in spiteful, self-destructive ways to enact and express his unprocessed anger. His dissociation owed much of its existence to surviving through submission to his mother's claustrophobic wishes.

Ben felt attacked by his own painful thoughts and avoided them at all costs. Initially, he refused to acknowledge he was overweight, as this was too upsetting. He insisted on thinking of himself as fit, despite being 90 pounds overweight. Ben shunned being known as he feared and associated relating with being shamed. While clothes shopping, he fooled himself into believing he could hide his large size by not asking for help. Feeling unknown by his mother, Ben clung to knowing himself in the only way his mother recognized him: as having unvaried and transparent goodness.

Ben related submissively to me as a constricted, rigid authority figure in order to avoid being responsible, and he tried to make me culpable for his well-being. Yet as a child, his mother's emotional needs eclipsed his own, and therefore he did not see me as a person whose thoughts and needs were separate from his own. In this way, Ben used our relationship to turn the tables, putting me in his place as little Ben. He attempted to overwhelm me with his unrecognized neediness and by playing his mother's role. Thus I was not allowed to have feelings, just as Ben was not allowed emotions that differed from those of his mother.

When Ben began analysis, he ate unhealthy foods high in cholesterol, salt, and sugar while seemingly remaining oblivious to the effects this diet had on his developing acid reflux and overall sluggishness. When we did discuss his diet's connection to his hypertension, he became enraged with me, as he insisted I was the all-knowing physician who should magically cure him. His mother had drowned him in her needs. She had expected him to save her. Now he expected me to save him. He became angry because I did not know the specific healthy foods uniquely suited to his physiology. I encouraged him to experiment with small amounts of healthy food to discover what felt beneficial. After several months of interpreting his rage over my lack of omniscience, he confessed that after leaving my office, he went straight to McDonald's for a high-calorie, fatty feast. His mother's anger that Ben could not save her from herself became Ben's rage that I could not save him from himself.

I saw Ben's relationship with food, hurting himself and disavowing the cause-and-effect relationship between his diet and health, as masochistic, the giving up of agency. He engaged in negative surrender, a self-destructive submission. I use "surrender" in accordance with Emmanuel Ghent's (1990) reframing of the term in a spiritual and Eastern philosophic sense as an antithesis to the submission of classical masochism. It has nothing to do with hoisting a white flag. Rather than carrying a connotation of defeat, it enables a liberation of the self by lowering one's defensive barriers.

After my mystical encounter, part of my spiritual practice was to meditate prior to seeing patients. On a blistering August day, while I was meditating in my office with the door closed, Ben was early and sat in the waiting room. A feeling of rage and agitation crashed in on my peaceful and relaxed state of mind. I tried to breathe into the rage, but I felt suffocated and was overcome with waves of panic and the feeling of being out of control. When I opened the door to welcome Ben into my office, I asked him how he was feeling and he responded, "Good." Upon my pointing out that he seemed agitated, Ben stated that he resented waiting in my warm, unairconditioned waiting room, while he imagined that I sat comfortably in my air-conditioned office. We explored his transferential feeling of being a puppet to me, based on his earlier relationship with his mother.

When I shared my experience of feeling his suffocating anger while he sat in the waiting room, something shifted between us. While maintaining my sense as an analyst, I experienced Ben's rage as if I was inside his mind for a moment, as if I was a part of Ben himself. Feeling his rage from the inside was uncanny. I had gained access to his experience of feeling suffocated and with that a deep sense of being connected emerged. This superconscious experience (Suchet, 2016) of feeling Ben's rage while meditating struck me as an extraordinary way of knowing that began the process of creating more space to know parts of Ben that were previously inaccessible. This uncanny experience of knowing required a silence, a moment of not trying to understand in words that allowed for the experience to be felt and known from the inside.

After my mystical awakening, which encouraged his own burgeoning awareness, Ben became able to take into account my existence outside of my professional life with less resentment. He non-verbally sensed and then commented on my spiritual awakening, saying I seemed "happier, serene, and peaceful." Before, when Ben occasionally sensed I was calm, he unconsciously resented it, as he had experienced my separateness as a loss of control and abandonment. Now he was able not only to become cognizant of my new-found equanimity but to find it comforting. He still at times regressed into defensiveness and feelings of shame, but he no longer thought of himself in reductive and purely positive terms, and became far less brittle. He also began to take initiative and risks, even though it petrified him, and to have more expansive experiences. Ben discovered joy in being a more involved grandparent and developed his significant artistic talent with less of the paralyzing fear of needing to be perfect.

Eventually, Ben surrendered his insistence on feeling like a puppet to his analyst and mother. He let go of his defensive relationship with food and began to take responsibility for what he ate. Radically changing his diet, he lost 90 pounds, which resolved his hypertension and need for medication. He transcended his need to be a victim, fulfilling what Winnicott (1965) described as the yearning to surrender the false self. In Ben's words,

> I was fed up with being oppositional and butting heads. It did feel like a revelation, the shift in me, that I'm responsible for my own feelings. Although it felt

sudden, it felt like a big container filling up with water but one drop makes a sudden difference and overflows.

Then he added, "It had something to do with feeling less judgmental. I associate spirituality with being non-judgmental, not that you were particularly judgmental prior." He expressed his new-found need

> to have a sense of community and belonging to something bigger than myself, like having a connection to my parent's religious practices of my past but with the new ability to take in the warmth and richness of the teachings, while leaving the exclusive, judgmental part.

Paradoxically, Ben and I had a meeting of our inner beings which allowed for a separation between us to grow and develop. Our being, allowed to become more separate, freed us from being drowned in Ben's previously unknown, unprocessed anger. Ben began to experience a sense of authentic identity where he became more self-aware rather than reflexively allowing "the other" to define himself. He learned how to surrender to the analytic process, which did not constitute a submission to interpretation but rather a release of emotional bondage that obscured his subjectivity and a turn to a much fuller, more hopeful story about who he was and what he could do. As we learned to relate as a contemplative psychoanalytic couple, there evolved space for Ben to become self-reflective. His hostile dependency shifted to a more loving interdependency where we could be two different people with varying interests.

Ben's transformation came to be reflected in his personal life as well, becoming more thoughtful and connected with others. He became able to take the leap of faith to "confess," which was his word, to his wife that he was working on becoming responsible in his analysis, which freed him from his shackles of clinging to the need to appear perfect. He was forging a path to having a more empathic, loving, intimate marriage.

One can learn about spiritual knowing, but it must be experienced and reflected upon to be fully understood. Even then, the experience of spiritual knowing is ineffable, revealing the limitation of words, as it is vast and limitless. Spiritual knowing can be seen from many different vantage points, but I will focus my discussion on spiritual knowing as it pertains to these clinical cases in terms of extraordinary knowing and the permeability of self-states.

SPIRITUAL KNOWING AS EXTRAORDINARY KNOWING

Superconscious states of knowing reside at the far reaches of the continuum of empathy and intuition. Superconscious states transcend space and time, and they are associated with a higher level of creativity and spiritual awareness that many of us have known albeit fleetingly. Examples of transcendent states are heightened moments in the arts and sports, as well as in drug-induced, religious, and meditative experiences. Superconsciousness involves a knowing at the higher levels of consciousness called universal consciousness, in which we are all one and have access to all knowledge. More simply put, superconsciousness is the attempt of human beings to understand the numinous. Subtler states of consciousness (Suchet, 2016) emerge as we go beyond our ordinary senses and we experience states of rapture, bliss, and equanimity. In these realms, subject and object dissolve and we experience states of grace and compassion that expand our ways of knowing and being.

My mystical and ecstatic moment with Molly gave me the sense of wholeness that characterizes spiritual knowing (Cerfolio, 2017). Molly's soulful gaze welcomed me into an infinite, blissful universe, where my internal introject shifted from a disappointing and critical one to a more loving, benevolent, attuned one. In Molly's recognition, I felt known with a new sense of an empathic internal other (Laub & Podell, 1995) so that I became better able to glimpse a more attuned introject and articulate an inner empathic dialogue.

This process has been further explored by Elizabeth Lloyd Mayer (2007), a classical psychoanalyst, whose process shifted to incorporate the art of extraordinary knowing. When her daughter's rare harp was stolen and despite all efforts could not be located, she hired a dowser, who specifically located lost objects. From Arkansas, the dowser told her the exact street in California the harp was on, and Mayer was able to retrieve it. This uncanny experience changed how she worked as a psychoanalyst. Mayer writes about Grace, a patient who had unusual intuitive capacities to survive a traumatic childhood with a violent alcoholic father. Grace suddenly knew, "by listening with my whole body, not my ears," that her father was 15 minutes away and driving home drunk. She would hustle her sister and herself into the closet to avoid his uncontrollable violence. She knew because she had to. Mayer describes patients similar to Grace, who developed extraordinary intuition through no known sensory means, in order to survive traumatic circumstances that required knowing more than people can usually perceive through the five senses.

Cynthia Bourgeault (2003), a Christian mystic who teaches how to know through meditation and breath, refers to the ensuing wisdom as "seeing with the eye of the heart." By slowing down the breath, one may surrender into a deeper state of relaxation that allows for a spaciousness to open and for a deeper empathic intuitiveness to develop. Bourgeault's "wisdom way of knowing" goes beyond one's mind, the intellectual and rational way of thinking, to embody the entirety of the person: body, mind, and spirit. Through contemplative practices and sitting still, one creates a safe place, apart from the chaos, to allow deeper insights to emerge. Tapping into one's "contemplative intelligence" is an authentic way of knowing, harnessing a deeper source of self.

While meditating prior to seeing Ben, I was close to being in Bion's "O" (1965/1984), although I only realized that in retrospect. By suspending my ego, memory, and desire for future hopes for Ben, the space for something unknown and new emerged which enlivened the analysis. Bion felt that even the therapist's wish for the patient to heal must be abandoned so as not to interfere with evolving truths within the present moment. He referred to those moments as transformations in O, where O is the unified single source in which all consciousness—known and unknown—arises.

SPIRITUAL KNOWING AS PERMEABILITY OF SELF-STATES

Having a mystical experience can involve not only a desire but an ability to surrender. Ghent (1990) referred to surrender as "reflective of some 'force' toward growth, for which, interestingly, no English word exists." Ghent reframed surrender as a longing to release ourselves from more rigid and bounded self-states; consequently, the sense of one's wholeness is enhanced by the resulting sense of unity with other living beings.

Ghent's (1995) goal was not insight, but transformation, as patients come in contact with frozen parts of themselves that are aching to be known, examined, and understood. Surrender allowed the release of precious dissociated self-states (Ghent, 2001) that prior to falling ill had been inaccessible to me. Through my spiritual growth, anthrax poisoning ironically allowed me the space to begin to wrestle with previously frozen parts (Mitchell & Aron, 1999) of myself, and of my patients and to come to peace with them. As a result of becoming ill, I learned to surrender, which required developing a certain pliability and lessening of my brittle defensiveness to have more faith to dive into the uncertainty of the unknown.

Now having more permeability between my different self-states, I may have conveyed more empathy for myself and my patients. Loosening the rigidity of my dissociative truth about myself may have allowed some of my patients to see me more as a whole person and also for them to become aware of their different self-states. Bromberg (2013) describes the patient/therapist relationship in the analytic treatment "as a journey in which two people must each loosen the rigidity of their dissociative 'truths' about self in order to allow 'imagination' to find its shared place." This creates a gradual greater communication of self-states both within each member of the analytic dyad and between them. As the self-states' permeability increases, so does openness to "state-sharing."

While the exact process in which Michelle and Ben became able to examine unknown aspects of themselves in a parallel process to my own remains somewhat mysterious, what follows are my hypotheses. In part, as I developed more of an internalized sense of an empathic other, I became more willing to puncture and relinquish my grandiose self-states and become more acquainted with my vulnerabilities with less fear of annihilation. Feeling inspired and changed by Molly, my mystical experience lent me a greater flexibility to examine, understand, and integrate previously disavowed and unknown self-states. In a parallel process, these patients seemed to begin to mirror a similar flexibility to articulate their authentic sense of self and unknown self-states.

Regarding Michelle, my new-found equanimity seemed to assuage her deeply embedded fear of delivering a defective baby. With Michelle, I was called on to more deeply examine my irrational anxiety that stemmed from childhood about feeling infectious, allowing me to contain and process what Bion describes as beta elements, that is, my own feeling of badness. This inner act of freedom (Symington, 1986) released me further from the shame of my irrational feelings. I became better able to stop repeating destructive interpersonal dynamics. Somehow, Michelle then became better able to mourn her childhood feeling of being unwanted and relinquish her fears of having a deformed baby.

Further, Michelle's insistence on being diminutive and relinquishing taking up any interpersonal emotional space reasserted the painful memories of my childhood upbringing, where my expressing an opinion was considered out of line. This resonance of our relationship helped move me toward both knowing about, and differentiating from, my irrational childhood fear of being infectious. Because I could more clearly see my noxious childhood upbringing reflected in Michelle's struggles, I made a decision to more freely allow myself to restore my expressiveness.

With Ben, before my spiritual awakening, my defensive stance of "warrior king" precluded me from having the fluidity of a full range of emotions; this greater fluidity may have been unconsciously and non-verbally communicated to him, and he began to take more responsibility for his actions.

My "warrior-king" stance related to Ben's false sense of self as "a ray of sunshine"; I was dissociated from my vulnerability and Ben was dissociated from his feelings of worthlessness and rage. These unknown aspects of ourselves kept us in an intersubjective deadlock. My brittle sense of "warrior king" interfered with knowing my other self-states, and may have colluded with Ben's not wanting to take agency in his life. As I acquired more fluidity in my self-states, I had a greater faith and took less responsibility for Ben's life. In Bion's sense, I relinquished some of my desire to heal Ben. This yielding liberated me to hold Ben more responsible for his struggles and for Ben to begin to have more agency to change them. As we became able to examine Ben's profound and unknown feelings of worthlessness, Ben became better able to glimpse his false sense of self. He began to have the courage to examine those unknown parts of himself, including his rigid defensiveness as a social Pollyanna persona (Jung, 1965/1966/2000), even though it terrified him, which was emotionally crippling both professionally and interpersonally. When I was more armored, Ben was more inclined to judge and disavow his dissociated anger. As I thawed with more pliability of self-states, Ben became more aware and able to articulate his anger. Prior to this, Ben's desperate neediness was acted out unconsciously by overeating. Eventually, Ben became more aware of his neediness and was even able to verbalize and enact it less.

The loosening of rigidities within the therapeutic dyad allowed Michelle, Ben, and me to better tolerate uncertainty. Estelle Frankel (2017) writes about how sitting with uncertainty can create openness and curiosity. After my transformation, I surrendered to a greater receptivity to the unknown, which created an enhanced spaciousness in the analytic relationship to allow Michelle's and Ben's becoming.

Marion Milner (1934) expressed that this practice, the idea of losing self to find self, is expressive of the paradoxical opening that comes with letting go of usual mindsets. This paradoxical finding is expressed by Dogen Zenji (2011), a Japanese Buddhist priest, in the Koan, "To study the Buddha Way is to study the self. To study the self is to lose the self. To forget the self is to be actualized by myriad things."

Spiritual knowing borrows from many sources including extraordinary, uncanny knowing and enhanced permeability of self-states, the latter put forth by the relational psychoanalytic model. These avenues of spiritual knowing came together psychodynamically to play an intricate role in both my transformation and the creation of the transcendent "third" in some of my psychoanalytic relationships. Michelle, Ben, and I became able to loosen our rigidities of dissociated self "truths," to have the faith to know previously unknown aspects of ourselves, and better sit with uncertainty. We were freed from old mindsets and better able together to experience a far-reaching inclusiveness and a greater sense of expansiveness, that eases and accelerates a path to wholeness and healing.

NOTE

1 Parts of this chapter appeared in an earlier version in Cerfolio (2019) and are gratefully reprinted with permission from Routledge, Taylor & Francis Group.

REFERENCES

Allik, T. (2003). Psychoanalysis and the uncanny: Take two or when disillusionment turns out to be an illusion. *Psychoanalysis & Contemporary Thought, 26*(1), 3–37.

Bass, A. (2001). It takes one to know one: Or, whose unconscious is it anyway? *Psychoanalytic Dialogues, 11*(5), 683–702. http://doi.org/10.1080/10481881109348636

Benjamin, J. (2007). Intersubjectivity, thirdness, and mutual recognition: A talk given at the Institute for Contemporary Psychoanalysis, Los Angeles, CA [Speech transcript]. https://terapia.co.uk/wp-content/uploads/2020/05/Reading-14-Jessica-Benjamin-Intersubjectivity.pdf

Bion, W. R. (1984). *Transformations.* Karnac Books (Original work published 1965).

Bollas, C. (1987). *The shadow of the object: Psychoanalysis of the unthought known.* Columbia University Press.

Bourgeault, C. (with Moore, T.) (2003). *The wisdom way of knowing: Reclaiming an ancient tradition to awaken the heart.* Jossey-Bass.

Bromberg, P. M. (1999). Playing with boundaries. *Contemporary Psychoanalysis, 35*(1), 54–66. http://doi.org/10.1080/00107530.1999.10746382

Bromberg, P. M. (2013). Hidden in plain sight: Thoughts on imagination and the lived unconscious. *Psychoanalytic Dialogues, 23*(1), 1–14. http://doi.org/10.1080/10481885.2013.754275

Buber, M. (1970). *I and thou* (W. Kaufmann, Trans.). Touchstone (Original work published 1923).

Cerfolio, N. (2015). Bulimia, separation anxiety, and finding the authentic self. *MOJ Addiction Medicine & Therapy, 1*(2), 37–40. http://doi.org/10.15406/mojamt.2015.01.00010

Cerfolio, N. (2016). Loss, surrender and spiritual awakening. *Palliative and Supportive Care, 14*(6), 725–726. http://doi.org/10.1017/S1478951516000304

Cerfolio, N. (2017). My mystical encounter with a wild gray whale. *Psychoanalytic Perspectives, 14*(2), 265–269. http://doi.org/10.1080/1551806X.2017.1304133

Cerfolio, N. (2019). Spiritual knowing, not knowing, and being known. In B. Willock, I. Sapountzis & R. C. Curtis (Eds.), *Psychoanalytic perspectives on knowing and being known* (pp. 117–130). Routledge. http://doi.org/10.4324/9780429454295-13

Dogen Zenji, E. (2011). *Dogen's Genjo Koan: Three commentaries.* Counterpoint.

Domash, L. (2020). *Imagination, creativity and spirituality in psychotherapy: Welcome to Wonderland.* Routledge. http://doi.org/10.4324/9780429299148

Ferenczi, S. (1980). Psychogenic anomalies of voice production. In J. Richman (Ed.) *Further contributions to the theory and technique of psycho-analysis* (J. Suttie, Trans., pp. 105–109). Karnac Books.

Ferenczi, S. (1988). *The clinical diary of Sándor Ferenczi* (J. Dupont, Ed., M. Balint & N. Z. Jackson, Trans.). Harvard University Press.

Frankel, E. (2017). *The wisdom of not knowing: Discovering a life of wonder by embracing uncertainty.* Shambhala Publications.

Freud, S. (1962). *The standard edition of the complete psychological works of Sigmund Freud* (Vol. 22, J. Strachey, Ed. & Trans.). The Hogarth Press (Original work published 1933).

Gallese, V., Eagle, M. N., & Migone, P. (2007). Intentional attunement: Mirror neurons and the neural underpinnings of interpersonal relations. *Journal of the American Psychoanalytic Association, 55*(1), 131–175. http://doi.org/10.1177/00030651070550010601

Ghent, E. (1990). Masochism, submission, surrender: Masochism as a perversion of surrender. *Contemporary Psychoanalysis, 26*(1), 108–136.

Ghent, E. (1995). Interaction in the psychoanalytic situation. *Psychoanalytic Dialogues, 5*(3), 479–491. http://doi.org/10.1080/10481889509539087

Ghent, E. (2001). Need, paradox, and surrender: Commentary on paper by Adam Phillips. *Psychoanalytic Dialogues, 11*(1), 23–41. http://doi.org/10.1080/10481881109348595

Jung, C. G. (1965/1966/2000). *Collected works* (Vols. 7 & 16). Princeton University Press.

Laub, D., & Podell, D. (1995). Art and trauma. *International Journal of Psycho-Analysis, 76*(5), 991–1005.

Marks-Tarlow, T. (2008). *Psyche's veil: Psychotherapy, fractals and complexity.* Routledge. http://doi.org/10.4324/9781315787480

Mayer, E. L. (2007). *Extraordinary knowing: Science, skepticism, and the inexplicable powers of the human mind.* Bantam Dell.

Milner, M. (with Bowlby, R.). (2011). *A life of one's own.* Routledge (Original work published 1934).

Mitchell, S. A., & Aron, L. (1999). Editor's introduction to Ghent, E. "Masochism, submission, surrender". In S. A. Mitchell & L. Aron (Eds.), *Relational psychoanalysis: The emergence of a tradition* (pp. 211–242). The Analytic Press.

Schore, A. N. (2011). The right brain implicit self lies at the core of psychoanalysis. *Psychoanalytic Dialogues, 21*(1), 75–100. http://doi.org/10.1080/10481885.2011.545329

Starr, K. E. (2008). Faith as the fulcrum of psychic change: Metaphors of transformation in Jewish mysticism and psychoanalysis. *The International Journal of Relational Perspectives, 18*(2), 203–229. http://doi.org/10.1080/10481880801909781

Suchet, M. (2016). Surrender, transformation, and transcendence. *Psychoanalytic Dialogues, 26*(6), 747–760. http://doi.org/10.1080/10481885.2016.1235945

Symington, N. (1986). The analyst's act of freedom as agent of therapeutic change. In G. Kohon (Ed.), *British psychoanalysis: New perspectives in the independent tradition.* Yale University Press.

Winnicott, D. W. (1965). Ego distortion in terms of true and false self. In *The maturational process and the facilitating environment: Studies in the theory of emotional development* (pp. 140–152). International Universities Press.

6

A Paradigm for Care

Multimodal Psychoanalytic Aid with Children Traumatized by the Second Chechen War[1]

Helping others **ultimately** saves ourselves.

DOI: 10.4324/9781032633497-7

History that is forgotten often repeats itself. What is not remembered influences us far greater than what is remembered. There are global consequences when the world turns a blind eye to Putin's unopposed 20 years of waging wars in Chechnya in 1994, Georgia in 2008, Crimea in 2014, and Syria in 2015. This historical lack of global resistance concerning this Russian aggression emboldened an alarming creeping normalization of Putin to continue with his tyrannical waging of wars and murdering of innocent civilians in Ukraine.

Russia is not alone in waging wars, as this is emblematic and a part of American history and mythology. In modern thought, we have married the relentlessly ubiquitous presence of evil, which is understood by the Shakespearean utterance, "The fault, dear Brutus, is not in the stars, but in ourselves." How do we come to terms with the realization of our own destructive tensions and motivation to create wars to destroy other humans? How do we understand evil and the dynamics of war which involves the killing and dying out of love of country? How do we bear witness to the Ukrainians' suffering and remain attuned to finding ways to support the challenges of Russian acts of terror that the Ukrainian people are enduring?

Richard Koenigsberg (2009) argues that war is a ritual process through which nations become alive and illustrates how genocide grows out of the logic of warfare. I would amend that this becoming alive of nations through waging war involves a generic attempt to repair feelings of weakness, fixing scarcity of resources, and revenging old wounds. Based on Hitler's speeches and *Mein Kampf*, Koenigsberg conceives of the Holocaust as the product of an ideology that demanded the sacrifice of both Germany's male population and European Jewry.

Although shocking to confront, wounding and fatally tarnishing to us Americans as exemplars of the shining star on the hill, it should come as no great surprise that the Nazis, whose crimes involved descent into radical evil, drew inspiration from American race law in creating their own program of racist persecution (Whitman, 2017). Andreas Rethmeier (1995), a German lawyer, wrote about the Nuremberg Laws that included an examination of some of the many Nazi references to American Law (Whitman, 2017). After reviewing his data Rethmeier arrived at a troubling verdict: America was, for the Nazis, the "classic example" of a country with racist legislation (Rethmeier, 1995). The fundamental racism at the heart of American life was a source and model worthy of emulation for Hitler, as he imagined a pure society devoid of Jews and other allegedly undesirable people (Whitman, 2017).

Similar to Hitler's desire to purify and unify Germany, Putin's virtue in justifying his war in Ukraine is the creation of a highly desired "sacred" empire based on Christian fascism and fundamentalism, which the Orthodox Church fully supports (Lifton, 2022). This Christian fascism centers on a unified, godly Russian empire achieved by Peter the Great that is pure in its virtue and absolute in its justified demands. The Russian leader said that one of the goals of the offensive was to "denazify" Ukraine, part of a long-running effort by Putin to delegitimize Ukrainian nationalism and sell the incursion to his constituency at home. The rhetoric around fighting fascism resonates deeply in Russia, which made tremendous sacrifices battling Nazi Germany in World War II. Critics say that Putin is exploiting the trauma of that war and twisting history for his own interests.

A deeper trigger for Russia's invasion may not have been "self-purification" but Putin's refusal to admit that neighboring Ukraine had become a flourishing democracy. The contrast of Ukrainian democratic success would have been intolerable for Putin, and may be one reason why he is trying to erase Ukraine. Putin was never going to let a Slavic Ukraine become a successful free-market democracy in the European Union next door to his stagnating Slavic Russian kleptocracy.

In response to Putin's invasion of Ukraine, the world became more unified as exemplified by the placing of global sanctions on Russia, the United Nations' condemnation of Russia's invasion of Ukraine, and many sympathetic countries granting temporary visas to Ukrainian refugees. This global outpouring of support and help was inspired in part by the brave resistance of the Ukrainian people, but also because we may more readily identify with the Ukrainians, who are a Slavic people of similar race and culture. Perhaps this identification with the Ukrainian people as opposed to the Chechen Muslims, allows the world to more readily recognize their suffering, open its heart, and offer help.

In sharp contrast to the current incredible outpouring of global aid in response to Putin's "special military operation" in Ukraine, in the past the world became inured to the brutality inflicted by Putin in the Russian wars in Chechnya, Syria, and Georgia. While doing first-hand humanitarian aid work during the Second Chechen War, I personally witnessed the sequelae of the world's laxness in not protesting Russian destructive war crimes against Chechens in the Second Chechen War. Similarly, Putin specializes in weaponizing refugees in an attempt to create resentment and destabilization of neighboring republics and countries. America seemed to cede Putin's waging war in Asia, in part, echoing 19th-century colonization and to skip past the specter of nuclear devastation. But then the world suddenly woke up and gave an intimation of unification protesting Putin's invasion of Ukraine. Although many countries have not followed through, the global resolve of citizenry remains unflinching and immovable.

When one cannot contain feelings like rage, vengeance, and envy, the Other may become the repository of these projected unwanted, disowned feelings. Despite decades of Putin's waging war and killing innocent Muslim civilians, our country "othered" this Muslim suffering. This is an echo of previous practices of our marginality: "Japs" in Japan, "Chinks" in China, and "Gooks" in Vietnam. When we inflict wars on our brothers and sisters in the world, we eschew the fact that reality is composed of multiplicity and the pursuit of virtue is a scarce commodity, further tattering our sense of community and spiritual connectedness. Othering creates a divisiveness that falsely insists that we are superior and that it is acceptable to humiliate and exploit the marginalized. This primitive tribalism foments much of the conflict in the world. Only by caring and bearing witness to the suffering of all, especially those from marginalized races and cultures, do we begin to reconnect severed social links and heal our world with the recognition of the unity of our planet (Davoine & Gaudillière, 2004).

A PARADIGM FOR CARE: MULTIMODAL PSYCHOANALYTIC AID WITH CHILDREN TRAUMATIZED BY THE SECOND CHECHEN WAR

This has all been a preamble for your understanding of my sentiments that galvanized me to go into the Second Chechen War to help—not a popular choice in my family. As mentioned previously, to address the suffering, in August of 2005 I visited Chechnya with a colleague to provide medical care to those stranded in Grozny and the Chechen refugees in Ingushetia. We also started a chapter for a New York disabled running club in Grozny to help those who became amputees as a result of the war, and to bring three disabled Chechen children to New York for further medical treatment (Cerfolio, 2009). Although our team helped many Chechens, both those who were refugees and living in neighboring Ingushetia and those trapped in war-torn Grozny receive medical and psychological care, I will primarily focus on our efforts with providing care to three Chechen children who we met in Grozny and were able to bring to New York to receive continued care. Being a volunteer in this running club, including serving on the Board of Advisors, the board of the Track Club for Disabled Iraqi War Veterans, and as an athlete due to a post-lenticular cataract that contributed to legal blindness in my right eye, I have experienced first-hand the empowerment of running to overcome life's obstacles and improve mental health. As a result of our visit, on September 11, 2005, 300 disabled Chechen children ran a 5-kilometer race in Ingushetia. It marked the first time a Muslim republic banded together officially to run against terrorism. In June 2007, after two years of emails and telephone calls, and six failures with their exit visas, the three children arrived for their six-week stay in New York. Thanks to the support of several nonprofit organizations, the children received prosthetics and medical care, and their transportation, airfare, and room and board were completely funded. The medical team consisted of two rehabilitation physicians, a medical internist, a prosthetist, a translator, and me, a psychiatrist.

With the translator, I saw the three children alone and as a group five days a week; I also ran with each of the children biweekly in scheduled workouts in Central Park, and saw them at other social and athletic functions. The medical team met weekly to define psychological and medical treatment guidelines for each child, and to set up daily activities, coordinate care, and identify and deal with the children's individual coping difficulties experienced by transitioning from a war-torn environment to a more peaceful one.

In the planning stages of our effort, our medical goal had been to bring back children with below-the-knee amputations (BKA), as we determined that BKA could be significantly medically addressed within the limits of both the six-week length of stay and the limited follow-up medical resources available in Chechnya. Despite our recommendations, and due to understandable circumstances beyond our control, two children were brought who had extensive injuries and who were limited in their recovery by both the practical and medical considerations of their six-week stay.

In an effort to contribute to the understanding of the psychological impact of war on children, we focused on Chechnya, since the Chechen war has been one of the most dangerous, least reported, and least understood in the world today. There is a tremendous need for medically and psychoanalytically trained aid workers in this area. The risk of non-intervention is that the next generation of Chechens will feel a deepening isolation as they struggle alone with the emotional and physical toll the war has brought. By this point in their history, the Chechen sense of vulnerability has increased as their struggle has been largely ignored internationally; much of the violence occurring in Chechnya was not reported by the world press due in part to the political agenda of the United States. The United States was eager to link the Chechens' fight against militant separatists in the North Caucasus with the international struggle against terror (Goldfarb & Litvinenko, 2007). Consequently, the Chechens' sense of hopelessness has left them vulnerable to the lure of terrorism as a means to create awareness of their struggle for survival. It was vitally important that other options be presented and our team found that by understanding the Chechen culture by engaging with individuals—listening and attending to their experience—we developed a deeper understanding. Reaching out to them, the medical team began to attend to their emotional, mental and physical needs to chip away at the hopelessness and despair that breeds terrorism. We hoped that this important therapeutic intervention presented a different paradigm that would take seed in these three Chechen children's lives to help them envision the possibility of a more peaceful and hopeful future and put them on a path of healing.

It was difficult to predict how survivors would respond to the reeducation and training required for them to work through potentially unrealistic expectations and accept the limitations of their medical situation. Our team needed to set realistic limits and boundaries, tolerate the child's (and in the third case, the parent's) potential anger, and avoid making unrealistic promises. Each child's situation needed constant re-evaluation to ensure that we clearly defined the medical limits of recovery and dealt with the child's emotional response. With this approach, feelings of betrayal were minimized and both the child and our team had a more rewarding experience.

REVIEW OF LITERATURE

When working with traumatized individuals, it is essential to be familiar with the multiple manifestations and reverberations of the traumatic event on both the child's and analyst's psyche. One of the key issues in working with traumatized individuals is that the neurological pathway of traumatic memory is different than for normal memory. Rather than being integrated through the mediation of the hippocampus and prefrontal cortex, traumatic memories are short-circuited and stored as somatic sensations and visual images in the amygdala (Boulanger, 2005). Consequently, traumatic memory can initially be expressed non-verbally. Memory for trauma has its own language and verbalization is not the primary one. Moreover, work with survivor testimonies demonstrates that unconscious and repressed memory traces are not preserved intact but are subject to complex modifications (Krystal, 2004).

Among the unique attributes of working with a traumatized individual is his/her altered sense of time. Trauma seems to fragment the individual's experience of continuous time. The past seems to coexist with the present and trauma is experienced as a current event, but it is not always consciously accessible. Memories of trauma are painful to remember as well as hard to forget. They may be remembered, forgotten, and then remembered over again (Alpert, 1997; Grand, 1995; Heim & Nemeroff, 2001; Hoffman, 2004; Nemeroff, 2004; Person & Klar, 1994; Rothe, 2008; Vinar, 2003). One of the major reverberations that results from these issues is that survivors of massive human-made psychic trauma frequently experience deficits in symbolic functioning affecting their capacity to think productively (Boulanger, 2005; Boulanger, 2007; Bromberg, 2000; Laub & Auerhahn, 1989; Laub & Auerhahn, 1993; Prince, 1998).

In the therapeutic milieu, affect dysregulation is a familiar problem for the analytic dyad when the patient is a victim of trauma (Boulanger, 2007; Bromberg, 2000; Krystal, 2004). The return of the traumatic memories with associated intense affect is understood as the product of dissociated affect and knowledge of the traumatic material, and it creates profound implications for patient, analyst, and the analytic relationship. Memory for trauma can come as an enactment rather than through the prefrontal lobe, as in normal memory. The centrality of the enactment of trauma in the clinical situation is well-recognized (Boulanger, 2005; Boulanger, 2007; Bromberg, 2000; Krystal, 2004; Prince, 1998). Indeed, the contribution of psychoanalysis to the human understanding of trauma may well be understood best through enactments. Affect dysregulation tests the ability of the analyst to withstand the patient's affective storms; in doing so, the analyst can reaffirm the patient's sense that one can survive those storms, thereby serving as a role model for the patient to withstand his/her own affect.

As a way of understanding the clinical material, it is essential to be familiar with the Chechen historical and cultural background. A 6,000 square-mile corner of the northern Caucasus, Chechnya is one of seven ethnic republics within the Russian Federation. The seven republics' history is closely intertwined; at the time of our visit, half of Chechnya's population was estimated to be living in refugee camps in Ingushetia, a neighboring republic. This placed a tremendous strain on the tiny republic and, in turn, adversely affected the Chechen–Ingush relationship.

Chechnya has struggled for centuries under Russian domination and its declaration of independence in 1991 led to the most recent war. One of the main cultural differences responsible for the ongoing conflict is religion. Instead of the Russian Orthodox religion practiced in much of Russia, the majority of Chechens are Sunni Muslims. The war was also based on longstanding hostilities that date back to 1785, when Catherine the Great's forces encountered Chechen mountain resistance fighters. In the 19th century, the Caucasus war created Chechen volunteer fighters who rose in patriotic defense of their homeland. The ongoing Chechen–Russian hostilities climaxed in February 1944, when Stalin ordered the deportation of the Chechens from their homeland to Central Asia. In the brutal cold, close to half a million people were crammed into freight trains. Between a quarter and a third of them did not survive the journey. The special emotional bond known to people subjected to genocide, that "never again" sentiment that reduces the whole world to the struggle for survival, has served to unify the Chechens over many generations (Politkovskaya, 2003, p. 16).

Monstrously echoed in Ukraine today, there was much commonality in the Russian atrocities committed in the First and Second Chechen Wars. Even though 30 years have passed, the same Russian barbaric tactics and mistakes are taking place in Ukraine. Thwarted from seizing several major Ukrainian cities, including the capital, Kyiv, the Russian military has regrouped to blitz them from afar. These cities are being pulverized into a scorched earth scenario, destroying infrastructure, including hospitals, maternity wards, bomb shelters and schools, even while thousands of Ukrainian civilians are trapped inside.

The next stage to Putin's grim playbook, well known by Chechens, is tragically now being seen in Ukraine. After releasing horrendous firepower and leveling Grozny to rubble was the strategic use of loyalist Chechen puppets to maintain Russian tyranny. Six years into the Chechen war, Putin appointed the chief mufti of Chechnya to betray the rebel cause. The mufti's son, Ramzan Kadyrov, became Putin's chief henchman and arrogantly bragged to supply Chechen civilians, including boys, and his own adolescent sons, to fight with Russian forces in Ukraine. Kadyrov rules Chechnya through despotism with forced disappearances and torture so widespread that they constitute crimes against humanity. This Russian method of squashing the will of the civilian Chechen population is hauntingly reminiscent in Ukraine. The terrifying ongoing systematic violence and attempts to squash the will of the civilian Ukrainian people is hauntingly reminiscent of the atrocities committed by Russia in the Chechen wars. The only major difference being that in Ukraine we have better-documented world media reports of possible mass Russian war crimes. Similar sinister Russian methods of suppression of the civil Chechen population have reoccurred in Ukraine including, the savage arrest and disappearance of local officials, the grisly detentions, torture, and mass graves of journalists and civilians, the appalling forced mass evacuation of Ukrainians to Russia, and the oppressive indoctrination and "reeducation" of Ukrainians into Russian society. The recent bloodcurdling Russian crackdown and infamous prison in the separatist districts of eastern Ukraine are yet another example of the recurring methods applied in Chechnya by Russia.

When we visited in 2005, the Consolidated Appeals Processes[2] estimated that the majority of the people living in Chechnya could not leave and more than 2,000 children under the age of 3 would die each year as a result of inadequate medical care. Although the numbers were not definitely known, it is estimated that more than 30,000 Chechen children have been injured or killed because of the war or the land mines spread throughout the country. They experienced acts of terrorism, kidnappings, and violence on a daily basis, which has further isolated them from the rest of the world. In addition to this horror, UNICEF reported that from 1994 up to 2008, 25,000 children in Chechnya have lost one or both parents (Seierstad, 2008).

Although Russia has a history of endured persecutions, famines, gulag camps, torture, and organized state murder for most of the 20th century, the notion of trauma is not easy to apply to its people. Historian Catherine Merridale observes with some wonder that the Russians strongly deny any notion of deep psychic damage originating from these events (Merridale, 2001). Post-Traumatic Stress Disorder (PTSD) is not a diagnosis that they seek, and not a label worn with pride. Two considerations may explain this attitude: the fact that mental distress, far from leading to compensation, has been stigmatized in post-Soviet Russia, and that in their earlier history there was no viable alternative than for the people to not discuss some of the things that troubled them.

Other cultural considerations may also play a role in the general Russian denial of trauma among those affected by it. In the Russian milieu, the individual mind is not viewed as the center of every human world, words like "collectivism" and "social effort" come up when former Soviet citizens attempt to explain why Stalin's Russia did not collapse under its burden of despair. It seems as if our Western concept of individuality strikes the Russian sensibility as amusing. Moreover, in Russian culture, the losses and persecutions may be tolerated due to a cultural history of suffering, so it is accepted as an honorable position that is part of the human condition. Rather than admit the level of suffering, though, there is a tradition in Russian culture to hide trauma and loss with fabricated versions of the truth. The Russian parent believes that if they deny that something bad has happened and prevent themself from showing their feelings they have about this trauma, they will save and spare their child the pain of these feelings (Konkov, 2002).

Merridale looked at the effects of trauma and shell shock in a group of people injured as children, under the age of 12, by landmines and stray bullets in 20th-century Russia (Merridale, 2000). She noted that for Russians, mutilation, far from being compensated for, was only the beginning of a lifelong struggle to be allowed to remain visible and lead a reasonably normal life. In fact, these innocent casualties of war were ostracized or suspected by neighbors of having inflicted injuries upon themselves. This served as a troubling example of how Russian culture has coercively suppressed the expression of trauma by this group of injured people.

Similar cultural values were evident to me in 2005 during our visit to Grozny where, despite block after block being a ravaged wasteland scarred with the detritus of ferocious bombings, the Chechens walked the streets prideful of what little they had, dressed as if they were going to their offices. It was in this squalor that 90,000 to 190,000 Chechens made their home. It was hard to imagine Grozny as a once-bustling modern city of education and culture; it became clearer that the attempts to erase the Chechen population from global consciousness had resulted in a cultural anxiety of intense pride and the need to appear "whole." This concrete and intrapsychic perception of wholeness was especially important to the sense of Chechen national pride.

Wars, in general, promote a regression from the depressive position and mobilization of the paranoid-schizoid mechanisms of splitting and projection, as defined by Melanie Klein (1975); there is also a regression to part-object relationships, which exclude empathy, compassion, and concern. The situation for the Chechens is compounded by other factors as well. In the case of the Chechen survivors, the processes of symbolization and sublimation were shattered by the enforced regression in refugee camps to the concreteness and realness of biological need. In addition, the Russian government's lack of acknowledgment of the whereabouts of Chechens who were kidnapped and disappeared has fostered a paranoid-schizoid position among the Chechen populace. Because of the lack of knowledge of how a loved one died and the lack of a body, it is more difficult to validate the death and mourn the loss and thereby achieving the depressive position. There is a sense of inner emptiness, which children experience during arrested mourning, when they feel they have been deceived about the death of their parents or grandparent. Survivor guilt and shame are often at the core of arrested mourning for these children (Valent, 1998).

AN EXAMPLE OF HOW TRAUMATIC LIFE-METAPHOR WAS RESOLVED AT AN EMBODIED, RATHER THAN AN EXCLUSIVELY VERBAL, LEVEL

Ali's story illustrates how effective aid work can be when both medical and psychological conditions are met. Ali was an unusually resilient 17-year-old male with a left BKA resulting from injuries caused by a landmine explosion when he was 8. It was medically recommended he come for treatment in New York, where he received a new prosthetic for his BKA. Ali was an architecture student and, since his father was killed during the war when he was 6, he lived with his mother. Appearing malnourished, Ali had soulful brown eyes beyond his years, a mass of dark curls, and a gentle expression; he was a handsome, engaging, and sensitive young man. He possessed a sense of humor and maturity well beyond his age. We developed an abiding relationship that was cemented when, functioning as his guide, I ran with Ali in the Hope and Possibility race in Central Park. Despite his exposure to oppression, starvation, and other conditions of living in a war zone and in sharp contrast to the materialistic abundance of the West, Ali flourished in New York. He was sociable, and had an amazing, inner flexibility and resilience.

Ali was somehow able to further manage his trauma while in New York and take in what was offered.

In Child Therapy in the Great Outdoors, Sebastiano Santostefano (2004) puts forth that for a child, traumatic life-metaphors may be resolved at an embodied rather than an exclusively verbal level. More specifically, they may be resolved as they are enacted between child and therapist in the outdoors. By running together in Central Park, relational psychoanalysts would argue, an understanding can be conveyed to a patient or analyst through non-verbal actions. For example, Ali seemed apprehensive of descending hills, and each time we approached a decline in our 5-mile loop in Central Park, we would slow down almost to a halt, his discomfort manifested by his facial and body movements. Even though Ali did not express his feelings verbally, seeing his physical expression of agitation led me to believe he was re-experiencing a previous trauma, possibly the landmine accident itself, during which he fell sideways down a ravine. Perhaps, by creating more space to experience his understandable distress in my presence, Ali was better able each time to process his painful emotions upon coming upon a descent and become more likely to construct an embodied solution to the meaning of this fear. Eventually, Ali was able to create a new way of descending with his two-arm crutches—he would swing them alternatively outwards, so that he descended the hill with his body being thrown in a zigzag motion. In this manner, his body would be thrown in the opposite direction of his arm crutch, and he would catch his body weight with the other crutch. As Ali internalized the solutions he enacted with me, his embodied self was revised and a new embodied self emerged. This new self enabled Ali to interact with human and nonhuman environments in ways that then promoted his further development. Ultimately, he was able to descend more confidently and with a newfound freedom. My embodied self was also revised as I internalized enactments experienced during our exercise regimen together, and relied on this revised matrix of embodied metaphors to help my other patients by being able to be more present with them. Taking our therapy to a revised matrix of an embodied life-metaphor, we relied on our non-verbal vocabulary to move from a relational crisis to an enacted solution.

By coming to New York, Ali was able to build upon the emotional and physical recovery that he had already started in his homeland, exemplifying the idea that "experiences wherein child survivors learn to validate their identities without shame, to retrieve memories, and to find their life-purpose have been found to be helpful" (Valent, 1998, p. 118). For instance, he recalled having lost what had brought him joy—Grozny's cultural and architectural treasures, describing how the national museum was bombed after Russian forces looted what they deemed worthy—European paintings—but Chechen art was blown to pieces. While in New York, Ali described and was able to further mourn the loss of buildings built in the 12th century that were leveled to the ground. Ali integrated his life through further emotionally confronting without shame his memories of what he had survived, and when he returned, he continued pursuing his dreams of becoming an architect to rebuild war-torn Grozny.

Ali seemed to have had a fortunate developmental history that facilitated more mature defenses and a flexible coping style that allowed him to deal with the extraordinary atrocities he had experienced. As though he was doggedly unwilling to wean, a noted idiosyncrasy of Ali was his shunning of all liquids at meals except for his notable dedication to milk with dinner. Using humor as a mature defense, Ali was able to take in what we offered and give of himself to others. Not only did he express overwhelming gratitude for what was provided, but he was empathic as well. Local papers covered the Chechen visit and interviewed us extensively concerning the historical context of the war. Upon learning that the news reports left out the atrocities of the Second Chechen War and its important contextual background, he empathized with my frustration, apologized for the paper's oversight, and understood that we had tried to help his case. He encouraged me to resist becoming demoralized and to continue to fight the good fight.

In Kleinian terms, Ali's ability to recognize his own aggression (expressed through empathic humor) and to experience and express mourning for his many losses was characteristic of the depressive position. Ali's gratitude was closely bound up with his ability to be generous and expansive. His good internal object allowed him an inner wealth to draw upon in a foreign environment. Being able to express his sadness and mourn his many losses, Ali was at a more highly integrated level of recovery. Auerhahn and Laub state that the survivors of atrocities, at best, oscillate between images of annihilation and nurturance (Auerhahn & Laub, 1984). Ali was impressively able to hold onto the brutal imagery of his past atrocities, but still maintain a nurturing connection to his caregivers, who offered some hope.

With the analytic process depending on the symbolic representation of experience, Ali and I shared the function of bearing witness to the war crimes that he lived through. The therapeutic position during witnessing is not that of holder, but that of accompanier, the one who stands by. While holding assumes merging, witnessing a painful internal truth requires the assumption of otherness. "In witnessing, we acknowledge the genuineness of what we grasp of the other, while at the same time acknowledging that we can never fully know or grasp what is essential in our patient's otherness" (Ullman, 2006, p. 195). Ultimately, witnessing and listening to Ali's story may have encouraged a way of further restoring his resilient sense of dignity and further undermining the split between self and enemy.

CULTURAL TRADITION AND RELATIVISM HAVING A SIGNIFICANT IMPACT ON ADDRESSING MEDICAL AND QUALITY OF LIFE ISSUES FOR THE CHECHEN CHILD

Ruslan's story illustrates the challenges involved when severe medical and psychological issues are complicated by a limited length of stay in the United States, and the difficulties in overcoming the lack of adequate technical resources in the home country. Ruslan was an 18-year-old male, a computer student, with a left above-the-knee amputation (AKA), right arm above-the-elbow amputation and part of his penis blown off, all resulting from injuries sustained by stray artillery fire that struck him in his backyard play area when he was 10 years old. Despite these circumstances and the Russian cultural value of rejecting the idea of psychological trauma and to coercively suppress the expression of trauma, we found that we were ultimately able to provide Ruslan with some medical care.

Even though we initially worried that his extensive medical needs could not be met given the time limit of his stay and the limited medical resources in Chechnya and had only encouraged those with BKA injuries to come to New York for medical care, Ruslan was brought to New York. Four years old when the first war started, he was only five when he saw his village destroyed and his father kidnapped, never to be heard from again. Not unexpectedly, Ruslan looked malnourished, walked with a limp, and had the wide-eyed stare of a small, hunted animal who expected nothing but trouble.

Ruslan was, as one could anticipate, guarded and depressed; he wanted to get married, but felt reluctant to approach girls due to profound unprocessed feelings of uneasiness about his injuries, which at first he tried to hide from us. Despite Ruslan's emotional withdrawal, he fortunately had bonded with Ali in the hospital in Grozny, and they became very close friends. But Ruslan seemed dissociated from his sadness when talking robotically about what had happened to him. Indeed, he spoke as though nothing that had happened to him had emotionally registered. For Ruslan to get the best coordinated medical care, I felt it was necessary to get the most current medical history from him. Perhaps it was an unfair expectation for us to ask him to be able to talk about his injuries. This situation required a deep intimacy which was foreign to Ruslan because I was asking him to talk about his medical illness which had been culturally ingrained in him to deny. Also, it may personally have served him to block the humiliation of his trauma. Perhaps overwhelmed with being exposed for the first time to a foreign culture, he exhibited an almost detached hostility in his interaction with us.

Seemingly exacerbating Ruslan's fear of being stigmatized and misunderstood as a result of his injuries, he struggled with the pain of fully confronting what had happened to him. When Ruslan attempted to talk about his horrific experiences in Chechnya, the impact of his trauma made his process of remembering and forgetting extremely complex. His significant trauma contributed to his expressing himself in stories containing elements that were fragmented, disjointed, nonsequential, and in actions loaded with symbolism. For instance, one day after visiting the Chechens, I happened to exchange eye contact with Ruslan while he was smoking outside on the street. But when I casually inquired about his smoking, he fervently maintained that he did not smoke, which corroborated that he continued to see me as a dangerous foreigner. Although I attempted to break up the tension with humor, Ruslan seemed to remain distrustful and keep me at a distance, most likely based on his past traumatic history; he may have felt concerned that I also would judge him adversely and abandon him. Perhaps, I was better equipped to withstand the vicissitudes of providing complicated medical care to Ruslan, because I could empathize as I also had difficulties asking for and receiving help from others due to growing up in a house where I often felt endangered. This is not meant to compare Ruslan's trauma, which was gargantuan to my much more minor trauma, but to emphasize that I could relate and understand his mistrustful feelings. His feelings of emasculation were further symbolized by his recurring need to camouflage his stumps, and emphasized by his lack of expression of feelings of loss, doubt, fear, horror, and despair in recalling his past traumatic events.

We attempted to take Ruslan from an environment of extreme degradation to one that offered some hope, but he had difficulty in not reenacting his past traumas. His prickliness seemed a cover to hide his grievous wounds, and to push us away before we could potentially reinjure him. Initially, in working with the prosthetist, he revealed being provided with one poor artificial leg made of wood and withheld information about being provided in Chechnya with a second, albeit poor, prosthetic to use for his leg when playing sports. The prosthetist noticed on race day that he was using this second prosthetic. When I attempted to discuss why he had never revealed having a second prosthetic, he became defensive and then emotionally shut down, refusing to tell us about his circumstance. We tried to reassure him that in order to best serve his medical needs, we needed full disclosure, which would not hinder us from remaining committed to offering him the best indicated medical help.

Despite numerous conversations with our medical team, Ruslan refused to grasp that if we fit him with the most advanced technical prosthetic, it would break down since it required constant maintenance and readjustments that were not available in Chechnya. Complicating matters, a team member, in denial of the limitations of the situation, made unrealistic promises. Nonetheless, we were able to fit Ruslan with two new prosthetics: one for his left leg and the other for his right arm. Both were suction-based and decreased his edematous stumps.

Due to his past shameful experiences with violence, Ruslan partly relived his feelings of hopeless deprivation while in New York. He showed his resentment because he seemed to feel that his close friend's medical needs were being met while his own more extensive injuries were not, as they were more difficult to address given the time limit and the lack of resources in Chechnya. Despite our team again trying to explain the limitations of his medical situation, he reverted to a concrete, presymbolic logic that interfered with his acceptance, a reversion that Laub and Auerhahn, who worked with concentration camp survivors, described as retaining "the memory of a basic deficit" that causes "a compromise in the empathic dyad" (Laub & Auerhahn, 1989, p. 378). As a result, there may no longer be a matrix of two people: self and resonating other. The survivor of genocide experiences an inability to affect the environment interpersonally so as to elicit a sense of mutuality. The survivor of genocide feels that there was no longer anyone on whom to count, as the link between self and other has been effaced by the failure of empathy. I found that I needed more extensive empathy because my do-gooder best intentions were met with profound suspicions.

The essence of Ruslan's psychic numbing was his inability to symbolize and find meaning as is common to other survivors of significant trauma. Ruslan's psychic numbing was a post-traumatic effect that was characterized by his detached feeling, his estrangement from us, and his loss of a spontaneous emotional experience while in New York. Ruslan's trauma seemed to lead to a defensive introjection of his malignant persecutory internal object that inflicted on him a pervasive, degraded, death-sentenced self-image. His memory of this basic deficit, a compromise in the empathic dyad between self and empathic other, a link first established by the expectation of mutual responsiveness in the mother–child bond and objectified in the maternal introject, led to his belief that he would not receive the same medical care that others would. The impact of Ruslan's trauma was an unraveling of this relationship between self and nurturing other. As a result of his traumatic experience of the genocide of the Chechens being erased, he revived this barbaric experience with us in that he felt he could not elicit a sense of mutuality, and that our medical team would only disappoint and abandon him. We were trying to provide the best medical care given his considerable medical injuries, but similar to other survivors of genocide, Ruslan could only reexperience his previous trauma.

The intensity of Ruslan's trauma experience, combined with his difficulty to function symbolically, led to quagmires in finding ways to navigate the turmoil each of us felt and sustain ourselves through his medical care. In reverting to the presymbolic mode of the paranoid-schizoid position, Ruslan distrusted and feared taking in what was being offered in New York and remained encapsulated in his rage. He exemplified what Klein describes when she states, "Deprivation increases greed and persecutory anxiety. The envious person is insatiable; he can never be satisfied because his envy stems from within and therefore always finds an object to focus on" (Klein, 1975, p. 183). In Ruslan's case, his inability to restore, or in Kleinian terms, to repair, the lost object transformed the fragmented pieces into persecutory objects. Relating to his defensive system as this was personally well known to me, I could empathize with Ruslan's struggle. I also grappled with assimilating any novel learning that would disrupt my past familiar persecutory experiences. I easily related to his feelings of being constantly betrayed and deserted. His regression to the paranoid-schizoid position was then manifested by the prevalence of persecutory anxiety rather than depressive guilt.

Our clinical interventions, however, surprisingly had a delayed impact on Ruslan's intersubjectivity. Several months after leaving New York, we received an email that provided news that Ruslan had married within two weeks of returning home. Ruslan's rehabilitation allowed him not only to appear more whole, and therefore be less ostracized and more integrated in his culture, but also to get back on his developmental track to marry and receive care for his emotional and physical needs.

We found the Russian cultural value of ostracizing amputees was circumvented in part by helping Ruslan to appear more "whole" to his community. This Russian cultural value enlarged and altered our Western sense of what could be "significantly" accomplished. Ruslan's sense of not being "whole" as a result of his injuries served as a life-metaphor for the extreme devastation, deprivation, and loss experienced by the Chechens. As he felt a renewed sense of "wholeness," made possible by his new prosthetics, Ruslan developed a new matrix of embodied life-metaphor. This matrix contained meanings that prescribed Ruslan to interact with a new fledgling acceptance, with a wider range of attributes that enabled him to continue negotiating his developmental needs and promoting his integration. What we had previously considered to be "insignificant" medical care, proved to be "adequate" medical care in the Russian culture. Due to the cultural importance of appearing "whole," Ruslan felt more confident and dared to submerge himself into a marriage and a more integrated life.

ANALYST FUNCTIONS AS RECOGNIZING WITNESS TO A PARENT'S TRAUMA; THE "BEING WITH" OF THE RELATIONSHIP FACILITATES THE AGENT OF THE PARENT'S CHANGE

This case illustrates the challenges involved in providing medical care for the child of a traumatized parent and the need to be multimodal psychoanalytically informed in withstanding the parent's affective storms, reshaping his trauma experience as an object of memory, and working through the enactments that accompany them. Even when the medical condition was suboptimal, the parent was still able to work through his maelstroms of anger toward further acceptance and gratitude.

Anzor was a dignified 53-year-old married man, father to five children, and caretaker of Malika, his disabled, nonambulatory daughter. He was a rather noble creature who had served in the Russian army and was single-mindedly directed in his mission to help his daughter. While I was in Grozny in 2005, Anzor was engaging and charming. He had shown me an earlier photo of Malika, an anodyne disguise for her horrendous medical history, which was proudly displayed on his desk. The photo revealed a plump, well-developed, and groomed, rosy-cheeked neonate, but her medical history was quite complicated. During the 2001 Russian bombing of Grozny, which killed over 100,000 civilian Chechens, Malika was delivered in an underground shelter. Her delivery was complicated by premature rupture of membranes and anoxic encephalopathy. Once her medical charts were translated, Malika's medical diagnosis was unclear since her Chechen medical work-up had been limited. We expressed our concern to her father at that time that we might not be able to significantly improve her medical status. Despite our medical recommendations against it, Anzor brought his now 7-year-old disabled daughter to New York.

When I first met Malika, she was being carried by her father. Malika was unable to walk, spoke only a few words of Chechen, and was incontinent of stool. She did not attend school and was carried, fed, and changed by her father. Tears filled my eyes as I was touched by the loving tenderness and devotion of this father to his disabled daughter. He tied Malika's disabilities to the struggle of his country, saying that for 300 years, we were fighting for freedom and independence, but now we're fighting to survive.

While in New York City, Malika received a diagnosis of Spastic Cerebral Palsy (CP). Her temperament was affable, sweet, and loving; she seemed alert, intelligent, and sensitive to her surroundings. Over the six weeks, Malika received a wheelchair and extensive medical care and rehabilitation. However, she would still need ongoing and intensive speech, cognitive, and physical therapy.

Despite his intelligence and sophistication in negotiating systems, Anzor's lack of medical knowledge and wish for his daughter to be healthy contributed to his having magical expectations for his daughter's cure. This was, in part, exacerbated by his romantic and idealized belief that America is "the land of freedom with the promise that everything is possible." After his daughter's initial medical visit, Anzor was visibly upset and angry. Despite struggling to hold back my tears as I felt responsible both for bringing them to New York and for his suffering, I struggled to approach him more assertively in order to try to explain the limited positive outcomes we could expect. He was convinced that his daughter needed "brain surgery by an American doctor" in order to reverse the damage caused during her traumatic birth. As this was not a reasonable outcome for Malika's condition, I tried to explain that the damage was permanent and that only a slow and constant rehabilitation could incrementally affect her development.

Feeling deflated and powerless, Anzor expressed anger and frustration toward the doctors caring for his daughter and did not want to be compliant with follow-up visits. Initially, Anzor was unable to overcome his feelings of hopelessness and felt resentment and anger. He asked me if the physician, a top-ranked and world-renowned New York City physiatrist, who was treating his daughter was "a real doctor?" At one point, he expressed his belief that his daughter's medical problems resulted from poisoning. Due to my own feelings of guilt and powerlessness, I found it necessary to take intermittent breaks in my attempts to be with Anzor's rage and to help him express his anger rather than reenact it, manage his disappointments, and be able to seek support for his daughter's medical care. Despite his resurgence of anger and resentment, I tried to encourage him to continue with the rehabilitation in order to gain a more realistic understanding of Malika's medical prognosis.

While in New York, we encouraged and provided the opportunity for Anzor to speak with the families of other disabled children, and in that milieu he seemed fortified to better confront the profound issues that fueled his anger. He expressed to me that in order for his family to survive during the war, he felt he had to shed his and his family's humanity for a while. He felt remorse for having submitted himself and his family to barbaric treatment by hiding in an underground tunnel to survive the Russian bombing in 2001. While watching the difficult and medically unattended birth of his daughter, he may have felt impotent because of his inability to have access to medical resources to intervene and help his daughter. I empathized with his sense of helplessness in having to turn himself and his family into "underground animals" in order to survive the bombings, which must have felt devastatingly dehumanizing. Some of his understandable difficulty with more fully accepting his daughter's condition was somewhat assuaged by his being in a caring environment while in New York and having the support of other American parents of disabled children with similar experiences.

Anzor's sense of humiliation was not unique to other peoples subjected to genocide, where the aggression is driven to destroy their personhood. Nor could his sense of shame in his survivor's psyche be wished away by our respectful ideas. The violence perpetrated in ethnic war and genocide is "purely to the identity and existence of the targeted group" (Hoffman, 2004).

It seemed that Anzor became somewhat more accepting of his daughter's condition. It may have been the cumulative influence of many physicians providing consistent medical information regarding his daughter's illness that contributed more to his ambivalent acceptance. Also, in our relationship, I functioned as a recognizing witness to his trauma. I would like to believe that "the being with" of our relationship was, in part, the agent of his change. From our initial meeting over two years earlier, Anzor was able to take the leap of faith toward a relationship with me and I toward him. I finally was able to struggle through my feelings of guilt and powerlessness to surrender to empathic attunement while still holding on to my sense of self.

Countertransferentially, I went through what Anzor experienced in a more condensed period of time. When Anzor pulled the tattered business card that I had given him in Grozny over two years earlier out of his shirt pocket and told me he had kept it close to his heart ever since, I felt an overwhelming sense of guilt, impotence, and responsibility for offering help and thereby exposing Anzor and his daughter to possible treatments that may never be available to them. The humiliation I felt at my inability to fix Malika's brain led me to reflect upon an earlier, concrete period of my own development where I felt inadequate.

During the middle of their stay, a medical internist expressed her anger that these Chechen children "should never have been brought to New York to receive medical treatment." This internist seemed to be expressing her anger and unprocessed feelings of guilt and remorse that we were able only to provide limited medical aid and could not erase the horrors that the Chechens had been exposed to and their suffering from these subsequent medical illnesses as a result of the war. Forgetting that at best we can only aspire in life, and like Moses none of us get to the promised land, this internist seemed to suffer the same hope in magic as Anzor.

By struggling through my own pain and working through my feelings of shame in therapy, I traveled to a more symbolic understanding and appreciation of what we did provide: helping to further slowly release Anzor from his trauma by offering medical information on Malika's condition, sharing his pain, empathizing, and bearing witness to their trauma. As a result, I became better able to emotionally remain with Anzor through his anger, the redirection of his potentially self-destructive behavior, and his beginning to mourn the loss of the hope that his daughter would fully recover, and help diminish his magical beliefs in a cure for acceptance of the efficacy of realistic help. The intensity of Anzor's trauma experience, coupled with my initial failure of symbolic understanding of what our team did offer, made it initially difficult for me to navigate his turmoil and sustain myself through his maelstroms. Multimodal psychoanalytic understanding was a rich resource for accompanying this man in attempting to reshape his trauma experience as an object of memory as opposed to reenactment.

One antidote to compensate for the feeling of hopelessness that inevitably results from war may be the empowering feeling of "I can." Illusory as it was, Anzor's grandiose defense that "he can" nevertheless served him to survive the atrocities of the war, pursue a faith in improving his daughter's illness and the tenacity to come to America. Both of us had to struggle through our grandiose sense of self in an attempt to overcome our mutual feelings of ineffectiveness to foster an acceptance of the limitations of my medical powers to cure, what we could medically provide, and the chronic nature of Malika's condition. Also, I unconsciously may have attempted to repair my long-held sense of impotence by a feeling of "I can" by going into the Second Chechen War to offer medical care. In both of us, our courage was a defense against feelings of helplessness. In order to submerge my anxious feelings of infectiousness, my grandiose defense, similar to Anzor's defense, helped me survive my childhood, and buoyed me into genuine accomplishments by becoming a physician and elite endurance athlete. And like Anzor, my defense also ultimately got in my way as I had to discover more realistic acceptance. My counterphobic delusion of being warrior king which covered my sad feeling of helplessness had to be dragged into the golden middle so that I could accept my own limitations but still deliver the best medical care to Malika, in spite of the unavoidable limitations. As we had not promised radical change, a "revolution" in medical care was not in the offering.

As Gerson has indicated, it is important for the analyst to work through shame in the transference, and that transference can be so shame-producing that it is avoided (Gerson, 1996, p. 190). Just as my mother did not recognize feelings of mine that were unimportant to her, I failed empathically in recognizing the feelings of Anzor. I over-identified with him and with the Chechens who were stranded, abandoned, and forgotten by the world. My feelings of being infectious all came sailing back for another slap in the face. My colluding with Anzor's feeling of shame and anger that we could not fix Malika's brain prevented me from staying in the moment with Anzor's anger and attempting to work it through. The Chechen fight for freedom and independence resonated in me through my lifelong struggle not to be "colonized" by my mother's intrusiveness and to define my own "country" and sense of self. Indeed, similar to the Chechens who are portrayed historically as "terrorists" and "bandits" in their attempt to separate and be independent from Russia, I was seen as "bad" when attempting to separate and individuate from my mother, as she felt abandoned.

Our team needed to be constantly mindful of being emotionally present while maintaining enough distance to work with the visiting Chechen patients and families and not inflate goals. We needed to be aware of their expectations and of our own desire to meet those expectations. Through his boundless spirit and energy, Anzor was able to begin to reshape his trauma experience as an object of memory as opposed to reenactment, better reflect on and be less ambivalent on accepting Malika's medical condition, and become more realistic regarding her treatment and the limits of her recovery.

Toward the end of their stay, we brought Ali, Ruslan, Anzor, and Malika to a Lighthouse Guild party for blind children. As the Chechen children and I entered the festive space decorated with balloons and food-filled tables, they suddenly morphed into familiar, giddy children, who could squeal at opening Christmas stockings. Their vibrant smiles were contagious. Momentarily suspended from their enveloping grief, the Chechens had an astonishing, innate, social ease that erupted in meeting other disabled children and enjoying the various food that was served. Their joyful spontaneity released the confines of my professional harness as a physician, medical advocate, and coordinator, allowing me to reveal myself as their playful companion. I no longer was in running clothes but wore my favorite blue dress and makeup. Ironically, the Chechen's levity was so infectious that it challenged my old nemesis of feeling infectious in a negative way that I transformed into an unburdened partier. Displaying a pure sense of gratitude, there was more of a flowing reciprocity of genuine connection and concern between us. I proudly introduced them to the other children and despite the language barrier, felt closely bonded to them. After the party, I ensured that they had transportation to where we had provided housing for them during their stay in New York City. They, in turn, showed their protective regard for my safety by inquiring how I was getting home after the party. Becoming part of my metaphorical family, the Chechens had forever entered my heart.

CONCLUSION

It is my hope with this chapter to illustrate the various challenges, potential pitfalls, and incredible fulfillment and healing possible while providing care to children ravaged by war. While the odds are heavily stacked against these survivors, we hoped that the progress initiated in New York could generate further growth when they returned to their homeland. For the larger Chechen population and for other societies ravaged by war, there is a tremendous need for organized, sustainable, therapeutic, and medical intervention, and for studies to be done that consider the larger need and the types of aid that can be achieved. It was a profound experience to try to balance the vicissitudes of the Chechens' enormous hope against our limited promise of help, while exposing them to basic rights and freedoms they may never have. In working with these survivors, there was a vast opportunity for all involved to learn and grow. Those engaged in this program were not only enriched by learning about the complex history and tradition of these people, but also by learning about the indomitable, independent, proud, and fiercely loyal Chechen spirit held within the frame of the infinite, complex human spirit—that endures even under the incredible deprivation and suffering that the war brought. Multimodal psychoanalytic and cultural sensitivity allowed us to attend to the unique and often unexpected ways these children organize their emotional responses to trauma and to the caregiver process; ultimately, these children were not only able to cope, but to flourish.

NOTES

1 Parts of this chapter appeared in an earlier version in Cerfolio (2009) and are gratefully reprinted with permission from Guilford Press.
2 The Consolidated Appeals Process includes numerous United Nations organizations like the International Organization for Migration, the Red Cross, and the United Nations International Children Fund (UNICEF).

REFERENCES

Alpert, J. (1997). Story-truth and happening-truth. In R. B. Gartner (Ed.), *Memories of sexual betrayal: Truth, fantasy, repression, and dissociation* (pp. 237–252). Jason Aronson.
Auerhahn, N. C., & Laub, D. (1984). Annihilation and restoration: Post-traumatic memory as pathway and obstacle to recovery. *International Review of Psycho-Analysis*, 11(3), 327–344.
Boulanger, G. (2005). From voyeur to witness: Recapturing symbolic function after massive psychic trauma. *Psychoanalytic Psychology*, 22(1), 21–31. http://doi.org/10.1037/0736-9735.22.1.21
Boulanger, G. (2007). *Wounded by reality: Understanding and treating adult onset trauma* (Psychoanalysis in a New Key Book Series, Vol. 6). Routledge.
Bromberg, P. M. (2000). Potholes on the royal road: Or is it an abyss? *Contemporary Psychoanalysis*, 36(1), 5–28. http://doi.org/10.1080/00107530.2000.10747043
Cerfolio, N. (2009). Multimodal psychoanalytically informed aid work with children traumatized by the Chechen War. *The Journal of the American Academy of Psychoanalysis and Dynamic Psychiatry*, 37(4), 587–603. http://doi.org/10.1521/jaap.2009.37.4.587
Davoine, F., & Gaudillière, J.-M. (2004). *History beyond trauma: Whereof one cannot speak, thereof one cannot stay silent* (S. Fairfield, Trans.). Other Books.
Gerson, B. (Ed.). (1996). *The therapist as a person: Life crises, life choices, life experiences, and their effects on treatment.* Routledge. http://doi.org/10.4324/9780203767184
Goldfarb, A., & Litvinenko, M. (2007). *Death of a dissident: The poisoning of Alexander Litvinenko and the return of the KGB.* Free Press.
Grand, S. (1995). Incest and the intersubjective politics of knowing history. In J. L. Alpert (Ed.), *Sexual abuse recalled: Treating trauma in the era of the recovered memory debate* (pp. 235–256). Jason Aronson.
Heim, C., & Nemeroff, C. B. (2001). The role of childhood trauma in the neurobiology of mood and anxiety disorders: Preclinical and clinical studies. *Biological Psychiatry*, 49(12), 1023–1039. http://doi.org/10.1016/S0006-3223(01)01157-X
Hoffman, E. (2004). *After such knowledge: Memory, history, and the legacy of the Holocaust.* PublicAffairs.
Klein, M. (1975). *Envy and gratitude and other works, 1946–1963.* The Free Press.
Koenigsberg, R. A. (2009). *Nations have the right to kill: Hitler, the Holocaust, and war.* Library of Social Science.
Konkov, F. (2002). Russia: An emptiness within. In J. D. Lindy & R. J. Lifton (Eds.), *Beyond invisible walls: The psychological legacy of Soviet trauma, east European therapists and their patients* (pp. 120–139). Brunner-Routledge.

Krystal, H. (2004). Resilience: Accommodation and recovery. In D. Knafo (Ed.), *Living with terror, working with trauma: A clinician's handbook* (pp. 67–83). Jason Aronson.

Laub, D., & Auerhahn, N. C. (1989). Failed Empathy—A central theme in the survivor's Holocaust experience. *Psychoanalytic Psychology*, 6(4), 377–400. http://doi.org/10.1037/0736-9735.6.4.377

Laub, D., & Auerhahn, N. C. (1993). Knowing and not knowing massive psychic trauma: Forms of traumatic memory. *The International Journal of Psycho-Analysis*, 74(2), 287–302.

Lifton, R. J. (2022, March 14). Is Putin beyond influence? How to stop a man on a mission. *Psychology Today*. https://www.psychologytoday.com/us/blog/the-guest-room/202203/is-putin-beyond-influence

Merridale, C. (2000). The collective mind: Trauma and shell-shock in twentieth-century Russia. *Journal of Contemporary History*, 35(1), 39–55. http://doi.org/10.1177/002200940003500105

Merridale, C. (2001). *Night of stone: Death and memory in twentieth-century Russia*. Viking.

Nemeroff, C. B. (2004). Neurobiological consequences of childhood trauma [Supplemental material]. *The Journal of Clinical Psychiatry*, 65 Suppl. 1, 18–27.

Person, E. S., & Klar, H. (1994). Establishing trauma: The difficulty distinguishing between memories and fantasies. *Journal of the American Psychoanalytic Association*, 42(4), 1055–1081.

Politkovskaya, A. (with Derluguian, G. M.) (2003). *A small corner of hell: Dispatches from Chechnya* (A. Burry & T. Tulchinsky, Trans.). The University of Chicago Press. http://doi.org/10.7208/chicago/9780226674346.001.0001

Prince, R. (1998). Historical trauma: Psychohistorical reflections on the Holocaust. In J. S. Kestenberg & C. Kahn (Eds.), *Children surviving persecution: An international study of trauma and healing* (pp. 43–53). Praeger.

Rethmeier, A. (1995). *"Nürnberger Rassegesetze" und Entrechtung der Juden im Zivilrecht* ["Nuremberg Race Laws" and disenfranchisement of Jews in civil law]. P. Lang.

Rothe, E. M. (2008). A psychotherapy model for treating refugee children caught in the midst of catastrophic situations. *The Journal of the American Academy of Psychoanalysis and Dynamic Psychiatry*, 36(4), 625–643. http://doi.org/10.1521/jaap.2008.36.4.625

Santostefano, S. (2004). *Child therapy in the great outdoors: A relational view* (Relational Perspectives Book Series, Vol. 29). Routledge.

Seierstad, A. (2008). *The angel of Grozny: Orphans of a forgotten war* (N. Chrijstensen, Trans.). Basic Books.

Ullman, C. (2006). Bearing witness: Across the barriers in society and in the clinic. *Psychoanalytic Dialogues*, 16(2), 181–198.

Valent, P. (1998). Child survivors: A review. In J. Kestenberg & C. Kahn (Eds.), *An international study of trauma and healing* (pp. 109–123). Praeger Publishers.

Vinar, M. (with Tylim, I.) (2003). Subjectivity under extreme conditions. In J. A. Cancelmo, I. Tylim, J. Hoffenberg, & H. Myers (Eds.), *Terrorism and the psychoanalytic space: International perspectives from Ground Zero* (pp. 171–172). Pace University Press.

Whitman, J. Q. (2017). *Hitler's American model: The United States and the making of Nazi Race Law*. Princeton University Press. https://doi.org/10.1515/9781400884636

7

Terrorism as a Perverted Negative Form of Attachment and Spirituality[1,2]

The wings of transformation take empathy and love.

Terrorism is one of the most pervasive complex problems of our time and combating violent extremism requires a deeper understanding of the unique social, political, religious, historical, and other factors for each terrorist act (Bongar et al., 2006). It is well known and documented that victims of violence experience feelings of powerlessness and impotence and may seek revenge. Further,

105

DOI: 10.4324/9781032633497-8

they can pervert religious principles in the service of hate for a twisted perceived sense of good. However, when we shine a brighter light on the human aggression and destructive instincts underlying terrorism, including cultural and spiritual aspects, a fuller, effectual picture is illuminated. International terrorists, for example, are usually motivated by reasons that may have little to do with the religious and political narratives they spin, and they always have a grievance that can be heard if you listen (Stern, 2003; Stern, 2010; Lotto, 2017). Many have documented the lack of mental or psychological disorder and how frighteningly "normal" the recruited, international terrorists can be (Silke, 2003; Post, 2005; Horgan, 2017; Gill & Corner, 2017). Terrorists may be driven by a multitude of factors: hate, trauma, humiliation, a search for identity, craving for attention (Stern, 2003; McCauley, 2017), and revenge. The power of terrorists is heightened by terrorist organizations, which are formed by radicalizers who, using oppression, isolation, and religion as both motivation and justification, can more easily recruit the disenfranchised. Another attraction of terrorism is the possibility of experiencing a profoundly thrilling, empowering, and spiritual intoxication (Stern, 2003; Cottee & Hayward, 2011).

"Why terrorism?" has become the modern-day version of the question "Why war?" that Einstein presented to Freud in 1932 (Einstein & Freud, 1981). Freud was absorbed in observing the impact of the collective violence of World War I on the human psyche. The psychoanalytic community, however, later became silent on the impact of the war, perhaps because of its own close encounter with the violence and loss experienced during World War II (Varvin & Volkan, 2018). As happened not only to Jews but also gay people, and the mentally or physically disabled during World War II, victimized groups today such as the Chechens suffer from dignity violations and a resulting sense of isolation, hopelessness, and humiliation which contributes to present-day terrorism.

Muslim humiliation by America and its allies is one of the driving forces of international terrorism and the ensuing cycles of violence. Both the Tsarnaev brothers (the Boston Marathon bombers) and Mohamed Atta (the 9/11 ringleader and pilot who crashed the American Airlines plane into the North Tower of the World Trade Center) identified as Muslim and may have been motivated by a sense of impotence in the genesis of their desire for violent retribution. Born in the shame of defeat, radical Islamists, like the Tsarnaevs and Atta, could be seen as sharing a fanatical determination to get on top of history after being underfoot for many generations. They have felt themselves to be victims of a history of violence and powerless to make the aggression stop, which is at the core of humiliating experiences. Their utter sense of certainty that they were right in committing horrendous terrorist acts of violence against Westerners, their perceived enemy, may have provided them with a sense of order and stability. In this chapter, the possible contextual motives of the Tsarnaevs and Atta are further explored as a means of deepening our understanding of their terrorist acts and ultimately to discover ways we could possibly avoid such tragic events in the future.

Susan Levine's *Dignity Matters* (2016) maintains that dignity is a basic human right, a vital need, that is a birthright to every human being. With that in mind, she examines the role of dignity violations in the understanding and treatment of trauma and the genesis of terrorism. When we treat others with indignity, a sense of humiliation results, which can be an important driver of retribution and terrorism. Acknowledging the loss and violation of a population's dignity and working to restore it can be a powerful force in conflict resolution. She refers to two interviews: one, an interview by a Black African from Cape Town, Pumla Gobodo-Madikizela with Eugene de Kock, the infamous white torturer of black South Africans during apartheid (Levine, 2016), and the other, Jessica Stern's interview with a terrorist imprisoned for life in Sweden (Levine, 2016). Levine maintains that helping perpetrators acknowledge the devastating harm they have done to others, as well as to their own selves, can restore dignity to both perpetrator and victim (Coen, 2018; Hicks, 2011; Gobodo-Madikizela, 2015; Stern, 2014).

Working in the field of international conflict resolution, Donna Hicks (2011) has applied these principles to facilitate dialogue between communities in conflict. When dignity is violated, the response is likely to involve vengeful violence. She describes an encounter with a member of an African guerilla organization representing an ethnic minority which was fighting for independence from the African majority government. The African guerillas were able to stay in control of their territory even when they were significantly outnumbered by the majority culture's army because the guerillas were fighting to protect the dignity of their people. This pattern of an unrelenting effort at empowerment by an ethnic minority is similar to that of the Chechen minority's attempt to restore the worth of its people despite being significantly outnumbered by the Russian army in their struggle for independence from Russia during the First and Second Chechen Wars. Hannah Arendt, in *The Origins of Totalitarianism*, described loneliness as the common ground for terror and explored its function as the chief weapon of oppressive political regimes. Arendt maintained that when people lose contact and are isolated from their fellow men, as well as the reality around them, their capacity for both experience and thought is diminished. Terror, she argues, can rule absolutely only over people who are isolated against each other (Arendt, 1968). This isolation and terror that Arendt describes also reflects the condition characterized in Chechnya during the Second Chechen War.

CHECHEN OPPRESSION AND THE ORIGINS OF INTERNATIONAL TERRORISM

When we lose sight of the fact that we are all inherently valuable and matter as human beings, we allow our dignity and our humanity to slip out of our hands. Inequality, discrimination, and injustice are all violent acts that have been perpetrated by Russia's policy in Chechnya. Although the Chechens' basic human dignity can never be abrogated, Russia's oppressive political regime in Chechnya has violated the Chechen's self-worth while subverting Russia's own dignity. When those of us in the rest of the world turn our backs on the suffering of the Chechens, we deny the respect of the Chechens, and we also lose our own humanity in the process (Cerfolio, 2021).

The devastating effects of the long-term full-blown imposed alienation Chechens experienced from their fellow man and the rest of the world is exemplified by the tyrannical Russian government's war in the First and Second Chechen Wars from 1994 to 2009. Starting in 1994, secret Russian black operations in Chechnya were attempting to keep the Soviet Union a single state (Dunlop, 1998), and as a result the international community knew little about what was happening in Chechnya (Lenkvist, 2010). The powerful Russian military waged decades of wars and destroyed the private lives of Chechens through endemic torture, poisonings, and murders. As a result of this isolation, a collective desperate Chechen sense of not belonging to humanity developed. I first became knowledgeable about Chechen history and their feelings of being forgotten and a sense of not belonging when I traveled to Grozny during the Second Chechen War to provide medical care to the Chechens.

During the Second Chechen War, the more fortunate Chechens that escaped before the Russian army occupation, nevertheless, lost their homes, culture, and familiar way of life (Cerfolio, 2009). Forced to live in camps, fields, or just the middle of nowhere, they lived in extreme hardship (Politkovskaya, 2003). Adding to the Chechen sense of helplessness is the fact that their struggle was largely ignored by the rest of the world; much of the violence occurring in Chechnya was not reported by the world press due in part to the political agenda of the United States, which further exacerbated the Chechens' sense of isolation. The United States was eager to identify the Chechens' fight as an example of international terrorism rather than as a fight for autonomy and defense against Russian oppression (Goldfarb & Litvinenko, 2007). Consequently, the Chechens' sense of hopelessness has left them vulnerable to the lure of terrorism, ironically, as a desperate means to create awareness of their struggle for survival.

OUR TEAM'S CHECHEN MISSION

You can't unknow what you know. The risk of non-intervention is that the next generation of Chechens will feel a deepening isolation—the obliteration of a sense of belonging and connection to humanity—as they struggle alone with the emotional and physical toll the war has brought. When young children, like the Chechens, grow up in a depraved environment of humiliating oppression with no possibility of stopping the bombings, shellings, torture, and "disappearances" and there is no accountability for these state-sponsored war crimes, their loss of dignity, alienation, and hopefulness multiplies. This violence perpetrated on innocent victims could lure them in the direction of terrorism in a desperate attempt to bring a voice to their plight. Extreme injustice leads to extreme measures. Impelled by our humanity and conscience, our team's humanitarian aid in Chechnya served to build bridges to the disenfranchised in the hopes of slowly assuaging their feelings of hopelessness which so often breeds terrorism and decreasing this cycle of violence. Even though there was a far greater need for intervention than we could provide, I believe that by reaching out to even one child and attending to their medical and psychological needs, we contributed to a sense of connection, helping the marginalized feel less alone. There is a tremendous need for medically and psychodynamically trained aid workers in Chechnya. We as psychoanalysts share the moral burden to help the surviving children of the genocide better digest their trauma.

Although the *New York Times* in 2005 did not widely cover the Chechen genocide or our group's humanitarian mission, *The New York Daily News* as well as local Chechen and Russian newspapers covered our humanitarian work during the Second Chechen War. The news coverage of our Chechen community outreach provided a glimpse into the Chechen sense of oppression by the more powerful Russian army, which had generated a deep sense of Muslim humiliation. The younger brother's social post "#chechnyapower" may have been a defensive reaction to his feeling of impotency and a reflection of his intimate knowledge of Russian's brutal oppression, specifically the barbaric torture of his father in one of the many Russian camps by KGB agents during the Chechen War. The many indignities of rape, bombing, torturing, and the "disappearances" of innocent Chechen civilians may be some of the motivating factors that drove the Tsarnaev brothers to recreate the atrocities that they had experienced as boys in Chechnya to commit their violent acts of retribution during the Boston Marathon bombings. The brothers were repeating their childhood experiences in Chechnya during the Boston Marathon bombing.

By slowly changing the environment of humiliation, hopelessness, and lack of opportunity and a sense of belonging, I believe it is possible to begin to slowly chip away at the present trends of violence. Toward this goal, we took one small step. We organized a 5-kilometer Hope and Possibility race from Nazran to Magas, Ingushetia. It took place two weeks after we left the North Caucasus. More than 200 Chechens, including invalid children and refugees, ran for Hope and Possibility on September 11, 2005. This race marked the first time a Muslim republic banded together to run on a notorious date in defiance of terrorism.

Despite our efforts of hope to slowly begin to lessen the cycle of violent retribution, there was a murder of a race participant. A deaf Chechen woman, a teacher and founder of a deaf school for the refugee Chechen children in Ingushetia, was run over by a speeding government car that left the scene of the crime. While we were in the North Caucasus, we visited her in her stark one-room school, while she proudly served tea. She told us about her deaf daughter who was also a student at the school. Taking this hit-and-run murder as a warning from the Russian government, the Chechens did not hold this race against terrorism in the North Caucasus again. This situation mirrored the more famous tragic stories of truth-tellers who tried to reveal the horrors of routine life in Chechnya. Alexander Litvinenko divulged Russian horrors such as the support of terrorism in Chechnya and worldwide by the KGB and FSB and their routine use of deadly poisons to kill dissidents (Litvinenko & Felshtinsky, 2007; Politkovskaya, 2006).

Litvinenko accused Putin of ordering the murder of Anna Politkovskaya, who resolutely reported on the torture of Chechens and political events in the Second Chechen War (Politkovskaya, 2004).

The murders of Alexander Litvinenko and Anna Politkovskaya, who both reported on the framing and torture of Chechens, served to deepen the Chechen sense of alienation, injustice, and loneliness (Cerfolio, 2021). The biographies of Litvinenko and Politkovskaya serve as the most well-known examples of how state-sponsored terrorism works to strip people of their personhood and dignity. Russian oppression in Chechnya has created a republic under immense stress about to explode. When there is no justice for the loss of basic human rights, how does this affect the young Chechens growing up? The destruction of war and the consequent reaction of rage, powerlessness, and shame with the burning desire for vengeance for the purpose of righting a wrong and to seek justice, is one of the most significant causes of international terrorism.

Nation-states have caused far more harm and suffering than non-state terrorists. Since 1999, in Chechnya alone, it was estimated that up to 200,000 Chechen civilians have been killed, while another 5,000 Chechen civilians are missing and 40,000 members of the Russian military have been killed.

Our team taking time to care for the Chechens, who had been ostracized and marginalized, may have helped plant a seed to diminish their feelings of humiliating isolation and begin to chip away at the cycles of retribution.

True belonging is initially fostered by good-enough parenting (Winnicott, 1973) creating a sense of justice, beauty, and love. This sense of belonging is needed whether we are in dire circumstances or just leading peaceful lives. With the United States and the international community becoming more aware and involved in providing stability in Chechnya, a sense of Chechen hopefulness and belonging—a bulwark against the lure of terrorism—will begin to develop. Our work as psychoanalysts is cut out for us.

In order to assuage the feeling of absolute loneliness that often breeds terrorism, we need to find, individually and in groups, the courage and passion to demonstrate that they are not alone and others care. Reaching out to the Chechens, the medical team aspired to slowly chip away at the chronic hopelessness and despair that often breeds desperate acts of violence. As Hillel the Elder, the famous Jewish leader, stated, "If you save one life, you save the entire world"; one person's effort to reach another who is suffering reverberates to assist all. We hoped that this important therapeutic intervention presented a different paradigm that would take root in at least one Chechen life and encourage her to envision a more hopeful future.

One key moment that obliterated the already tattered Chechen sense of belonging occurred in 1999—a phenomenon called the Russian apartment bombings, which killed hundreds and injured thousands of Russian civilians, spreading a wave of terror across the country. The defected Russian KGB agent, Alexander Litvinenko, revealed that the 1999 apartment bombings were manufactured acts of terrorism and were actually planted and staged by FSB (former KGB) agents and not Chechen terrorists, so that Russia could wage war on "terrorism" in Chechnya to bring Putin into the presidency (Litvinenko & Felshtinsky, 2007; Dunlop, 2014; Satter, 2016; Anderson, 2017). The Chechens' sense of hopelessness in response to being framed by Russia for the 1999 apartment bombings and then invaded by the Russian military has deepened their embedded depiction as terrorists and redoubled their sense of not belonging to humanity.

The bombings triggered the Second Chechen War. The handling of the crisis by Putin, who was prime minister at the time, boosted his popularity greatly and helped him attain the presidency within a few months. The attacks were officially attributed to Chechen terrorists, even though this was never proven. A suspicious device resembling those used in the bombings was found and defused in an apartment block in the Russian city of Ryazan on September 22, 1999. Despite there being vigilant Ryazan inhabitants witnessing three FSB agents planting the bombs at Ryazan and only the FSB having access to the specific bomb material used, the FSB continued to claim that the incident had been an anti-terror drill by the FSB and the device found there contained only sugar (Dougherty, 1999).

Former FSB agent Alexander Litvinenko, who defected and divulged that the FSB had in actuality planted the Russian apartment bombings, was subsequently poisoned and killed in London in 2006. A British inquiry conducted on the behalf of Litvinenko's widow later determined that Litvenenko's murder was carried out by two FSB agents with Putin's approval (Addley et al., 2016). The UK inquiry said former KGB bodyguard Andrei Lugovoi and another Russian, Dmitry Kovtun, deliberately poisoned Mr. Litvinenko, probably by putting the radioactive substance into his tea. Litvinenko's widow took the case against Russia to the Strasbourg-based rights court, which agreed with the UK inquiry's conclusion. Supporting the UK inquiry and Strasbourg-based high rights court ruling, and despite the attacks by Russia being officially attributed to Chechen terrorists, many historians and journalists have maintained that the bombings were coordinated by state security services to bring Putin into the presidency (Knight, 2012; Satter, 2016; Felshtinsky & Pribylovsky, (2008); Salter et al., 2021; Stein, 2022; VPRO Documentary, 2007).

THE BOSTON MARATHON BOMBERS

The Chechen sense of not belonging—not sharing in the inherent rights of mankind, a history of betrayals, and an eye-for-an-eye mentality—are exemplified by the events in April 2013 in the Boston Marathon bombings.

The Tsarnaev brothers' background was one of dislocations and not belonging. Their father was Chechen, while their mother was Avar, another Muslim ethnic group, indistinguishable from the Chechens in the eyes of their Russian rulers, but a different Muslim population, nevertheless. The mother was never fully accepted into the Tsarnaev family because of these Muslim ethnic differences (Murphy, 2015).

The family continuously moved around in a desperate attempt to find violence-free areas, financial stability, and opportunity for autonomy: from Siberia to Kyrgyzstan, from Kyrgyzstan to Kalmykia, back to Kyrgyzstan, then to Chechnya, back to Kyrgyzstan to flee the Chechen War, then to Dagestan, then to the United States. The parents emigrated in 2002 via refugee status to the United States and settled in Cambridge, Massachusetts.

During one of the Chechen wars in the 1990s, their father was tortured in Chechnya in one of the many Russian camps, and as a result often suffered flashbacks that KGB agents were following him. Given the father's history of Russian torture, he and his family were granted asylum in the United States (McPhee, 2017). The Tsarnaev's father was later diagnosed with Post-Traumatic Stress Disorder by an American psychiatrist, who testified to the father's torture in a futile effort to change Dzhokhar Tsarnaev's death sentence to life in prison (CBS, May 5, 2015).

My goal is not to condone the Tsarnaev brothers' horrible act of human destruction but to provide a background of the Chechen psychological, historical, and political milieu that contributes to a sense of humiliating powerlessness; that impotency that obliterates a sense of belonging which in turn can breed terrorism. The despicable killing of innocents did nothing to further the brothers' cause. The brothers not only demeaned their victims in order to carry out the killings, but dehumanized themselves in the process. They disconnected from the part of themselves that felt the horror of taking someone's life.

James Jones (2008) points out that to the extent that one is identified with those who are victims of violence, the humiliation that results from a sense of not belonging can be experienced vicariously. An example of this vicarious identification is the Tsarnaev brothers were descendants of ethnic Chechens deported to Central Asia in the Stalin era (Gessen, 2015).

The brothers struggled to assimilate in the United States. Dzhokhar, the younger brother, was charming but was a master of mirroring everyone's expectations of him, and he was foraging for some sense of self and connection to others. Few people noticed his slow deterioration into a stoner who was failing out of a mediocre college. Perhaps in an attempt to create a sense of stability, connection, and belonging, he began to forge a Russian-speaking, Chechen-centric identity. Living a marginalized immigrant existence and feeling like outsiders (Murphy, 2015), the brothers grew to hate the United States, which led to their growing rage and radicalization. As their radicalization developed, they became even more embittered, enraged, and vengeful.

Tamerlan, the older brother, was the perfect candidate for recruitment by the US government with a promise in regard to his citizenship. Broke, desperate, and with a new American wife and baby girl to take care of, he spoke fluent English, Russian, and a dialect of Chechen. Despite being on several terrorist watch lists, he was recruited by the FBI as a "mosque crawler" to inform on radical separatists here and in Chechnya during the six months he spent in Russia. However, upon his return to the United States, the FBI broke their promise of granting him citizenship (McPhee, 2017).

And to top it off, the US betrayal of the promise of citizenship, which occurred previous to the Boston Marathon bombing, may have destroyed his already fractured final hope to belong. A basic human primitive reflex when humiliated is to humiliate the perpetrator. Already having a fragile sense of self, Tamerlan's response to the government's broken promise of US citizenship may have decimated him enough to rev up his avenging rage, exploding into the bomb he presented at the Boston Marathon. His desperate attempt to deal with his chaotic feelings was to inflict his terror on the perpetrators, the United States. When one feels there is nothing left to live for, the will to die through murder is kindled (Merari, 2010). The sense that the Tsarnaevs might have felt that they did not belong is evident in the younger brother's writing a note scrawled on the interior of a boat in Watertown where he was hiding from the FBI that stated the Boston Marathon bombings were "retribution for the United States' military action against innocent Muslims in Afghanistan and Iraq." He called the Boston Marathon victims "collateral damage."

Tamerlan's inability to integrate into American society, his sense of not belonging, combined with his sympathy for the rebellion in the Caucasus region, contributed to his motivation for retaliation in the Boston bombing. Through the bombings, the brothers may have seen a chance to not only lessen their intrapsychic sense of emasculation but to create a sense of significance and belonging to a cause greater than themselves by waging war on the United States. The brothers may have felt a collective sense of shame as a result of the United States' wars waged against Muslims that was compounded by the international community largely ignoring the Chechen War. The Tsarnaev brothers' sense of despair may have left them more vulnerable to the lure of terrorism as not only a means to bring awareness of the globally ignored Chechen struggle for survival against a much more powerful Russian adversary, but also for retribution for all the violence they endured.

The terrorist's push is to reconstitute a distorted sense of belonging. The Tsarnaev brothers' hatred served as a prosthetic device to maintain a steady relationship with an object, the United States, which they could hold on to by seeking revenge. Hate was a device that stabilized the brothers' tattered psyches with a malignant sense of object constancy. The brothers' hatred may have created a pseudo-sense of purpose, stability, self-organization, and equilibrium for their unsettled lives.

In addition to being inspired by the Chechen political, historical, and psychosocial issues, the Tsarnaev brothers' violence may have been driven by a need to demonstrate and reconstruct their sense of masculinity. The brothers were psychologically steeped in the traumatic violent history of the Chechens, including the two wars waged by the Russian military in Chechnya during their childhood in the 1990s, in which tens of thousands of civilians were killed (de Carbonnel, 2013). Tamerlan may well have felt emasculated by his failure to achieve the American dream; his boxing career and studies at a junior college did not work out, he never found a full-time job, and family members say his wife supported him while he stayed home with his child (de Carbonnel, 2013). Demonstrating bravado helped the Chechens to keep their identity in the face of Russian oppression and the perception of their history as being one of constant powerlessness and subjugation; the younger Tsarnaev tweeted, "#chechnyapower" and "A decade in America already, I want out" (de Carbonnel, 2013, p. 18). The younger brother said of his terrorist killings: "This is easy to do. These tragedies happen all the time in Afghanistan and Iraq" (de Carbonnel, 2013, p. 22).

As Ruth Stein notes in her book, *For Love of the Father*, defensive rephrasing of evil and hate as love is what constitutes perversity. Terrorism, in which the drive to kill in the name of God is present, involves false religious love. The brothers were radicalized online by the Muslim fundamentalist Anwar al-Awlaki, who was a member of al-Qaeda. Prior to his being sentenced to death, Dzhokhar spoke in court about his love of and devotion to Allah and that there was only one God. Their radicalization permitted them to relinquish accountability for killing as they were disavowing their will; they were acting in the name of God.

There is a significant amount of evidence that violent criminals come from broken families and that serial killers often grew up in abusive and cruel conditions (Miller, 1990; Reavis et al, 2013; Gilligan, 1996). The criminal incorporates his abuser as an internalized persecutory object. Rittenberg (1987) points out that perverse thinking is linked to modern forms of violence and can be used in the service of propaganda. Steiner (1982) describes perversity of character in which a "bad," ganglike part of the psyche takes over; it dominates other healthier parts of the self. Lowenstein (2017) maintains that the perverse or destructive part is motivated by a sense of omnipotence, envy, and hatred; it attacks links of trust and dependency on good objects.

Klein's internalized persecutory object and Fairbairn's inner saboteur address the perverse parts of the brothers' personalities, which may have allowed them to choose to become terrorists and murder others. Then the simultaneous identification with the persecutor leads to abuse of the external victim, which allows for murder. The external victim has to be annihilated as a symbol of the internalized victim, which then attempts to alleviate the individual's self-loathing. In a vicious cycle of violence, the former victim becomes the perpetrator, who inflicts violence on a new victim, who will then become the perpetrator.

MOHAMED ATTA: KILLING IN THE NAME OF GOD AND THE DIVINE ALIBI

Similar to the Tsarnaevs' obsessional, shamed sense of self, the perverse part of Atta's personality allowed him to kill in the name of Allah in an attempt to restore his masculine dignity. Both the Tsarnaev brothers and Atta committed their vengeful acts with utter certainty, which may have given them a sense of order and stability.

The experiential quality of psychic pain is the awareness, at varying levels of consciousness, of the gap between one's "actual" self and one's "idealized" self

(Sandler, 1963). The emotional work of coming to terms with this traumatic loss and guilt can be an essential part of psychoanalytic work. Working between awareness of what is causing pain and protective dissociation from this realization, the patient learns to mourn. Psychoanalytic acknowledgment of the loss of achieving the idealized self keeps the gap from becoming an abyss, while omnipotent denial of this realization of a gap between the actual from the idealized self can be a driving force in some terrorist acts.

Ironically, in the mind of the terrorist, when one detaches from one's human moral judgment, one tragically merges with "God" (Stein, 2010). The enemy becomes the depository of the unconscious rejected parts in oneself and a negative binding link between the believer and his God. The shared fantasy of symbiosis with the omnipotent and idealized persecutory object creates a myth that enhances this perverted imagination. Relinquishing the responsibility to find one's own moral judgment parallels the avoidance of the vital internal process of developing one's own autonomous ethics and contributes to mindless obedience to authority.

Jihadi terrorism unveils a narrow and exclusive belief system where any deviation results in lethal punishment because difference and indecision threaten its existence. The call to dominate the world by the sword and to eradicate non-believers involves the conscious shelving of the central core of a humanitarian moral code. The abusive, tyrannical misogynistic practices toward women and moderate Muslims exhibit a totalitarian mindset of evil posing as righteousness. Westerners came to represent the terrorists' own "bad boy" self in projection and had to be killed off for such unforgivable sins as listening to music and enjoying sex (deMause, 2002). In a perverted effort to expel the unwanted part of themselves that is drawn to "Western pleasures," the suicide bomber is created.

The self-deceptive reliance on a "divine alibi" (Stein, 2010) to justify attacking the different "other" illustrates a part of this moral responsibility. Stein (2003) describes a simplistic, concrete "horizontal" division between good and evil and right and wrong that characterizes all fundamentalist religion's sensibility and creates two phenomena at the same time: a gross emotional intensity that endows experience with a stark quality of grandiosity and abjection and a "vertical" division that constitutes the basic inequality between God and man. The "vertical" difference between the believer and his God intensifies longing and mystical desire. By renouncing his individuality and autonomy, the believer longs to merge with a perfect and cruel God. In his regression and merging with an archaic Father, a dangerous process of de-differentiation occurs, so that the believer becomes a submissive supplicant. The images of father regression, which includes extreme asceticism, martyrdom, sacrifice and renunciation of sexuality, and the banishment of the mother are the fantasies that propel terrorism that can lead to explosive self-destruction.

The radicalization of Atta and his horrendous violent acts demonstrate this regression and merging with the Father in a dangerous process of de-differentiation, where Atta became a submissive supplicant. Atta was born in Egypt, the youngest son of a strict, austere, reclusive lawyer. His father kept the family insulated and forbade the already shy Atta from playing with neighborhood children. His father felt that Atta was spoiled by his mother and that she raised him as a girl (Yardley, 2001). In 1990, Atta obtained an engineering degree from Cairo University. Under pressure from his father, he continued his studies at the Hamburg Technical University in Germany. Atta was socially isolated and struggled with hopelessness, guilt, and shame (Lankford, 2012). Physically, there was a feminine quality to him; Atta was elegant and delicate (Benjamin, 2015). Atta's shame may have been related to his sense of being effeminate.

While in Germany, he became more religious, following Muslim dietary restrictions and abstaining from alcohol and women. During his Islamic lessons each Sunday at the Turkish mosque in downtown Hamburg, several acquaintances noticed Atta's mounting interest in the political struggles and oppression of Muslims and *jihad* in the Middle East, North Africa, Indonesia, and Chechnya (Crewdson, 2004). Ironically, for all his malice toward Israel, for he believed that the Jews had planned the Muslim-waged wars in Bosnia, Kosovo, and Chechnya and were the group that planned to extinguish Islam and control the world, Atta spoke not of murdering Israelis and Americans rather a desire to kill Russian soldiers in Chechnya (Crewdson, 2004, p. 93). In late 1999, Atta arrived at a bin Laden al-Qaeda training camp in Afghanistan in search of paramilitary training and assistance in reaching Chechnya. While in Germany, he began researching flight schools in the United States (National Commission on Terrorist Attacks Upon the United States, 2004). Where there's a will there's a way.

In the will left in his luggage, Atta insisted that "No women be allowed to attend his funeral or visit his grave site." In these misogynistic fundamentalist families, women are regarded as polluted and one is encouraged to reject and disown feminine vulnerabilities. His father nicknamed Atta "Bolbol," Arabic for a little bird and described him as "a very sensitive man ... soft and extremely attached to his mother" (Cloud, 2001). Words used to describe Atta were mostly feminine ones, "like a soft girl, kind and nice, very delicate, elegant" and not physically imposing or ever aggressive (Crewdson, 2004). Enacting his father's master script of reifying masculinity, the American Airlines Boeing 767 airplane that crashed into the World Trade Tower silenced once and for all Atta's despised, fluttering, feminine wings. Atta's behavior can also be seen as exemplifying a simplistic, concrete fundamentalist sensibility on a horizontal division where the impure feminine, soft, and timid aspects of the self are purged and there is a celebration of the cherished masculine, potent, doer self.

Hallmarks of a coercive and violent fundamentalism are a sense of utter certainty, hermetic consistency, and highly rhetorical reiterations of truths (Stein, 2006; Gilligan, 2017). This simplification of complexities into binary oppositions of good and bad attempts to create order out of vagueness and constitutes a "vertical" homoerotic quest for God's love, an ecstatic reunion with Allah. In Islamic thought, there have been attempts to explain *jihad* as an inner struggle against the baser elements of the self. The *jihad* struggle is conceived as the purification of the contaminated inner self.

Atta's letter to the hijackers found in his luggage in his car that was left at Logan Airport prior to the World Trade Center attack is illuminating. The letter is a testimony of rituals to transform young Muslims into warriors through spiritual practices that create inner calm, fearlessness, obedience, and a dissociation of feeling during the killing. Atta's voice is calm and reassuring; it encourages thoughtful control for a heightened consciousness. The letter does not mention hate or the act of killing the non-believing infidel and themselves. Atta's letter informs the terrorists to wash and perfume their bodies and clean and polish their knives. It encourages the terrorists to be confident and serene in carrying out their continued attentiveness and devotion to God. The letter stipulates what needs to be done for the terrorists to gain entry into Allah's eternal paradise. The letter does describe a spiritual ritual at the end of which the supplicant is to receive God's approval. The merger with God by performing their acts accurately and mindfully is stressed.

Atta's letter details a perverse love of a dutiful intimacy between a son and his father to finally obtain the father's previously withheld approval. This murderous martyrdom is a symbiotic killing and dying, where achieving God's will means becoming one with the victims in death. This transformation of self-hatred and envy into God's love allows for the obliteration of those unwanted, contaminated parts of self that require purification. Ironically, purification means killing the corrupted parts of self so as to wring sanctity out of death. The 9/11 terrorists were taught to perform numerous rituals of washing themselves prior to the attacks. While washing was seen by Atta as a key element of purification, fire also played a role in his vision; fire is regarded as a more radical and stronger cleansing agent than other means in many religions, including Islam. The fire generated from the World Trade Center attacks brought elevated purification status for the terrorists as the baseness of their and their victims' souls was burned away and an exalted spiritual transcendence was thought to be obtained.

IMPLICATIONS FOR THERAPEUTIC INTERVENTIONS

Richard Galdston, in *The Longest Pleasure: A Psychoanalytic Study of Hatred*, maintains that hatred affords a homeostatic adaptation of the impulsive reaction of retaliation. Hatred enables the ego to retrieve aggression through a process comparable to incomplete mourning of a disappointing object, so that those who hate do not process the loss. Hatred can be distinguished from anger, which is a time-limited response to a proximal irritation which passes. The ability to hate is a skill indicative of ego development to the level of object constancy (Galdston, 1987).

The ability to hate can provide a distorted sense of object constancy to terrorists who have suffered narcissistic injuries severe enough to threaten their sense of survival. David Lotto (2017) examines terrorism through the lens of Heinz Kohut's (1972) theory of narcissistic injury and rage with the desire for revenge. The narcissistic injury and the consequential reaction of fury and desire for vengeance for the purpose of righting a wrong is an important cause of terrorism (Lotto, 2017). How do we acknowledge and begin to lessen these downward cycles of revenge and violence?

Lotto (2017) argues that the sequence of humiliation leading to revenge is helpful in understanding the United States' response to the events of September 11, 2001. Our customary sense of invulnerability was shattered. It marked the end of American innocence and the beginning of a way of life we had fooled ourselves into believing that we were immune from and could avoid (Cerfolio, 2019). We were attacked for the first time by our own planes in our homeland and suffered a major loss and defeat. Robert Lifton's book (2003), *Superpower Syndrome: America's Apocalyptic Confrontation with the World*, describes the process of mutual narcissistic injury and humiliation followed by retaliatory violence as one of the primary ways that Americans have responded to the trauma of September 11, 2001. Lifton (2003) also points out that Osama bin Laden, al-Qaeda, and the Islamist fundamentalists have engaged in a parallel process and cycle of revenge (like Russia and America).

The Tsarnaev brothers and Atta may have unconsciously sought radicalization as an ideological, sacred object to effect an environmental transformation that they hoped would deliver personal, familial, economic, social, and moral change (Cerfolio, 2020). Christopher Bollas (1979) maintains that in adult life there is a wide-ranging collective search for a transformational object to effect a self-metamorphosis. In this aesthetic moment, an individual feels a deep subjective rapport and uncanny fusion with an object (which can be a new partner, painting, poem, or religion) that generates renewed vision, hope, and confidence. As an ego memory of the ontogenetic process, this fusion with the object recalls the kind of ego experience that constituted the individual's earliest experience. Once the ego memories are identified with a contemporary object, the subject's relation to the object can become fanatical, as occurs with radicalization. The Tsarnaev brothers and Atta may have been unconsciously searching to lessen their sense of marginalization through a transformational object by becoming radicalized to create a sense of belonging, meaning, and potency.

The Tsarnaev brothers and Atta may have felt that they had little effective voice in society and were encouraged by radicalizers to display their aggression. They became socialized to see terrorist organizations as legitimate and America and its policies as evil. Although exploring the unique and complex underlying factors that drive individual terrorist acts is vital, focusing solely on these individual acts misses the importance of group phenomena.

Ultimately, the best long-term policy against terrorism is prevention, which is made possible by respecting the dignity and humanity of others, encouraging socioeconomic equality and self-determination, and helping protect all individuals and societies from the effective threats of shame and humiliation.

Deleuze and Guattari (1983) put forth three criteria required for liberation from oppression: lessen the force of unconscious prejudices, increase in the investment in marginalized people by the social field, and remove and disinvest from repressive structures. The restoration and respect for all people is necessary to begin to change the social field of oppression. A recognition of the humanity of others slowly decreases the cycles of retribution and violence. Equality of man is not just economical; it is treating "others" with respect and dignity. Psychoanalysts could consider revisiting the work of Immanuel Kant, who espoused the theory of "the kingdom of ends" in which no person is treated as a means to an end but in which each merits deep respect for the sanctity of his individual life. Respecting the dignity of other people is vital to creating space for dialogue and understanding.

While the political solutions to oppression are worth addressing, the need for psychoanalytic understanding is paramount to help build bridges between groups and view one another as human beings from varying cultures and having experienced different realities. When we lose contact with strangers, we lose our sense of interconnectedness and humanity. The self is social in nature and begins its reflection from a sense of relationality.

There is a great need to work with marginalized groups to restore the emotional meaning of the violent events that were ruptured by the traumatization. Whether for individual victims or groups, the need for greater reflection about terrorism and the feelings engendered by it, is required in order to encourage psycho-political dialogue. It is unprocessed losses and psychological trauma that perpetuate the divide between warring communities. Further psychoanalytic exploration of the trauma of loss, which addresses the societal compulsion to repeat cycles of violence, is needed. By working through these catastrophic displacements, new psychoanalytic perspectives of hope can unfold.

NOTES

1 Parts of this chapter appeared in an earlier version in Cerfolio (2020) and are gratefully reprinted with permission from *The Journal of Psychohistory*.
2 Parts of this chapter appeared in an earlier version in Cerfolio (2021) and are gratefully reprinted with permission from Taylor & Francis.

REFERENCES

Addley, E., Harding, L., & Walker, S. (2016, January 21). Litvinenko 'probably murdered on personal orders of Putin.' *The Guardian*. https://www.theguardian.com/world/2016/jan/21/alexander-litvinenko-was-probably-murdered-on-personal-orders-of-putin

Anderson, S. (2017, March 30). None dare call it a conspiracy. GQ. http://www.gq.com/story/moscow-bombings-mikhail-trepashkin-and-putin

Arendt, H. (1968). *The origins of totalitarianism*. Harcourt, Brace, Jovanovich.

Benjamin, J. R. (2015). *Inside the mind of Muhammad Atta*. https://jrbenjamin.com/2015/04/14/what-did-muhammad-atta-believe-about-the-world/

Bollas, C. (1979). The transformational object. *International Journal of Psycho-Analysis*, *60*(1), 97–107.

Bongar, B., Brown, L. M., Beutler, L. E., Breckenridge, J. N., & Zimbardo, P. G. (Eds.). (2006). *Psychology of terrorism*. Oxford University Press. http://doi.org/10.1093/med:psych/9780195172492.001.0001

CBS News. (2015, May 5). *Doctor: Boston bomber's dad claimed he was tortured, had PTSD*. https://www.cbsnews.com/news/boston-marathon-bomber-dzhokhar-tsarnaevs-father-had-ptsd-doctor-testifies/

Cerfolio, N. (2009). Multimodal psychoanalytically informed aid work with children traumatized by the Chechen War. *The Journal of the American Academy of Psychoanalysis and Dynamic Psychiatry, 37*(4), 587–603. http://doi.org/10.1521/jaap.2009.37.4.587

Cerfolio, N. (2019, May 23). Trauma two times over: Developing breast cancer as a result of being a first responder during 9/11. *Terror. House Magazine.* https://terrorhousemag .com/trauma/

Cerfolio, N. (2020). Terrorism and the psychoanalytic origins. *The Journal of Psychohistory, 47*(4), 256–274.

Cerfolio, N. (2021). The origins of terrorism: The obliteration of a sense of belonging. In R. C. Curtis (Ed.), *Belonging through a psychoanalytic lens* (pp. 45–57). Routledge.

Cloud, J. (2001, September 30). Atta's odyssey. *Time, 158*(16), 64–67. https://content.time .com/time/magazine/article/0,9171,176917,00.html

Coen, S. J. (2018). Between action and inaction: The space for analytic intimacy. *Journal of the American Psychoanalytic Association, 66*(2), 312–336. http://doi.org/10.1177 /0003065118769617

Cottee, S., & Hayward, K. (2011). Terrorist (e)motives: The existential attractions of terrorism. *Studies in Conflict and Terrorism, 34*(12), 963–986. http://doi.org/10.1080 /1057610X.2011.621116

Crewdson, J. (2004, September 12). From kind teacher to murderous zealot: Acquaintances saw hijacker transform. *Chicago Tribune.* https://www.chicagotribune.com/news/ct -xpm-2004-09-12-0409120328-story.html

de Carbonnel, A., & Simon, S. (2013, April 23). Special report: The radicalization of Tamerlan Tsarnaev. *Reuters.* https://www.reuters.com/article/us-usa-explosions -radicalisation-special/special-report-the-radicalization-of-tamerlan-tsarnaev-idU SBRE93M0CZ20130423

Deleuze, G., & Guattari, F. (1983). *Anti-Oedipus: Capitalism and schizophrenia* (R. Hurley, M. Seem, & H. R. Lane, Trans.). University of Minnesota Press (Original work published 1972).

deMause, L. (2002). *The emotional life of nations.* Other Press.

Dougherty, J. (1999, September 24). *Russian bomb scare turns out to be anti-terror drill.* CNN. http://edition.cnn.com/WORLD/europe/9909/24/russia.bomb.01/

Dunlop, J. B. (1998). *Russia confronts Chechnya: Roots of a separatist conflict.* Cambridge University Press. http://doi.org/10.1017/CBO9780511612077

Dunlop, J. B. (with Knight, A.) (2014). *The Moscow bombings of September 1999: Examination of Russian terrorist attacks at the onset of Vladimir Putin's rule.* Ibidem Press.

Einstein, A., & Freud, S. (1981). *Why war? An exchange between Albert Einstein and Sigmund Freud* (6th ed.). Shalom Press International.

Felshtinsky, Y., & Pribylovsky, V. (2008). *The age of assassins: The rise and rise of Vladimir Putin.* Gibson Square Books.

National Commission on Terrorist Attacks Upon the United States. (2004). *The 9/11 Commission report: Final report of the National Commission on Terrorist Attacks Upon The United States* (Authorized ed.). W. W. Norton & Company.

Galdston, R. (1987). The longest pleasure: A psychoanalytic study of hatred. *The International Journal of Psychoanalysis, 68*(3), 371–378.

Gessen, M. (2015). *The brothers: The road to an American tragedy.* Riverhead Books.

Gill, P., & Corner, E. (2017). There and back again: The study of mental disorder and terrorist involvement. *American Psychologist, 72*(3), 231–241. http://doi.org/10.1037/ amp0000090

Gilligan, J. (1996). *Violence: Reflections on a national epidemic.* Vintage Books.

Gilligan, J. (2017). Toward a psychoanalytic theory of violence, fundamentalism and terrorism. *International Forum of Psychoanalysis, 26*(3), 174–185. http://doi.org/10.1080 /0803706X.2017.1333145

Gobodo-Madikizela, P. (2015). Psychological repair: The intersubjective dialogue of remorse and forgiveness in the aftermath of gross human rights violations. *Journal of the American Psychoanalytic Association*, *63*(6), 1085–1123. http://doi.org/10.1177/0003065115615578

Goldfarb, A., & Litvinenko, M. (2007). *Death of a dissident: The poisoning of Alexander Litvinenko and the return of the KGB*. Free Press.

Hicks, D. (with Tutu, D.) (2011). *Dignity: Its essential role in resolving conflict*. Yale University Press.

Horgan, J. G. (2017). Psychology of terrorism: Introduction to the special issue. *American Psychologist*, *72*(3), 199–204. http://doi.org/10.1037/amp0000148

Jones, J. (2008). *Blood that cries out from the Earth: The psychology of religious terrorism*. Oxford University Press. http://doi.org/10.1093/acprof:oso/9780195335972.001.0001

Knight, A. (2012, November 22). Finally, we know about the Moscow bombings. *The New York Review of Books*. https://www.nybooks.com/articles/2012/11/22/finally-we-know-about-moscow-bombings/

Kohut, H. (1972). Thoughts on narcissism and narcissistic rage. *The Psychoanalytic Study of the Child*, *27*(1), 360–400. http://doi.org/10.1080/00797308.1972.11822721

Lankford, A. (2012). A psychological autopsy of 9/11 ringleader Mohamed Atta. *Journal of Police and Criminal Psychology*, *27*(2), 150–159. http://doi.org/10.1007/s11896-011-9096-9

Lenkvist, A. (2010, November 18). Book "The Colour of War" shows the war in Chechnya by eyes of Russian soldiers. *Caucasian Knot*. http://www.eng.kavkaz-uzel.eu/articles/15234/

Levine, S. S. (2016). *Dignity matters: Psychoanalytic and psychosocial perspectives*. Routledge. http://doi.org/10.4324/9780429473753

Lifton, R. J. (2003). *Superpower syndrome: America's apocalyptic confrontation with the world*. Thunder's Mouth Press.

Litvinenko, A., & Felshtinsky, Y. (2007). *Blowing up Russia: The secret plot to bring back KGB terror*. Encounter Books.

Lotto, D. (2017). On the origins of terrorism. *The Journal of Psychohistory*, *45*(1), 12–22.

Lowenstein, E. A. (2017). Dystopian narratives: Encounters with the perverse sado-masochistic universe. *Psychoanalytic Inquiry*, *37*(1), 3–15.

McCauley, C. (2017). Toward a psychology of humiliation in asymmetric conflict. *American Psychologist*, *72*(3), 255–265. http://doi.org/10.1037/amp0000063

McPhee, M. R. (2017). *Maximum harm: The Tsarnaev brothers, the FBI, and the road to the Marathon bombing*. Forest EngineeringEdge.

Merari, A. (2010). *Driven to death: Psychological and social aspects of suicide terrorism*. Oxford University Press.

Miller, A. (1990). *For your own good: Hidden cruelty in child-rearing and the roots of violence* (H. Hannum & H. Hannum, Trans.). Farrar, Straus, Giroux (Original work published 1980).

Murphy, C. (2015, April 7). From Chechnya to Boston: Tracing the Tsarnaev brothers' motivation. *Vanity Fair*. https://www.vanityfair.com/news/2015/04/the-brothers-masha-gessen-tsarnaev-brothers-book

Politkovskaya, A. (with Derluguian, G. M.) (2003). *A small corner of hell: Dispatches from Chechnya* (A. Burry & T. Tulchinsky, Trans.). The University of Chicago Press. http://doi.org/10.7208/chicago/9780226674346.001.0001

Politkovskaya, A. (2004). *Putin's Russia: Life in a failing democracy* (A. Tait, Trans.). The Harvill Press.

Politkovskaya, A. (2006, March 1). Poison in the air. *The Guardian*. http://www.theguardian.com/world/2006/mar/01/russia.chechnya

Post, J. M. (2005). When hatred is bred in the bone: Psycho-cultural foundations of contemporary terrorism. *Political Psychology*, *26*(4), 615–636. http://doi.org/10.1111/j.1467-9221.2005.00434.x

Reavis, J. A., Looman, J., Franco, K. A., & Rojas, B. (2013). Adverse childhood experiences and adult criminality: How long must we live before we possess our own lives? *Permanente Journal*, *17*(2), 44–48. http://doi.org/10.7812/TPP/12-072

Rittenberg, S. M. (1987). *Creativity and perversion: By Janine Chasseguet Smirgel.* W. W. Norton and Company, Inc. 1984. pp. 172. *International Review of Psychoanalysis,* 14, 130–132.

Salter, L., Lopez, L., & Kakoyiannis, A. (2021, April 7). How the 1999 Russian apartment bombings led to Putin's rise to power. *Business insider.* https://www.businessinsider.com/how-the-1999-russian-apartment-bombings-led-to-putins-rise-to-power-2018-3

Sandler, J., Holder, A., & Meers, D. (1963). The ego ideal and the ideal self. *The Psychoanalytic Study of the Child,* 18(1), 139–158. http://doi.org/10.1080/00797308.1963.11822927

Satter, D. (2016, August 17). The unsolved mystery behind the act of terror that brought Putin to power. *National Review.* https://www.nationalreview.com/2016/08/vladimir-putin-1999-russian-apartment-house-bombings-was-putin-responsible/

Silke, A. (Ed.). (2003). *Terrorists, victims, and society: Psychological perspectives on terrorism and its consequences.* Wiley. http;//doi.org/10.1002/9780470713600

Stein, J. (2022, February 3). *Russian. 'false flag' Ukraine plot wouldn't be its first.* SpyTalk. https://www.spytalk.co/p/russian-false-flag-ukraine-plot-wouldnt

Stein, R. (2003). Vertical mystical homoseros: An altered form of desire in fundamentalism. *Studies in Gender and Sexuality,* 4(11), 38–58.

Stein, R. (2006). Fundamentalism, father and son, and vertical desire. *The Psychoanalytic Review,* 93(2), 201–229. http://doi.org/10.1521/prev.2006.93.2.201

Stein, R. (2010). *For love of the father: A psychoanalytic study of religious terrorism.* Stanford University Press.

Steiner, J. (1982). Perverse relationships between parts of the self: A clinical illustration. *The International Journal of Psychoanalysis,* 63(2), 241–251.

Stern, J. (2003). *Terror in the name of God: Why religious militants kill.* HarperCollins.

Stern, J. (2010). *Denial: A memoir of terror.* HarperCollins.

Stern, J. E. (2014). X: A case study of a Swedish neo-Nazi and his reintegration into Swedish society. *Behavioral Sciences and the Law,* 32(3), 440–453. http://doi.org/10.1002/bsl.2119

Varvin, S., & Volkan, V. D. (2018). *Violence or dialogue? Psychoanalytic insights on terror and terrorism.* Routledge.

VPRO Documentary. (2007, May 31). *In Memoriam Aleksander Litvinenko - VPRO documentary – 2007* [Video]. YouTube. https://www.youtube.com/watch?v=PnkYo9TuBIQ

Winnicott, D. W. (1973). *The child, the family, and the outside world.* Penguin.

Yardley, J. (2001, October 10). A portrait of the terrorist: From shy child to single-minded killer. *The New York Times.* https://www.nytimes.com/2001/10/10/world/nation-challenged-mastermind-portrait-terrorist-shy-child-single-minded-killer.html

8

Underlying Psychological Motives for Putin's Sponsoring of State Terrorism

Victim Morphs into Perpetrator

History that is forgotten is often repeated.

123

DOI: 10.4324/9781032633497-9

S tate terrorism involves acts of terrorism, which a state commits against an individual or another state. It is similar to non-state terrorism in that it involves politically, ideologically, or religiously inspired acts of violence against individuals or groups. Similar to non-state terrorism, state terrorism is not only about the destruction of those targeted, but also driven by an aspiration to intimidate and terrorize more widely. Russian Intelligence, including in the Soviet era, has a long history of deploying murder as a deterrent against voicing any opposition or criticisms of the state or a particular leader. However, authoritarian states do not have a monopoly on state terrorism. An example is the 1985 state-sponsored terrorism by the American Central Intelligence Agency allegedly sponsoring a car bomb in Beirut in an effort to kill a cleric connected to Hezbollah. The explosion missed its intended target, murdering 80 people instead.

By being poisoned by a FSB agent, I lived the experience of how state terrorism is about the intended destruction of being targeted, but if you are fortunate enough to survive, how these violent acts linger to psychologically intimidate you to have a voice. After being poisoned and eventually fighting to regain my health, I then had to confront my feelings of apprehension and fear of retaliation, in order to have the fortitude to write about my experience of being targeted and the other atrocities that I witnessed in the Second Chechen War. I refused to be terrorized and silenced. My writing this book is a willful act against tyranny. My defiance and determination allow me to not merely survive, but to flourish. While the emotional sequelae of experiencing terror are complex, they mostly have served to deepen my sense of gratitude for being alive and for all of my blessings.

Yet another terrifying example of a state sponsor of terrorism is Russia's invasion of Ukraine. On February 24, 2022, Putin announced a "special military operation" in Ukraine, marking the start of a full-scale military invasion of Ukraine, which created the biggest refugee crisis since World War II and tens of thousands of deaths. The Internal Displacement Monitoring Center (IDMC) is a Ukrainian organization that documents the number of refugees during periods of time as the war progresses. In 2022, the IDMC estimated that nearly 7.9 million Ukrainian refugees and 8 million internally displaced Ukrainians, as well as a large number of persons in host countries, will face anxiety, confusion, mourning, exploitation, prejudice, and difficult real-life and large-group identity issues (Akhtar, 2014; Varvin, 2021; Volkan, 2017).

After more than 20 years of Putin's circle of impunity in Chechnya, Georgia, and Syria, in November 2022 the European Parliament finally designated Russia as a state sponsor of terrorism, arguing that its military strikes on Ukrainian civilian targets such as energy infrastructure, hospitals, schools, and shelters violated international law (Siebold et al., 2022). Putin's delusional justification (Volkan & Javakhishvilli, 2022) for war was his claim that there was a genocide of Russians by Ukraine, which he needed to stop by waging war and occupying Ukraine. Similarly in Chechnya, Putin portrayed and accused Chechens as terrorists through the twisted, false, and unproven accusations that Chechens were responsible for the Moscow apartment bombings in September 1999; he perversely justified waging the First and Second Chechen Wars as a fight against this "Muslim terrorism," which resonated with the West after 9/11.

HISTORY OF THE UKRAINE WAR

Just as Mohamed Atta's perverted rationale for the 9/11 terrorist attacks was, in part, a need to purify the corrupted Western soul, the "purification" and "denazification" of Ukrainians is Putin's distorted justification for his unprovoked unleashing of evil upon Ukraine. Russia's professed motivation also trumpets this quasi-mystical interpretation that takes one above individual needs and catapults a jingoistic impulse into a transcendent war of holy dimensions. Similar to Russia's many invasions of Georgia to impose totalitarian rule since the 1920s, Ukraine has a long history of suffering from Russian annexation which may contribute to the Ukrainian unified, valiant, fighting spirit as it has century-old legs. Ukraine is a highly desirable land to possess; it has rich, black, fertile soil, which contributes to being one of the largest grain producers and a breadbasket of the world. Earlier in 1932 through 1933, in order to suppress resistance and aspirations of independence from the population, Joseph Stalin, then head of the Soviet Union, confiscated the entire grain supply from eastern and central Ukraine, restricted freedom of movement by closing roads, and inflicted a man-made famine named the Holodomor (Jones, 2017) or Terror-Famine (Davies, 2006; Baumeister, 1997).

Holodomor is a compound word combining the word "*holod*" meaning hunger, with the verbal root "*mor*" meaning to exterminate. Estimates of between 3.5 to 5 million Ukrainians died (Marples, 2007; Mendel, 2018) as a result of the famine. Since 2006, the Holodomor has been recognized by the European Parliament, Ukraine, and 22 countries as a genocide against the Ukrainian people implemented by the Soviet regime (Dahm, 2022). Understandably, the widespread psychological impact of intergenerational transmission of terror caused by the famine persists in Ukraine to this day.

Since the collapse of the Soviet Union, and Ukraine's regaining of independence, the Russo-Ukrainian war has been renewed and ongoing since February 2014. In early 2014, the Revolution of Dignity, also known as the Ukrainian Revolution, occurred as the result of protests over then pro-Russian president Viktor Yanukovych suspending political association and free-trade agreements with the European Union, which culminated in Yanukovych being ousted from office. In response, covert, unmasked Russian troops, who were "little green men" without insignia on their green uniforms, moved into Ukraine's Crimea and took control of government buildings and strategic infrastructure. The Kremlin continued fomenting a separatist war with false claims that Russian-speaking Ukrainians were under threat from pro-Western, pro-democracy protesters. After a highly disputed Crimean status referendum, Russia soon illegally annexed Crimea. In April 2014, pro-Russian backed separatists declared war in Ukraine's eastern Donbas region, proclaiming the establishment of the Donetsk People's Republic and the Luhansk People's Republic with clandestine Russian support. Although

Russia continued to deny involvement, Russian troops directly participated in the covert war.

Robert Jay Lifton (2022), a psychiatrist and scholar of psychological issues on the effects of war and political violence, is convinced that Putin's deeply destructive and self-destructive mindset is based on a religious and political ideology that is based on the work of the 20th-century Russian philosopher, Ivan Ilyin. Ilyin's influence on Putin has also been well-documented by Yale historian Timothy Snyder (2018). Ilyin, a Russian jurist and dogmatic religious and political philosopher, was an ultra-nationalist with utopian ideas of a transfigured Holy Russia emphasizing Russia's autocratic heritage. He criticized individualism, liberalism, and neutrality, and was an enemy of intellectualism and Western analytic philosophy. Ilyin was a mystic who believed in Christian fascism based on a unified, sacred, godly Russian empire that is pure in its "virtue" and absolute in its justified demands (Lifton, 2022; Snyder, 2018; Kripkov, 1997). Lifton insightfully points out that it is difficult to invade a sovereign country and kill a large number of people without claiming a "virtue" (Lifton, 2022). Lifton (2022) maintains that the "virtue" driving Russia's waging war in Ukraine was a totalistic ideology based on Ilyin.

There are three types of political regimes: democracies, totalitarian, and sitting in between these two, authoritarian regimes (Linz, 2000). Totalitarian regimes are characterized by political repression and human rights violation, widespread personality cultism around the person in power, absolute control over the economy, large-scale censorship and mass surveillance systems, and widespread usage of state terrorism and secret police. For instance, totalitarian regimes in Germany under Hitler, Italy under Mussolini, and the Soviet Union under Stalin, had initial origins in the chaos that followed in the wake of World War II. Totalistic ideologies may result from distorted convictions. An example is Hitler's *Mein Kampf*, in which he states his belief that the Nordic race, once strong and dominant, was poisoned and weakened by the influence of the Jewish race, so that Jews had to be removed in order to heal the Nordic race (Lifton, 1986; Lifton, 2022).

In 2005, Putin ordered the repatriation of Ilyin's remains from Switzerland to reburial in Moscow and referred to Ilyan as his historical mentor, encouraged the republication of his writings, and assigned his work to subordinates (Lifton, 2022). In Ilyins's totalistic ideology, the mysticism is overt and primal, where the Russian state is conceived as a manifestation of God's plan (Kripkov, 1997; Snyder, 2018; Lifton, 2022). Ilyin also expressed his concern and remorse for Russia's loss of Christian purity. Ilyin envisioned a Russian empire as a large, inclusive entity that should not be "subject to arbitrary dismemberment" or "diseased disintegration" which would bring "a universal infection" (Grier, 1994; Lifton, 2022). In his 2005 State of the Nation address, Putin promoted Ilyn's language of dismemberment with the breakup of the Soviet Empire, when he stated, "the demise of the Soviet Union was the greatest geopolitical catastrophe of the century" (NBC News, 2005).

Freud's analysis of both the "unknown Russian patient"—a young Ivan Ilyin—(Ljunggren, 2014); Sergey Pankeev—the Wolfman; and his writings on

Dostoyevsky, acknowledges the Russian tendency toward repression and projections of evil in an attempt to purify the self, especially toward the "corrupt" West. As Ilyin's analysis in 1914 partly coincided with the final phase of Freud's treatment of the "Wolfman," Freud probably had Pankeev and Ilyin in mind when he began his work on Dostoevsky. In Freud's analysis of the Wolfman, psychic splits were observed in Pankeev where his Russian religious moralizing and conservatism contrasted with an enthusiasm for violent oppression (Freud, 1918; Yakushko, 2023). According to Freud, the Wolfman sublimated his sadism into a penchant for military affairs, weapons, and violence and sanitized religiosity, which were related to his same-sex desires. In Freud's (1928) "Dostoyevsky and Parricide," Freud acknowledges Dostoyevsky's creativity but focuses on his management of sin and neurotic moralism (Yakushko, 2023). Describing Russia's longstanding tendency toward their denial of aggression and colonization overlain by a strict veneer of religious moralism, Freud noted that a characteristic Russian trait is similar to the barbarians of the great migrations, who murdered and did penance … till penance became an actual technique for enabling murder to be done (Einstein & Freud, 1981). Dostoyevsky's (1919) *A Writer's Diary* is marked by Russophilic glorifications of an innocent Russia but contains sadistic aggressive projections of those perceived as adversaries, especially Jews, Western Europeans, and radicals (Yakushko, 2023). While the Russians pedaled their illusion of conservative moralism to mask their violent aggressiveness, Freud calling a spade, a spade, pulverized any pretense of Russian sanctimonious motivation to expose their underlying horrific barbarism used to unify, guarantee submission, and project hatred to those outside its frontiers (Einstein & Freud, 1981).

Lifton in *Thought Reform and the Psychology of Totalism: A Study of "Brainwashing" in China* (1961/1989) writes that totalistic ideologies desire complete control over human behavior and most importantly thought. He finds two common motives in totalistic movements: the fear and denial of death, channeled into violence against scapegoated groups that are set up to represent a metaphorical threat to survival, and a reactionary fear of social change. Borrowing from the rhetoric of Josef Stalin, Putin perversely likened Ukrainians to "gnats" and "demons" who were taken over by neo-Nazis who present a security threat to Russia's sovereignty at the behest of the West (CBS News, 2022). By competing with Stalin, Putin may be displaying his desire to be more well-known than other Soviet leaders and emphasizing his exaggerated narcissism (Volkan & Javakhishvili, 2022).

Ilyin lamented Russia's loss of Christian purity (Kripokav, 1997) and maintained that Russia had endured "1000 years of historical suffering" (Snyder, 2018; Lifton, 2022) at the incursions of corrupted Western liberalism. He denounced democratic procedures and insisted that Mother Russia had a special transcendent soul that negated their more reasonable quotidian sentiments (Snyder, 2018; Lifton, 2022). In Ilyin's ideology, the Russian nation is an organism of nature and soul (Snyder, 2018; Lifton, 2022) and it was "conceived in the eternal Christian spirit as a manifestation of God's plan" (Kripkov, 1997). Based on Ilyin's notion of Christian fundamentalism, Putin continues with Ilyin's rhetoric by expressing the need to self-cleanse and denazify Ukraine as a "natural and necessary self-puri-fication of society that will strengthen our country, our solidarity, our cohesion and readiness to respond to any challenges" (CBS News, 2022). These mystical notions, distorted as they are, have resonance for the Russian people through their exceptionalism earned by their tremendous Russian sacrifices battling Nazi Germany in World War II. More sanguine critics say that Putin is exploiting the trauma of World War II and twisting history for his own interests.

The colonial genocide (Snyder, 2018) of Ukraine is multifaceted and involves: Putin denying the very existence of Ukraine as a sovereign nation; the forced deportation of between 13,000 (Ministry of Reintegration of Temporarily Occupied Territories, 2022) to 307,000 (Le Monde, 2022) Ukrainian children to Russia, without any indication when they could return home; the interroga-tion, detainment, and forcible deportation (similar to Russian filtration opera-tions in Chechnya) between 900,000 to 1.6 million Ukrainian citizens to the isolated regions in the Far East of Russia; and the deliberate Russian separat-ing of Ukrainian children from their parents or abducting Ukrainian orphans before putting them up for adoption inside Russia. From this perspective, Putin's "denazification of Ukraine" may have less to do with the Nazi killing of Jews than with his refusal to admit that neighboring Ukraine had become a flourishing democracy transplanting Ukraine into the bed of the West, his mortal nemesis. Becoming preoccupied with burial and graveyards, Putin has linked Russia and the image of the Soviet Union to his family's brutal hardship during the Siege of Leningrad (Volkan & Javakhishvili, 2022). Putin's attempt to decrease his sense of humiliation over the historical dissolution of the Soviet Union and to resurrect the Soviet Empire by land grabbing, including a sovereign Ukraine, is fully supported by this Christian fascism, which also assaults all forms of homosexuality. Similarly, this reiteration of Christian fascism supports the wish of the Russian Orthodox Church to secretly absorb, assimilate, and revise the Ukrainian Orthodox religion.

In another perspective, Uzlaner (2017) uses a Lacanian interpretation to better understand Russia's turn to "perverse conservatism" (Uzlaner, 2017). This "per-verse conservatism" incorporates: anti-Westernism; an insistence on tradition that is highly focused and narrow; a concern for maintaining traditional values for the sake of symbolic figures who are the millions of "children" and "simple Russians"; and the persecution of symbolic figures of moral decay who are homosexuals, per-verts, liberals, and foreign agents (Uzlaner, 2017). Similar to the Roman emperor Constantine's adoption of Christianity in 300 AD to strengthen his rule, Putin perversely rationalizes his virtual mafia state through a narrow despotism and a Russian conservatism that he maintains is sanctified by an Orthodox Christian God.

The Orwellian message of this future Russian dystopian totalitarian state, which was solidified in the Chechen Wars, reverberates in the continuing chilling signs of Russia's war in Ukraine. Russia's post-invasion scenario used in Chechnya and now Ukraine is to terrorize the local population by creating a climate of fear and chaos. This terror, which is the traditional tool of despots, is accomplished by: committing civilian atrocities of rape, torture and murder to terrify the local population; abducting local officials; appointing sham councils; and enlisting collaborators to set up pro-Russian puppet regimes. These civilian atrocities committed by the Russian military are illustrative of Putin's callous disregard for human suffering, life, and death.

In Chechnya, Putin road-tested a doctrine of hybrid warfare, a mix of weapons and words to create fictions that sowed confusion and division that he then reapplied in Ukraine. Russians excel at revisionist history; their defensive denial, deflection, and projection may inflict more harm than Russian military firepower as they create prolonged schismatic divisions. Justifying his aggression in Chechnya as a "war against terrorism," Putin rationalized his war in Ukraine with a bombardment of similarly twisted propaganda, perhaps an earlier version of fake news. Some of Putin's absurdist justifications for invading Ukraine are: that Ukraine, with a Jewish president, is ruled by Nazis; that Russian atrocities, thoroughly captured in photographs, videos, and witness accounts, are Ukrainian false-flag attacks; that Ukraine is preparing to detonate a dirty bomb, even as Moscow strokes global fears of a Russian nuclear attack. But in contrast to the largely internationally ignored Chechen Wars, the events unfolding in the Ukrainian war have been globally covered, raising worldwide alarm, and contributing to unification of the West due to many factors. Some of these contributing factors are: the sudden emergence of an unlikely diminutive Ukrainian leader, a previous comedic actor, who speaks English, and understands how to negotiate the media in his appeal to the West; the Ukrainians seem better at documenting the war crimes which have been caught on security camera footage and traced by phones; they also have documented arbitrary detentions and disinformation through government records; and used phone records as digital fingerprints when Russian soldiers stole the phones of Ukrainian victims to call home to Russia, often only hours after they were killed, all to chip away at the veneer of Putin's mastery manipulation.

The lack of documentation of Russian war crimes in the Chechen Wars as opposed to other wars waged by Putin is exemplified by following the barbarous acts against civilians committed by Igor Girkin. Igor Girkin, also known as "Igor the Terrible," a Russian army and former FSB officer, played a key role in the wars in Bosnia, Chechnya, and in the annexation of Crimea and Donbas in Ukraine. In his role in the annexation of Ukraine, Dutch prosecutors held Durkin accountable for his actions, charged him, and found him guilty with three other men of the 2014 shooting down of Malaysia Airlines Flight 17 killing 298 mostly Dutch civilians. In 2014, The Prosecutor General's Office in Ukraine charged Girkin with terrorism, and Ukraine crowdfunds raised a US $150,000 bounty for his capture. He also was accused by the Bosnian media of having been involved in the Visegrad massacres in which thousands of civilians were killed in 1992. But in contrast, in Chechnya sadly none of his war crimes were solved by official investigations. In 2014, Anonymous International disclosed Girkin's personal emails, which he sent to some friends for review and contained his diaries from the wars in Bosnia and Chechnya in *The Moscow Times* (Nechepurenko, 2014). When asked why he did not publish them Girkin explained that when he served in the FSB from 1999 to 2005 in the Chechen Wars he was regularly involved in operations of capturing and questioning Chechen civilians after which they almost always disappeared without court, without a trace, and this is why they could not be openly published. When there is an accumulation of no accountability and a presumed blindness toward appalling atrocities, this disregard could have motivated Putin to feel that he could continue his land grab with impunity, a situation reminiscent in America's midst.

A similar psychology to Putin's sense of humiliation, and incidentally not unrelated to the Germans, is noted in the study of Nazi soldiers during World War II, conducted by British psychiatrist Henry Dicks. Dicks concluded that Hitler's idea of *Lebensraum*, which involved land grabbing (ironically much of it in Ukraine), that Germans claimed belonged to them was based on an underlying sense of inadequacy (Pomerantsev, 2022). A twisted sense of victimhood, also claimed by Putin to justify Russia's aggression, is seen in the Nazi's claim of victimhood that became a rationale for their assaults in World War II. The German psychoanalyst, Erich Fromm's (1973), study of the Nazi mind noted how for the Nazis their claim that they were victims became an excuse to victimize and attack others (Pomerantsev, 2022). This pervasive feeling of inadequacy is currently seen in Putin's resentment toward the West, which includes his accusing United States presidents of hypocrisy, double standards, and attempts to shame Russia to justify his attempt to grab land beyond its border in Ukraine in an endless cycle of a culture of humiliation, a sense of inadequacy and compensatory aggression. Both Russia and Germany's grabbing of land may be, not just a geopolitical idea, but also a compensatory attempt to satiate their boundless sense of shame.

In sharp contrast to the inhumane oppression of the Ukraine war, and the day prior being on the front lines in Bakhmut to support Ukrainian forces, President Zelensky delivered a heroic speech before a joint meeting of Congress on December 21, 2022. Just as British Prime Minister Winston Churchill did more than 80 years ago, Zelensky's electrifying, historic address as a charismatic wartime leader appealed for continued American military support in the face of Russia's unprovoked attacks. Dressed in his now trademark green military fatigues with an official emblem for the Ukraine Armed Forces, Zelensky was a living symbol that the fight was far from over. In his words, against all odds and doom scenarios, Ukraine was "still alive and kicking." Zelensky pointed to several moments in US history and recalled Americans to their revolutionary history as a way to ensure continued American support in fending off Russia's invasion of Ukraine. Reminding Americans of our heritage as a birth of a nation, Zelensky compared Bakhmut's struggle to hold back the Russian army to the Battle of Saratoga, which gave a decisive victory to the Americans over the British in the Revolutionary War. For the past 20 years however, the United States has seen a democratic recession, where anti-democratic predators gaining power and momentum through an inflated, dangerous perversion of nationalism with slogans such as "Make America Great Again" used to displace international cooperation and collective security. In contrast, Zelensky encouraged a strengthening unified partnership among democracies where its people have more confidence and faith in themselves and their government. He astutely encouraged the Russian people to free their minds from the tyranny of Putin, reminding them that this is Putin's desperate war to stay in power and not a Russian war. As much as a fight for minds as for land, his rousing and inspirational rally was to remind the West and the European Union of Ukrainians' courage and resolve to endure the heartbreak and devastation of fighting Putin. The Ukrainians fight because they must as they are defending their lives as they were invaded by Russia. But the Ukrainians also fight not just for themselves but also for the rest of the world in defending democracy, freedom, and the values of the West.

PUTIN AND THE RUSSIAN CHARACTER

In order to better elucidate the complexities of the ferocity with which Putin presides over the Ukrainian war, it is necessary to examine Putin's brutal childhood. Putin's birth was preceded by the death of two brothers—the first died in infancy, and the second to starvation and diphtheria during the Siege of Leningrad in World War II. Putin was born in 1952 in Leningrad, a city that lived under a nearly three-year siege by the Nazis during World War II that wiped out most of the population of more than 3 million people. One million people starved to death. The Siege of Leningrad, termed as a genocide, is described as the world's most destructive siege of a city. From 1941 to 1944, Hitler's Nazi forces sought to pummel the city known today as St. Petersburg; during this siege, Putin's mother barely survived (Wood, 2022; Weiss, 2022).

Breathtakingly reminiscent of using the same tactics of Russia's military operation in Ukrainian cities today, rather than assault the city directly, the Germans systematically starved, shelled, and froze its Russian civilians into oblivion. Pleas to allow humanitarian relief to reach the city were rebuffed; refugees fleeing along the one escape route were gunned down. During the first winter when the outside temperature fell to 40 degrees below Fahrenheit, 100,000 Russians a month died of starvation and cold. When the siege was lifted, only 700,000 Leningraders of the city's prewar population of 3.5 million remained alive.

Like thousands of other Russian mothers, Putin's mother, Maria Shelomova Putin, had left her young second son Viktor in a children's shelter, while she scavenged for food. But despite her efforts, Viktor eventually died of diphtheria and starvation and his burial place to this day is unknown. Maria, weakened by a lack of food, fainted near a pile of corpses. Her husband, Vladimir Spiridonovich Putin, was badly wounded at the front lines of World War II by a German grenade but survived. The day Putin's father returned from the hospital, he saw his wife being dragged with other corpses into a mass grave. But his father noted that his wife was still faintly breathing, narrowly preventing her from being buried, and took her home (Weiss, 2022). Toward the end, Maria was too weak to walk. But she and Leningrad's other survivors grimly held on and lived. Other losses in Putin's family during World War II were the death of his mother's mother, who was shot by Germans when they occupied Tver City. Also, five of his paternal uncles and two maternal relatives died during the war. Seven years after the war ended, the Putins had their third son, Vladimir Vladimivovich (Volkan & Javakhishvili, 2022).

During Putin's childhood, Leningrad had not yet recovered and life was extremely difficult. His parents shared a room in a run-down apartment with two other families, with no hot water, no bathtub, and little heat (Stevens, 2022). His father worked in a factory, his mother found any odd job she could. His parents had to leave him with another family. Putin was left to fend for himself and was often bullied by other children in their apartment building.

In *First Person: An Astonishingly Frank Self-Portrait by Russia's President* (Putin, Gevorkyan et al., 2000), Putin wrote about his childhood. He recalled that his father mostly did not want to discuss the family's war losses, but sometimes his parents included him in conversations about what the family endured during World War II. He remembers his mother as gentle and his father beating him with a belt as a child for going out with his friends on a train away from home. This punishment resulted in Putin losing his desire to travel without his parent's permission (Volkan & Javakhishvili, 2022). We do not know if physical punishment was a regular occurrence in his childhood.

Putin was a horrible student and a street hoodlum (Weiss, 2022). But at least two experiences kept him from living on the street. He learned judo to defend himself and after a rough time during his elementary school years, a sixth-grade teacher took interest in him and brought out his intellect. As an adolescent, Putin became preoccupied with becoming a KGB agent and eventually obtained a law degree and joined the KGB. While enrolled at the famed Red Banner Institute, an elite KGB training program, Putin recklessly got into a brawl with a subway rider who was bugging him, and pulverized him. Putin had been waiting a decade to get into the program, plodding away in the bowels of the lower ranks of the KGB. That impulsivity sabotaged his lifelong dream of a glamorous foreign assignment. His rash behavior nearly derailed his KGB career.

Being diminutive in stature, Putin cultivated a cult personality of a macho, take-charge superhero (Rawnsley, 2011). We have all seen the photographs of a tough Putin: horseback riding shirtless in the Siberian mountains; staged ice hockey games in which, in full uniform and pads, well into his 60s, despite stumbling on his skates, the leader is allowed to score a goal; practicing judo as a black belt despite the editor of Lawfare, an American blog dedicated to national security issues, disputing Putin's martial arts skill; and sitting at the head of a long table isolating him from would-be collaborators (Hawkins, 2017). The frequency of these virile displays suggests anxiety about Putin's sense of self.

Putin's unimaginably harsh childhood deprivations including a lack of food, inadequate housing, bullying, neglect, parental depression, and a wartime trauma perpetrated by Nazi forces may have shaped his compulsion to repeat this violent aggression. If one does not resolve their violent childhood experiences, they are often fated to repeat their trauma. The unspeakable reality of his childhood certainly could twist his vision; bereft of any of the ingredients necessary for a child to flourish, he was instead flooded with experiences of loss, betrayals, brutality, and inhumanity, all too nightmarish to metabolize. Such crippling violence may have contributed to his distrustful, unpredictable behavior. A cultivator of half-truths and disinformation and a former KGB agent, he remains culturally and psychologically obsessed with a Soviet Union that no longer exists. Russia during World War II sacked beyond imagination, perhaps Putin's avatar, is demanding the restoration of its sacrosanct destiny.

Most years Putin commemorates the horrific German stranglehold by visiting the Piskariovskoye Cemetery. In 2019, Putin publicly shared the narrative of his family's World War II experience during a memorial ceremony for those who had died in the siege, which was held at the city's Piskariovskoye Cemetery. Seventy-five years later, the president of Russia laid a bouquet of roses and stated, "I don't know where my own brother is buried, whom I never saw, never knew" (Wood, 2022). Describing the brutal suffering of Leningraders inflicted by the Nazi siege, Putin declared, "This is what is called a crime against humanity." One may wonder why Putin does not recognize his own war crimes in Chechnya, Georgia, Syria, and Ukraine; but he may feel that it is a justified restitution, an eye for an eye (Pasha-Robinson, 2016). In 2000, the organization, "We Remember Them All by Name," attempted to find where Victor had been buried in 1942. In 2014, this organization concluded Victor most likely was in one of the mass graves. Putin (2015) felt assuaged when strangers "on their own initiative" discovered documents about his brother (Volkan & Javakhishvili, 2022).

Interestingly, Polish journalist Krystyna Kurczab-Redlich's (2016) book provides a different version of Putin's background. The author claims that she visited Putin's biological mother who is still alive, in her 90s, and lives in the Republic of Georgia. According to this author, who maintains that the story is well-known in Poland, Putin, who is referred to as Vovka, was the product of a love affair that his mother had with a married man. His mother initially left the baby with her parents near the Ural Mountains. When his mother married a man from Georgia, she reclaimed him and they all moved to Georgia. Because his stepfather was a violent person, his mother sent Vovka back to her maternal grandparents. In turn, the grandparents gave the boy to a family who were relatives living in St. Petersburg who had lost two sons.

In this shocking version of Putin's background, can we hypothesize that Putin has an unconscious rescue fantasy? He went from a displaced, changeling child to become a vehemently ferocious fighter. As he returns the scorched earth Ukraine back to Mother Russia, is he symbolically restoring a destroyed part of himself that was violently torn away? In a more grandiose version, is Putin also comparing himself to Peter the Great as a leader "returning" and "strengthening" Russian lands (Roth, 2022), an unconscious attempt to become heroic to undo his puniest baby self, repeatedly handed off to multiple takers?

Replacement children, like Putin, involve a mother's internalized image of her deceased child, in this instance Victor, Putin's older brother. This image is then deposited and transgenerationally transported (Kogan, 1995; Laub & Auerhan, 1993) and becomes the developing self-representation of her next-born child. The replacement child (Cain & Cain, 1964; Poznanski, 1972; Volkan & Javakhishvili, 2022) has no actual experience with the dead sibling. But the mother keeps the dead child alive by treating the replacement child as the repository of the image of the dead child. Mostly unconsciously, the mother bequeaths certain ego tasks to the second child to protect what has been deposited in this child (Volkan & Javakhishvili, 2022). The mother also deposits her traumatized self and traumatized object images into the replacement child's self-representation. How the child handles what has been deposited by the traumatized adult into his internal world determines if it becomes a source of psychopathology.

The postwar Leningrad of Putin's desolate childhood was a community version of a type of childhood experience widely recognized as a prelude to adult violence (Gessen, 2012). Victim no more. Putin morphs into perpetrator. Is this a possible second restoration of identifying with a brutal mother – according to Kurczab—Redlich's version of Putin's childhood – and rectifying their separation by becoming her? Putin may be acting out his deeply repressed childhood deprivations in a repetition compulsion to unconsciously inflict similar inhumane circumstances of hegemony in Chechnya, Georgia, Syria, and Ukraine. Identifying with another grandmaster, he lifted from Stalin's playbook by collecting political and economic power, often crushing political opponents through poisoning and imprisonment – like Alexi Navalny, Vladimir Kara—Murza, and Mikheil Saakashvili. Like a rapacious octopus, the tentacles of Putin can attack and seize any dissident in any country. Poisoning opponents is his trademark calling card, a perfect crime informing that the Kremlin was responsible, but yet remaining difficult to prove as poisonings are ambiguous, covert, and concealed. Putin may feel he must defend himself from being the victim of the corrupted West, just like the way he had to protect himself from being bullied by learning judo as a child. Interestingly, similarities between Putin and Donald Trump have been noted in their twisted sense of shunned victimization to justify their violence and authoritarian rule—for Trump, a lack of connection between himself and other people, and for Putin, no separation between a sense of self and his dedication to his dreams of restoring Russian greatness (Fisher, 2022).

Similar to the feelings of shame and need for retaliatory violence that some terrorists experience, like the Tsarnaev brothers and Mohamed Atta, Putin's unconscious reenactment of his childhood trauma, including his family going through the Siege of Leningrad, could be seen as his attempt to abolish past wrongs and triumphantly restore Russia's glorious hegemony. How do we better metabolize and not repress, forget and then repeat acting out our past traumas and fears? How do we better contain this human malevolence, within us all, but now being unleashed by Russia to murder Ukrainian women and children?

Putin is also known for his often rough and sharp language, especially toward those he wishes to oppress. During the 1999 Russian apartment bombings, while pointing his finger at framed Chechen terrorists, Putin made the hooligan statement, "We'll get them anywhere. If we find terrorists in the shithouse, then we'll waste them in the shithouse" (Hearst, 2016). But he needed more than a mobster image to become well-known in times of turmoil. He needed something big like waging war in Chechnya. Madeleine Albright (2022), who served as United States Secretary of State from 1997 to 2001, described Putin as small, pale, and so cold as to be almost reptilian. She wrote that he was unemotional but determined to resurrect Russia's economy and squash the Chechen rebels.

We witnessed a Putin who seemed disconnected from reality during his speech about Ukraine not having a tradition of statehood (Ferreri, 2022). His bizarre and grievance-filled speech also publicly humiliated his foreign policy aides, demonstrating not only a discord between Putin and his core leadership in invading Ukraine but also his paranoid resentment and obsession to be recognized as tough. Putin does not seem to care about the cringeworthy displays of his masculinity, humiliating his senior colleagues or killing hundreds of thousands of innocent civilians. Without global intervention, Russia will continue with its annihilistic march into the obliteration of the Ukrainian people. NATO and the world must continue to have the strength to face and oppose this malevolence with intensified military support to Ukraine and increased sanctions against Russia to help end the war with a Ukrainian win. It may be the only way that Russia acknowledges that Ukraine exists is for Russia to lose the war (Snyder, 2018).

MALIGNANT POLITICAL PROPAGANDA AND DESTRUCTIVE RESCUE FANTASIES

Malignant political propaganda and destructive rescue fantasies (Volkan & Javakhishvili, 2022), such as Putin's obsession with the resurrection of the Soviet Empire, involve a chosen trauma that is shared by a large group's ancestral history in which the large group suffered an undigested humiliation and catastrophic losses at the hands of the enemy. This malignant political propaganda involves the creation and exploitation of a shared mental image of the large group's trauma, making it a major large-group identity marker, involving a shared sense of victimization followed by a collective sense of entitlement for revenge. Putin's malignant political propaganda and destructive rescue fantasies is linked to both his individual psychology and Russia's unmourned traumas of the World War II period. Similar to Putin's inflaming of Russia's collective past losses in World War II, Adolf Hitler in *Mein Kampf* (Ford, 2009) was a master puppeteer of the art of political propaganda to exploit the emotions and psychology of the German masses.

According to Volkan (1997), part of this malignant propaganda involves a large group narcissism that is contaminated with an entitlement ideology where the large group feels privileged to regain what their ancestors lost centuries ago.

Illustrative of that is both the Germans' sense of injustice meted out to them by the Versailles Treaty of World War I and similarly by the Japanese who felt robbed of their spoils of war at the close of the Russo-Japanese war in 1905, so their enmity boiled over into explosions of World War II. In the Russian version, a geopolitical concept and entitlement ideology that influences a national concept of Putin's Russia is "Eurasianism," which states that Russian civilization does not belong to the European or Asian categories, but is unique and special. Lev Gumilyov (1990), a Soviet historian and ethnologist, was an exponent of "Eurasianism," and regarded Russians as a "super-ethnos" who need to oppose the destructive influences from Catholic Europe that posed a threat to the integrity of Russia (Clover, 2016; Volkan & Javakhishvili, 2022).

A similar entitlement ideology that Russia is special is "Russkiy Mir" or Russian World. "Russkiy Mir" is the concept of an encompassing social totality associated with Russian culture and the Russian diaspora with its influence on the world. In 2007, Putin in cooperation with the Russian Orthodox Church, created the Russkiy Mir Foundation. The now familiar regilding of the Russian halo is Putin's promotion of the Russian World concept.

"Russkiy Mir" is even frighteningly incorporated as an ideology that is promoted by the leadership of the Russian Orthodox Church to provide a spiritual cover for the invasion of Ukraine. Patriarch Kiril of Moscow, who is a Russian Orthodox bishop, takes this ideology of "Russkiy Mir" and twistedly elevates its status by burnishing it with spiritual dimensions. For the Russian Orthodox Church, "Russkiy Mir" is a reminder that through the baptism occurring in Kievan Rus – which dates back to the year 988 when Vladimir the Great was baptized in Chersonesus located in the Crimean Peninsula and proceeded to baptize his family and the people of Kyiv – that God consecrated these people to the task of rebuilding a Holy Russia (Petro, 2015; Volkan & Javakhishvili, 2022). This term, "Russkiy Mir" epitomizes an expansionist and messianic Russian foreign policy, which involves the perverse intertwining of the interests of the Russian state with the Russian Orthodox Church. This close relationship between church and state sanitizes Putin's barbaric foreign policy with a defendable moral luster.

REFERENCES

Akhtar, S. (2014). *Immigration and acculturation: Mourning, adaptation, and the next generation.* Jason Aronson.
Albright, M. (2022, February 23). Putin is making a historic mistake [opinion]. *The New York Times.* https://www.nytimes.com/2022/02/23/opinion/putin-ukraine.html
Baumeister, R. F. (1997). *Evil: Inside human violence and cruelty.* Henry Holt.
Cain, A. C., & Cain, B. S. (1964). On replacing a child. *Journal of the American Academy of Child Psychiatry, 3*(3), 443–456. http://doi.org/10.1016/S0002-7138(09)60158-8
CBS News. (2022, March 18). *Putin calls opponents "scum and traitors" as Moscow announces new crackdowns on "false information."* https://www.cbsnews.com/news/putin-opponents-scum-traitors-repression/
Clover, C. (2016). *Black wind, white snow: The rise of Russia's new nationalism.* Yale University Press. http://doi.org/10.12987/9780300223941

Dahm, J. (2022). *EU parliament votes to recognise 'Holodomor' famine as genocide.* Euractiv. https://www.euractiv.com/section/agriculture-food/news/eu-parliament-votes-to-recognise-holodomor-famine-as-genocide/

Davies, N. (2006). *Europe east and west: A collection of essays on European history.* Jonathan Cape.

Le Monde Group Letter. (2022, August 5). *Deporting Ukrainian children and "Russifying" them is jeopardizing the future of Ukraine.*

Dostoyevsky, F. (1919). *A writer's diary.* Northwestern University Press.

Einstein, A., & Freud, S. (1981). *Why war? An exchange between Albert Einstein and Sigmund Freud* (6th ed.). Shalom Press International.

Ferreri, E. (2022, February 24). Putin's invasion of Ukraine reveals leader 'disconnected in many senses from reality,' expert says. *Duke Today.* https://today.duke.edu/2022/02/putin%E2%80%99s-invasion-ukraine-reveals-leader-%E2%80%98disconnected-many-senses-reality%E2%80%99-expert-says

Fisher, E. (2022). The psychology of Vladimir Putin. *Chicago Tribune.* https://www.chicagotribune.com/opinion/commentary/ct-opinion-vladimir-putin-russia-ukraine-personality-20220321-7rlrzfvdvvcsrit2vmmej7o63i-story.html

Ford, M. (2009). *Mein Kampf: A translation controversy.* Elite Minds.

Freud, S. (1955). *The standard edition of the complete psychological works of Sigmund Freud* (Vol. 17, J. Strachey, Ed. & Trans.). The Hogarth Press (Original work published 1918).

Freud, S. (1961). *The standard edition of the complete psychological works of Sigmund Freud* (Vol. 21, J. Strachey, Ed. & Trans.). The Hogarth Press (Original work published 1928).

Fromm, E. (1973). *The anatomy of human destructiveness.* Henry Holt and Company.

Gessen, M. (2012). *The man without a face: The unlikely rise of Vladimir Putin.* Riverhead Books.

Grier, P. T. (1994). The complex legacy of Ivan Ilín. In J. P. Scanlan (Ed.), *Russian thought after communism: The recovery of a philosophical heritage* (pp. 165–186). M. E. Sharpe.

Gumilyov, L. (1990). *Ethnogenesis and the biosphere.* Progress Publishers.

Hawkins, D. (2017, July 18). Is Vladimir Putin a judo fraud? *The Washington Post.* https://www.washingtonpost.com/news/morning-mix/wp/2017/07/18/is-vladimir-putin-a-judo-fraud/

Hearst, D. (2016, January 24). Putin's war in Syria is Chechnya revisited. *Vocal Europe.* https://www.vocaleurope.eu/4021/

Jones, A. (2017). *Genocide: A comprehensive introduction* (3rd ed.). Routledge. http://doi.org/10.4324/9781315725390

Kogan, I. (with Chasseguet-Smirgel, J.) (1995). *The cry of mute children: A psychoanalytic perspective of the second generation of the Holocaust.* Free Association Books.

Kripkov, O. D. (1997). *To serve God and Russia: Life and thought of Russian philosopher Ivan Ilyin* (Order No. 9909601) [Doctoral dissertation, University of Kansas]. ProQuest Dissertations Publishing.

Kurczab-Redlich, K. (2016). *Wowa, Wolodia, Wladimir: Tajemnice Rosji Putina* [*Vova, Volodya, Vladimir: Secrets of Putin's Russia*]. W.A.B.

Laub, D., & Auerhahn, N. C. (1993). Knowing and not knowing massive psychic trauma: Forms of traumatic memory. *The International Journal of Psycho-Analysis, 74*(2), 287–302.

Lifton, R. J. (1986). *The Nazi doctors: Medical killing and the psychology of genocide.* Basic Books.

Lifton, R. J. (1989). *Thought reform and the psychology of totalism: A study of "brainwashing" in China.* The University of North Carolina Press. (Original work published 1961)

Lifton, R. J. (2022, March 14). Is Putin beyond influence? How to stop a man on a mission. *Psychology Today.* https://www.psychologytoday.com/us/blog/the-guest-room/202203/is-putin-beyond-influence

Linz, J. J. (2000). *Totalitarian and authoritarian regimes.* Lynne Rienner Publishers. http://doi.org/10.1515/9781685850043

Ljunggren, M. (2014). Poetry and psychiatry: Essays on early twentieth-century Russian symbolist culture. Academic Studies Press. https://doi.org/10.1515/9781618116963-014

Marples, D. R. (2007). *Heroes and villains: Creating national history in contemporary Ukraine.* Central European University Press. http://doi.org/10.1515/9786155211355

Mendel, I. (2018, November 24). 85 years later, Ukraine marks famine that killed millions. *The New York Times.* https://www.nytimes.com/2018/11/24/world/europe/ukraine -holodomor-famine-memorial.html

Ministry of Reintegration of Temporarily Occupied Territories. (2022). *Children of war.*

NBC News. (2005, April 25). *Putin: Soviet collapse a 'genuine tragedy'.* https://www.nbcnews .com/id/wbna7632057

Nechepurenko, I. (2014, May 15). Santa-for-hire, soapmaker run insurgency in Ukraine's east. *The Moscow Times.* https://www.themoscowtimes.com/2014/05/15/santa-for-hire -soapmaker-run-insurgency-in-ukraines-east-a35496

Pasha-Robinson, L. (2016, October 9). Putin's brother died in the Siege of Leningrad, which bears striking resemblance to the Syrian crisis. *International Business Times.*

Petro, N. N. (2015, March 23). *Russia's Orthodox soft power: U.S. global engagement initiative.* Carnegie Council for Ethics in International Affairs. https://www.carnegiecouncil.org /media/article/russias-orthodox-soft-power

Pomerantsev, P. (2022, February 26). Vladimir Putin: What's going on inside his head? *The Guardian.* https://www.theguardian.com/world/2022/feb/26/valdimir-putin -russia-ukraine-inside-his-head

Poznanski, E. O. (1972). The "replacement child": A saga of unresolved parental grief. *The Journal of Pediatrics, 81*(6), 1190–1193.

Putin, V. (with Gevorkyan, N., Timakova, N., & Kolesnikov, A.). (2000). *First person: An astonishingly frank self-portrait by Russia's president* (C. A. Fitzpatrick, Trans.). PublicAffairs.

Rawnsley, A. (2011, May 26). Pow! Zam! Nyet! 'Superputin' battles terrorists, protesters in online comic. *Wired.* https://www.wired.com/2011/05/pow-zam-nyet-superputin -battles-terrorists-protesters-in-online-comic/

Roth, A. (2022, June 10). Putin compares himself to Peter the Great in quest to take back Russian lands. *The Guardian.* https://www.theguardian.com/world/2022/jun/10 /putin-compares-himself-to-peter-the-great-in-quest-to-take-back-russian-lands

Siebold, S., Trevelyan, M., Hunder, M., & Meijer, B. (2022, November 23). European Parliament declares Russia a state sponsor of terrorism. *Reuters.* https://www.reuters .com/world/europe/european-lawmakers-declare-russia-state-sponsor-terrorism -2022-11-23/

Snyder, T. (2018). *The road to unfreedom: Russia, Europe, America.* Tim Duggan Books.

Stevens, J. (2022, March 1). *How Vladimir Putin's childhood is affecting us all.* Paces Connection. https://www.pacesconnection.com/blog/how-vladimir-putin-s-childhood-is -affecting-us-all

Uzlaner, D. (2017). Perverse conservatism: A Lacanian interpretation of Russia's turn to traditional values. *Psychoanalysis, Culture and Society, 22*(2), 173–192. http://doi.org/10 .1057/s41282-016-0036-6

Varvin, S. (2021). *Psychoanalysis in social and cultural settings: Upheavals and resilience.* Routledge. http://doi.org/10.4324/9781003206057

Volkan, V. D. (1997). *Blood Lines: From ethnic pride to ethnic terrorism.* Farrar, Straus, Giroux.

Volkan, V. D. (2017). *Immigrants and refugees: Trauma, perennial mourning, prejudice, and border psychology.* Routledge. http://doi.org/10.4324/9780429475771

Volkan, V., & Javakhishvili, J. D. (2022). Invasion of Ukraine: Observations on leader-followers relationships. *The American Journal of Psychoanalysis, 82*(2), 189–209. https:// doi.org/10.1057/s11231-022-09349-8

Weiss, A. S. (2022). *Accidental czar: The life and lies of Vladimir Putin* (B. Brown, Illus.). First Second.

Wood, D. (2022, March 21). *Putin's parents survived the siege of Leningrad. Why does he presume an independent Ukraine won't?* Backbencher. https://timothynoah.substack.com/p/putins -parents-survived-the-siege

Yakushko, O. (2023). *Freud on "The Russian Character" and the war against Ukraine* [Manuscript submitted for publication].

9

Terrorism and Mass Shootings Springing from Ideology

A Monolith That Denies the Existence of the Problem of Humanity[1]

How many elephants will it take?

DOI: 10.4324/9781032633497-10

UNDERLYING ETIOLOGICAL ROOTS IN FAR-RIGHT GROUPS AND RUSSIA: CHRISTIAN FASCISM AND FUNDAMENTALISM

Hopefully, this chapter will further contribute to a deepening understanding that the origins of domestic terrorism and mass shootings have deep, complex roots in people and groups who have been marginalized, traumatized, lack a sense of belonging, and/or have undiagnosed, untreated mental illness. With the recognition of the burgeoning hope for a more equitable distribution of opportunities and goods, white people at the margins of society project their fears of further degradation by the introduction of any and all new groups. I am including the ideological monolith that is Christian fundamentalism that swoops in to the marginalized whites, exploiting their underlying psychological issues of impotency under the eager wings of their dogma. This has become all too prevalent today within our current political landscape and technology, enabling leaders such as Putin and far-right groups a larger platform to communicate and glorify the perceived advantages promised through fascist and fundamentalist ideologies as a means to mollify the perceived marginalized. Consider this: the enthusiasm that American and European far-right groups have for Putin is based on Christian fascism and fundamentalism. Putin's superman image and disdain for anything liberal has turned him into the beacon of salvation for American white nationalists. Many far-right groups in America favorably view Putin's hardline totalitarian rule to inflict suffering and death in Ukraine based on their perceived perception of a debased Ukraine as having the same societal degradation as a permissive Western society. In this light, in 2004, David Duke, longtime leader of the Ku Klux Klan, described Russia as crucial to white survival (Olmos, 2022). On the evening of the Russian invasion, Steve Bannon, Trump's chief strategist, commended Putin as "anti-woke" and a fellow nationalist and crusader against cosmopolitanism. Bannon believes that movements with Japan's Shinzo Abe, India's Narendra Modi, Russia's Vladimir Putin, Saudi Arabia's Mohammad bin Salman, China's Xi Jinping, Turkey's Recep Tayyip Erdogan, and America's Donald Trump are part of a global shift toward nationalism. Expressing his belief that traditionalists see Russia as an ally, Bannon has praised Trump's ties to Putin. According to Teitelbaum's *War for Eternity* (2020), Bannon met infamous Russian Aleksandr Dugin in Rome in 2018 to discuss traditionalist philosophy and advocate for closer relations between the United States and Russia.

For the past decade, Alexandr Dugin, referred to in the media as "Putin's brain" and a Russian political philosopher, disapproves of Western liberalism, human rights, and individualism while supporting the rule of Stalin and the Soviet Union. Dugin's fascist ideology has found a home in American white nationalist circles. Dugin's "Eurasianist" ideology, which is anti-American globalization, has been constructed on the refusal to allow Western liberal values to infiltrate and corrupt

Russia. His thinking is fascism a-la-russe, which includes a series of far-right ideologies including Traditionalism and the European New Right. Not surprisingly Dugin's *Russia's Manifest Destiny* expounds an ideology that is imbued in Russian Christian nationalism and has resonated with the worldview of Putin and American far-right groups. White nationalists are drawn to Putin's aggressive repression, military invasions, and his brand of traditional Christianity with attacks on the homosexual community. At the same time, it reverberates much of the Christian nationalist activism in the United States, where liberal values, gay rights, and a desire to keep religion out of the state are all regarded as degenerate and responsible for American decline.

Despite the Russian attempt to undermine the 2016 democratic presidential election, Trump's frisson of recognition with Putin resulted in Trump's praising him as a "genius" and "smart" at the beginning of the Russian invasion of Ukraine, but then withdrew his praise later as the Russian military floundered and casualties mounted. Frighteningly, some extremist right-wing militias view the war in Ukraine as a framework to model by repeating this brutal scenario by creating urban warfare in America. Similarly, insisting on their view of our societal disintegration, these right-wing militias have become obsessed with preparing for an impending civil war in the United States. As exemplified by the January 6 insurrection, the possibility of sustained political violence in our country and civil war have become commonplace in far-right groups. But distressingly, we now see the narrative of the far-right groups growing hostility toward the federal government and continued call for an organized battle to overthrow the American government infiltrating into the mainstream.

DOMESTIC TERRORISM AND MASS SHOOTINGS

Donald Trump's "Make America Great Again" appeals to right-wing groups, just as German right-wing populists and Adolf Hitler were dedicated to restoring Germany economically and culturally to its pre-World War II status as one of the leading nations in Europe. On January 6, 2020, Trump's slogan to save America, which served as a dog whistle to appeal to the delusions of lost white privilege, eventually led to the deadly assault by a pro-Trump mob on the US Capitol. This organized attack on our Capitol was the first time in more than 200 years that our government was ransacked under our watch. Perhaps the most shocking example of domestic mass terrorism in America's history was the January 6 insurrection led by right-wing extremists, including QAnon, Oath Keepers, Proud Boys, and the Three Percenters. As of January 2023, eight of these right-wing leaders, who attempted to dismantle authority and democracy, were found guilty of seditious conspiracy for efforts to stop the transfer of power following the 2020 Presidential election. One of the convicted rioters was photographed reclining with his foot on then Speaker of the House Nancy Pelosi's desk having deposited a quarter, even though he said she was not worth it, as well as leaving a note referring to the congresswoman as "biatch"; both are demeaning gestures, reminiscent of dysfunctional patriarchal family dynamics. These defendants perverted the constitutional order by using violence to impose their distorted view of the electoral process on the rest of the country.

According to the findings of the House select committee investigating the insurrection, the insurrection resulted from a seven-part plan by Trump to overturn the 2020 presidential election. Five people died either shortly before, during, or following the attempted coup. Many were injured, including 138 police officers. In addition, four officers who responded to the attack killed themselves within seven months. Only after being pressured by his cabinet, the threat of removal, and many resignations, Trump finally committed to a transition of power.

If we examine the history of activist movements, peaceful protest is a hallmark of democracy, and has been a vital necessity for ensuring equality and progression in our society. American protest has been usually accomplished without violence; however, it has also been accompanied by violence, sometimes engendered by law enforcement officers themselves, as we remember with Selma, Alabama. Another example is the Chicago demonstrations in 1968 which involved the accusations of violence against the Chicago Seven, which proved to be the work of the fists and mace of the Chicago police, and led to the exoneration of the activists.

But terrorism, such as the January 6, 2021, siege of our Capitol, is quite another matter where the attack is often planned. Currently, most terrorist incidents in the United States are committed by domestic groups. The result is escalating violence in US cities between extremists from opposing sides, a major break from historical trends. In 2021, the most frequent targets of attacks were government, military, and law enforcement agencies, which are increasingly at the center of domestic terrorism by extremists of all ideologies. In the past decade, 66% of acts of domestic terrorism have ended "successfully" i.e., are less likely to be disrupted by law enforcement vs 22% of international terrorism. An illustrative example is, despite the FBI increasing the reward money, the unidentified perpetrator who was caught on tape planting pipe bombs outside the Republican National Committee and Democratic National Committee on January 5, 2021, still remains at large. As discussed previously, research has shown that many terrorists suffer from a sense of alienation and disenfranchisement and use their violence as a misguided attempt to gain a distorted sense of belonging (Cerfolio, 2021).

Even though Trump lost by over 7 million votes, he refused to accept the defeat. Perhaps experiencing a sense of powerlessness and impotency, the Trump-inspired seditionists exhibited a common defense of identification with the aggressor, which is a defense utilized in traumatized people when they feel that they cannot stop a terrifying situation in which they feel victimized (Ferenczi, 1988). Exhibiting a maneuver often employed in authoritarian takeovers, the insurrectionists contended that they were just faithfully protecting Trump's lie of a stolen election (Snyder, 2017). Seemingly unable to tolerate defeat, Trump and the seditionists instead split and projected into the "other" to deny this feeling of loss (Pivnick, 2021).

According to Lee (2020), narcissistic symbiosis and shared psychosis were two emotional drives behind Trump's destructive behavior and what motivated some of his followers who sieged the Capitol. Narcissistic symbiosis refers to developmental wounds that make the leader–follower relationship alluring. The leader, hungry for glorification to counteract feelings of inadequacy, projects invincibility, while the followers, rendered needy due to feelings of powerlessness and lack of productivity, crave a parental figure. Shared psychosis refers to the infectiousness of induced delusions of a highly symptomatic leader's symptoms spreading through a population through emotional bonds, heightening existing pathologies and inducing paranoia and violence.

Similarly, Rudden (2021) maintains that psychotic, projective, and introjective group defenses may be seen to have increasingly developed within far-right groups leading up to and involved in the insurrection. These defenses were then heightened by undermining a sense of truth and trust in the government and an amplification of false messages by social media sites. Endorsing the QAnon conspiracy theory movement, which falsely and violently claims that Democrats are baby-eating devil worshippers, Trump shared a post on the Truth Social Network with an image of himself wearing a pin in the form of the letter Q along with a phrase closely associated with the QAnon movement, "The storm is coming" (Bensinger, 2023). Seemingly promoting regression and fantasy in his followers, Trump's authoritarian leadership often strayed from logic and demonstrable fact. There are connections between psychological problems and belief in conspiracy theories, such that the election was stolen. For example, anxiety, social isolation, and loneliness increase the propensity for conspiratorial thinking. Many QAnon followers revealed that they suffer from bipolar depression, anxiety, and addiction (Moskalenko, 2021). In court records of QAnon followers arrested in the wake of the Capitol insurrection, 68% reported they had received mental health diagnoses.

Yet, as of December 2021, Robert Pape, who directs the Chicago Project on Security and Threats at the University of Chicago, has been analyzing the identities of the more than 700 people arrested for breaking through the barricades that grim day. He estimates that 87% of the capital rioters were not members of violent groups but were part of mainstream white-collar workers such as business owners, architects, doctors, and lawyers (Tong & McMahon, 2022). These rioters came from counties that lost their white, non-Hispanic population. This loss of white representation has been amplified by right-wing conspiracy, voiced by mainstream political leaders, known as the great white replacement of white people by minorities (Tong & McMahon, 2022). Aggrieved entitlement refers to this gendered sense of entitlement felt by mostly white men, which has been thwarted by larger economic and political shifts in the United States. Mass shootings are an extremely violent example of this much larger socio-cultural issue.

As previously mentioned, white supremacist beliefs, violence, and murder are deplorable and result in part from the inability for symbolic functioning, which often results from trauma, and represent the de-symbolization of our culture (Pivnick, 2021). These insurrectionists demonstrated the concept of "the banality of evil" (Arendt, 1968) as they maintained that their violent actions resulted, not from a sense of personal responsibility and agency, but from being "loyal" to the president who had invited them to take over the Capitol. Many individuals of these far-right groups experience themselves as under the foot of the government and their violence is justified to push off the yoke of oppression. Trump appealed to the rioters as victims, and ignited them by counterphobic manipulation to "fight like hell" in an attempt to restore their wondrous efficacy and their countries' lost glory.

Nations have highlighted mass shootings as one of the gravest threats in the world today. Recently, almost on an epidemic level, there has been a rash of domestic mass shootings. The Gun Violence Archive (GVA) is a nonprofit research group that tracks gun violence using police reports, news coverage and other public sources. According to the GVA, the United States had 692 mass shootings in 2021, with 28 involving four or more fatalities and 648 mass shootings in 2022, with 21 involving five or more fatalities (GVA, 2023). The scenes of agony and horror are all too increasingly familiar. As of January 24, 2023, there have already been 39 mass shootings across the country. At least 70 people have been killed and 167 wounded in mass shootings so far in 2023.

Gill et al. (2014) defined *terrorism* as the threat or use of action designed to intimidate the public or government to advance a political, religious, or ideological cause. *Mass shootings* did not have an official definition until 2013 when the US government defined "mass killing" as three or more killings during an incident, excluding the death of the assailant (US Code, 2013). The GVA defines mass shootings as having a minimum of four victims shot, either injured or killed, not including any shooter who may also have been killed or injured in the incident.

Yet, there is a lack of a universally accepted definition of either terrorism or mass shootings. Rather, there are multiple definitions of these terms, and they may overlap. For example, mass shootings that have political or ideological causes generally are considered forms of terrorism. Further confounding the literature is that differing studies and databases of mass shootings use different definitions of mass shootings.

Although many narrative, qualitative literature reviews exist on mass shootings and terrorism (Cerfolio, 2020; Gill & Corner, 2017; Stone, 2017; Silke, 2003; Victoroff, 2005), there is a dearth of rigorous systematic, quantitative evidence that explains the role of psychiatric disorders in mass shootings and terrorism (Marazziti & Stahl, 2018; Vad, 2018). Most of the scholarship on mass shootings and terrorism (63%) comes from the political science and international relations field (Sheehan, 2014; Horgan, 2017). By contrast, only a small proportion of the research on mass shootings and terrorism (5%) has been conducted by psychiatrists (Sheehan, 2014).

Early research on the relationship between mass shootings and mental illness has been characterized by inconsistent data collection and a lack of methodological rigor. Collectively, misconceptions led to false ideas that mental health problems have nothing to do with mass shootings (Corner & Gill, 2016). The general reluctance that pervades the culture over the importance of child development, early experience, and mental health restricts much of the population in Plato's cave. We can at times recognize the relevance of gun control (although America fails to legislate effectively), but we have dimmed our vision to recognize the more nuanced world of mental health's impact on this grim phenomenon.

More recently, research on the psychology of mass shootings has evolved, providing new information on the backgrounds of offenders. Despite the claim of some researchers that mass shooters and terrorists are rarely mentally ill (McCauley, 2002; Atran, 2003; Pape, 2005; Dvoskin, 2016), when studies conducted extensive background investigation and interviews with perpetrators, researchers found a high prevalence of mental illness (Lankford, 2014, 2016). With their extensive resources, the Secret Service conducted interviews with numerous perpetrators and assigned criminal investigators and social science researchers to study the case materials from each incident. Using this additional information, they concluded at least 61% of school shooters were depressed (Vossekuil et al., 2004). Subsequent research with rampage school shooters between 1974 and 2008 found evidence that more than 90% were mentally ill (Newman et al., 2004; Newman & Fox, 2009). Similarly, the FBI released a report on a study of the pre-attack behaviors of active shooters in the United States between 2008 and 2013 which found that 25% of active shooters were diagnosed with mental illness prior to the attack (Silver et al., 2018).

Another study that noted mental illness in mass shooters was by the US Secret Service National Threat Assessment Center (Alathari et al., 2019), which released a report on mass attacks in public spaces. It analyzed 27 mass shootings that occurred in public spaces in the United States between January and December 2018, in which three or more persons were killed or injured. The study found that two-thirds of the attackers experienced mental health symptoms, the most common being depression and psychosis. Additionally, nonpsychiatric studies have noted that the incidence of mental illness is much higher in lone-actors than in group-actors (Gruenewald, 2013; Corner & Gill, 2015; Corner et al., 2016).

The relative dearth of rigorous systematic psychiatric studies that examine the role of psychosocial variables and psychiatric disorders in mass shootings and terrorism, in part, contributed to my feelings of frustration and sense of urgency in better understanding these cycles of violence. But my passion was also inspired by several other personal factors. My serving victims of terror at Ground Zero during 9/11 in 2001 and in the Second Chechen War and genocide in 2005 contributed to my commitment to more deeply comprehend how a world could create the firmament for the kinds of destructive aggression that is now a daily occurrence. In addition, my surviving two terrorist attacks, developing breast cancer from being a first responder at Ground Zero and being poisoned by a FSB agent with suspected anthrax in the Second Chechen War, furthered my desire to understand this violence. How is there such a global paucity of spirituality and compassion for those who are marginalized and isolated? How is there such a rigid divide and lack of empathy in our country and our world? To attempt to address these questions, I along with my colleagues, Ira Glick MD, Danielle Kamis MD, and Michael Laurence JD, conducted the first-ever systematic psychiatric study utilizing standardized instruments to examine the psychosocial determinants and psychiatric diagnosis of domestic mass shooters.

OUR STUDY OF PSYCHOSOCIAL DETERMINANTS AND PSYCHIATRIC DIAGNOSIS OF MASS SHOOTERS IN THE UNITED STATES: THE FIRST-EVER SYSTEMATIC PSYCHIATRIC STUDY UTILIZING STANDARDIZED INSTRUMENTS

We designed a retrospective observational study of mass shooters, defined as those who killed four or more people with firearms between 1982 and 2012 or who killed three or more people with firearms between 2013 and 2019 (Cerfolio, 2022). We sought to determine the prevalence of psychiatric diagnosis and various psychosocial variables among those who have committed mass shootings in the United States.

Given the limitations of the small number of studies of perpetrators of mass shootings and terrorism conducted by psychiatrists, we conducted the first-ever systematic psychiatric study utilizing a standardized interview, the DSM-5, and a Sheehan MINI (2016) standardized scale. We obtained all psychiatric and psychosocial information available on these mass shooters. The psychiatric interviewers evaluated the clinical evidence obtained by interviewing forensic psychiatrists, who had assessed the assailant following the crime and/or reviewing psychiatric court evaluations conducted during the post-crime judicial proceedings to determine the prevalence of psychiatric illness.

We examined the assailant's background including identifying whether the assailant was isolated from their family, friends, neighbors and school, the assailant's history of childhood uprootedness and poor psychosocial support, whether the assailant's perceived grievances were radicalized online, and whether stigma prevented the assailant from receiving psychiatric care.

We used the Mother Jones database, which consists of 115 persons identified as committing a mass shooting in the United States between January 1982 and September 2019 (Follman et al., 2023). In most of the incidents in the database, the perpetrator died either during or shortly after the crime. We first examined every case, which was 35 cases, in which the assailant survived and criminal proceedings were instituted.

For each of these 35 mass shootings, we interviewed forensic psychiatrists/psychologists, who examined the perpetrator following the crime, and/or collected the testimony and reports by psychiatrists/psychologists at trial or in the post-conviction proceedings contained in the court record. In addition, we reviewed available information from the court proceedings, neuropsychological testing, brain CT and PET scans, public records, videotape interviews of assailants by law enforcement, social media videotaped verbal declarations, and postings and writings of the assailants.

In addition to using the data from the 35 assailants who survived, we then randomly selected an additional 20 cases from the remaining 80 incidents where the assailant died. For these 20 cases, no forensic psychiatric evaluation had been conducted and coding of the questionnaire was based upon gathering available news reports of the perpetrator's mental health, background, and behavior, so our data and diagnostic evaluations were less reliable.

We developed a uniform, comprehensive 62-item questionnaire to compile the data collection from multiple sources and record our psychiatric assessments of the assailants, using DSM-5 criteria. Of course, the diagnosis of mental illness is best determined by a clinical assessment of the assailant. In 26 of the 35 cases in which the assailant survived, our evaluation was based on such clinical psychiatric assessments. Thus, in many of the cases, we were able to exercise our clinical judgment by applying the diagnostic criteria to information collected from interviewing forensic psychiatrists/psychologists and/or reviewing judicial documents of mental health professionals who clinically assessed the perpetrators close in time to the criminal act. When such data was unavailable, as mentioned, we relied on clinical information obtained through the media. These media reports often consisted of forensic reports by psychiatrists/psychologists who had interviewed the assailant post-crime and the statements of family members, coworkers, friends, and neighbors who observed the assailant's mental functioning prior to the crime. When the information was insufficient, or the presence of diagnostic criteria was unclear, we did not make a diagnosis.

Of the 35 cases in which the assailant survived and criminal proceedings were instituted, 32 cases had sufficient information to make a diagnosis. We determined that 87.5% had the following psychiatric diagnosis: 18 assailants (56%) had schizophrenia, while 10 assailants (31%) had other psychiatric diagnoses: 3 bipolar I disorders, 2 delusional disorders (persecutory), 2 personality disorders (1 paranoid and 1 borderline), and 2 substance-related disorders without other psychiatric diagnosis and 1 PTSD (Post-Traumatic Stress Disorder).

Figure 9.1 depicts our findings concerning psychiatric disorders among the 32 surviving assailants. Of the 87.5% of perpetrators of mass shootings who survived and were diagnosed with major psychiatric illness, none were treated appropriately with medication at the time of the crime (Glick et al., 2021). Four assailants (12.5%) had no psychiatric diagnosis that we could discern. The percentage of those suffering from a psychiatric illness may be higher, as in many cases the available clinical information suggested a mental illness diagnosis, but there was insufficient information to definitively make a clinical diagnosis.

Table 9.1 shows the case information for each incident of mass shooting by the assailants who survived. All were male, except for one case in which the assailant

Prevalence of Untreated Psychiatric Disorders Among Mass Shooters
Who Survived the Crime, Excluding Unknowns (n=32)

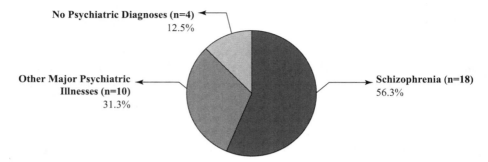

FIGURE 9.1 Prevalence of untreated psychiatric disorders among mass shooters who survived the crime, excluding unknowns (n=32). (Originally published in *Psychodynamic Psychiatry* 50(3), Fall 2022 and used by permission of The Guilford Press.)

was female. The primary and secondary sources are listed for each case in which we gathered information from multiple sources to determine the presence of a DSM-5 psychiatric diagnosis.

As depicted in Table 9.1, case 517 involved a 42-year-old male who, after writing a will at work, opened fire and killed seven coworkers. He was found by police sitting calmly but disorganized. Despite everyone speaking English, he stated entirely out of context that he did not speak German. He did not understand why his company had to comply with the garnishment of his salary due to a tax lien. According to an interviewed forensic psychiatrist, the assailant heard an archangel's voice during the shootings, "to prevent the Holocaust by taking six of the architects of the Holocaust." According to the assailant's court records, he had a long history of auditory and visual hallucinations, but he kept the problem to himself due to fear of being "locked up." Although two prosecutorial experts stated that he was "faking a mental illness for an insanity defense," two defense experts opined that the assailant was psychotic and did not understand the wrongfulness of his violence. According to the interviewed forensic psychiatrist and media reports, the assailant had a long history of apathy and social downward drift with poor interpersonal functioning and difficulty maintaining work and social relationships. We confirmed the diagnosis of the interviewed defense forensic psychiatrist, as the DSM-5 criteria for schizophrenia was met and the Sheehan diagnostic scale confirmed psychosis.

Similar to the above case, many perpetrators as illustrated in Table 9.1—503, 504, 507, 508, 510, 513, 514, 516, 518, 520, 522, 526, 529, 533, 534, 535—had perceived grievances, typically for their inability to function in society and/or maintain a job often due to many factors, including underlying psychiatric illness. They felt deeply humiliated by their marginalization and were often drawn to grievance cultures or ideologies that identified an enemy responsible for their humiliation.

Table 9.1 Case information of perpetrators who survived mass shootings. Originally Published in *Psychodynamic Psychiatry* 50(3), Fall 2022 and Used by Permission of The Guilford Press

CASE	AGE AT TIME OF CRIME	GENDER	PRIMARY DSM-5 DIAGNOSIS	MINI	PRIMARY SOURCE	ADDITIONAL SOURCES OF INFORMATION	# KILLED	IDEOLOGY	APPROPRIATELY MEDICATED FOR DIAGNOSIS
501	25	Male	Schizophrenia	P	E	EC, M	12	None	No
502	19	Male	Schizophrenia	P	EC	EM, M, W, V	17	FR, AB, AM, AS, AGay, AI	No
503	35	Male	Schizophrenia	P	EC	EM, W	6	AW, AI	No
504	26	Male	Schizophrenia	P	EC	M	5	None	No
505	43	Male	Bipolar I	NP	EC	M	6	None	No
506	21	Male	Unknown	NE	M	M	5	None	Unknown
507	43	Male	Schizophrenia	P	EM	M	7	None	No
508	29	Male	Schizophrenia	P	EM	M	4	AGov (Sovereign citizens), AS	No
509	20	Male	Substance-related disorders	NP	M	N	5	None	No
510	19	Male	Bipolar I	NE	EC	EM, NP	4	None	No
511	22	Male	Schizophrenia	P	EM	W, V	6	AGov, AWom, AS, AT	No
512	15	Male	Schizophrenia	P	EC	M, PET, W	4	None	No
513	21	Male	None	P	M	W	23	FR, WS, AI(Great Replacement)	NA
514	36	Male	Schizophrenia	P	M	N	5	None	No
515	57	Male	Delusional Disorder: Persecutory Type	N	EC	M, W	3	AAbort	No
516	38	Male	None	NP	EM	M, W	5	None	NA
517	42	Male	Schizophrenia	P	E	EC, M	7	None	No
518	43	Male	Paranoid Personality Disorder	P	E	EC, M	4	None	No

(Continued)

Table 9.1 (Continued)

519	46	Male	Schizophrenia	P	M	W	11	FR, WS, AS	No
520	44	Female	None	N	M	N	4	None	NA
521	21	Male	Schizophrenia	P	E	EC, M, W, P	9	WS(neo-Nazi)	No
522	20	Male	Bipolar I	NE	EC	NP, EM, IP	4	None	No
523	47	Male	Schizophrenia	P	M	N	3	None	No
524	22	Male	None	NP	M	N	4	AB, AGay, AWom	NA
525	40	Male	Schizophrenia	P	EC	CT, W	13 (Plus Unborn child)	AAM (Jihadism)	No
526	40	Male	Schizophrenia	P	EC	M	7	None	No
527	45	Male	Substance-related disorders	NP	M	None	8	None	No
528	17	Male	Unknown	NE	M	P	10	WS (Nazi)	Unknown
529	39	Male	Delusional Disorder: Persecutory Type	P	EC	M	7	None	No
530	42	Male	PTSD	NP	M	N	8	None	No
531	13	Male	Borderline Personality Disorder	P	EC	ID, M	5	None	No
532	39	Male	Schizophrenia	P	EM	M, W	4	AW (Nation of Islam, Reactionary Black Nationalism), AGov	No
533	38	Male	Schizophrenia	P	EC	EM, M	3	None	No
534	39	Male	Unknown	NP	M	None	6	None	NA
535	59	Male	Schizophrenia	P	EC	M	6	None	No

MINI: Mini International Neuropsychiatric Interview; P=Psychotic Disorder (Current); NP=No Psychosis; NE=Not Enough Information; EC=Experts Information from Court Records; EM=Experts Information from Media; M=Information from Media; W=Writings; V=Verbal declarations; P=Posting of photos; IP= Videotaped interrogation by police; ID= Videotaped interview at deposition; NP=Neuropsychological testing; PET=PET scan brain; CT=CT scan brain; FR=Far-Right Extremism; WS=White Supremacy; AAbort=Anti-Abortion; AAM=Anti-American; AB=Anti-Black; AGay=Anti-Gay; AGov=Anti-Government; AI=Anti-Immigrant (Hispanic, Asian); AM=Anti-Muslim; AS=Anti-Semitic; AT=Anti -Theist; AW=Anti-White; AWom=Anti-Women.

For white supremacists, the enemy includes people of color, Jews, and the liberals who allegedly promote them. Many of our perpetrators who felt a grievance often found others with similar ideologies and posted on these various related websites. Organizing with others online gave these perpetrators who often felt psychologically impotent due to lost status a sense of purpose and significance.

Despite many of the shooters we studied having psychiatric illnesses and being psychotic, I was struck by the fact that many perpetrators still possessed enough cognitive functioning to permit them to plan their violent acts in a methodical manner. Although each mass shooting is unique and complex, three mass shootings are highlighted here to represent key ideas, including some of the specific factors that prompted two school mass murders (National Research Council, 2003).

The first perpetrator, which is case 512 from Table 9.1, demonstrates an adolescent male shooter who was psychotic, but could still plan and execute violent acts, because parts of his cognitive functioning were relatively unaffected by his underlying psychopathology. Tragically, only after being properly psychiatrically treated while incarcerated was this adolescent able to have his chronic auditory hallucinations commanding him to kill to stop.

At the age of 15, this hapless adolescent, TS, first shot his father at home, who was seated at the kitchen counter drinking coffee. He then dragged his father's body into the bathroom and covered it with a sheet. When his mom arrived home, TS met her in the garage, told her he loved her, and shot her twice in the back of the head, three times in her face and once in her heart. Throughout the day TS repeatedly played a recording of "Liebestod," which means "love death" from Wagner's opera.

The next day TS engaged in a high school shooting that left 2 students dead and 25 others wounded. Similar to the history of many of the adolescent domestic shooters we reviewed, TS had high intelligence, suffered from a learning disability, and was bullied by other students. He was diagnosed with dyslexia in the second grade.

Starting at the age of 12, TS suffered from auditory hallucinations of three distinct male voices. The first voice would put him down, call him names, and deride him. The second voice told him to kill. The third voice would comment on the two other voices. TS also had delusions that the government placed a chip in his brain and believed that the brain chip caused his auditory hallucinations. Prior to the shooting, TS had a history of violence, using explosives in a futile attempt to stop his auditory hallucinations.

TS looked normal and hid his psychotic symptoms from judges, attorneys, and doctors because this tormented adolescent was terrified of being labeled mentally ill. Prior to the shootings, his parents also hid their extensive mental health illness on both sides of their family from TS's treating psychologist. Perhaps, because of his father's denial of the extent of mental illness in his family and feelings of shame for his son's need for mental health treatment, his parents stopped TS's therapy a few months before the shooting, because they felt he was doing "well" and no longer needed Prozac and psychological care. His father admitted to a friend that he was "terrified" of what his son might do but felt he "was out of options." The father threatened to send TS to a military school.

After shooting and killing both his parents, TS left a note in which he described his motive for his violence,

> I've just got two felonies on my record. My parents can't take that. It would destroy them. The embarrassment would be too much for them. My head doesn't work right. God damn these VOICES inside my head … I have to kill people. I don't know why … I have no other choice.

The ironic tragedy of TS and many of the other shooters we examined in our study was that their schizophrenia responded well to antipsychotic medication and their violent acts could have been prevented if they had received proper psychiatric medication prior to their shooting spree. Tragically, in the aftermath of the shooting, just ten days after receiving antipsychotic medication, TS expressed remorse for having killed his parents and fellow students. Currently, TS, who is incarcerated, is compliant with psychiatric treatment and antipsychotic medication, and he is no longer violent or has a behavioral problem.

Since being in prison, TS finished his GED and BA degrees, obtained his electrical license and become the prison's electrician. He has become a voracious reader, including *Ulysses* and *Crime and Punishment*. He teaches yoga in the mental health ward of the prison. TS maintains a daily spiritual practice, where he meditates and prays for those he harmed.

We found that the clinical misdiagnosis and mistreatment of early-onset schizophrenia was associated with the worsening of many of these assailants' psychotic symptoms. Many of our adolescent shooters prior to the massacre had been misdiagnosed with Attention Deficit Disorder, Major Depression Disorder, or Autism Spectrum Disorder (Schatzberg, 2019). The second mass shooting serves as an example of this clinical misdiagnosis and mistreatment of schizophrenia as "depression."

ML, a 16-year-old male assailant killed two family members and then drove to school where, waving and grinning, he shot randomly, leaving ten dead and several students wounded, before committing suicide. His family attributed ML's violence to being treated with Prozac for "depression." Although antidepressants may lower the threshold for acting on underlying psychotic symptoms, the assailant's violence seemed more attributable to a constellation of factors, including his undiagnosed and mistreated schizophrenia, as indicated by his chronic auditory hallucinations and paranoid delusions. Struggling with chronic negative symptoms, the assailant had poor interpersonal functioning and was marginalized in school.

ML suffered from paranoid delusions that his American Indian classmates were diluting their racial purity by listening to rap music. Although his belief may be viewed in a cultural and historical context, it had psychotic qualities such that the assailant felt he had to kill to avenge this racial dilution. His favorite quote, which he attributed to Hitler, was, the law of existence requires uninterrupted killing, so that the better may live. Experiencing a kinship with Hitler, ML began blogging on neo-Nazis websites. Similar to ML's obsession with violence which was fanned by reading extremist material on neo-Nazi websites that discussed Hitler's politics of racial decline, many of our assailants also suffered paranoid delusions and used political themes as a substrate for their delusions.

In addition to suffering undiagnosed psychosis, ML, born an unwanted child to an alcoholic, adolescent, emotionally/psychically abusive mother, endured profound childhood instability, trauma, and loss. While being frequently shuffled between his ambivalent parents and while ML was 8 years old and living with his father, his father committed suicide by shooting. Although intimidating in his outsized appearance, ML was ridiculed by classmates for wearing black eyeliner and goth clothing, expelled for behavioral issues in high school, and had two previous suicide attempts.

As school shooters are often victims of unacknowledged psychological turmoil, the momentous responsibility attached to raising children is thrown into high relief. The internal role of malignant shame, compulsive fantasies of retaliation, and deficiencies in the capacity to mentalize play an important role in their assaults. It is not only the nightmare of their childhood, but the sequela of that catastrophic background that adversely cognitively affects them. Severe childhood trauma often precludes the ability to possess the flexibility of cognitive scanning, so the adolescent perpetrator is more likely to grow into a brittle adult only capable of reflexively reenacting his childhood violence. Often there is a history of disorganized attachment and false-self pathology that render them ripe for radicalization. Trying to salvage some sense of being, they spin into a shame–rage cycle, in which their mordant rage floods their being and propels them into justified retribution and necessary violence. Again, as hate is the binder that these assailants experience, their violence may be understood in that it preserves perverted collective ties, sense of belonging and social recognition (Cerfolio, 2021). Focusing on external factors, Cartwright (2013) maintains that the abuse/neglect, school failures/expulsions, and bullying that these boys experienced shed light on the unconscious dynamics evident in the buildup to the rampage attack.

The vengeful state of mind often experienced by these adolescent shooters can be seen as a psychological fixation that is instigated by the workings of suppressed shame dynamics, which in extreme cases transform a prodromal disorganized shame state into a relentlessly vengeful state of mind (Lansky, 2007). Vengefulness is one example of a shame–rage cycle that can be understood as unacknowledged humiliation that provokes rage. Triggering rage by unconscious humiliation is an indication of the defense of splitting.

Although these assailants were rarely in psychotherapy, resolution could be possible, I would like to suggest, through psychoanalytic working through vengefulness by creating a greater sense of perspective and emotional distance from the trauma, so the violence becomes less likely to be reenacted. Creating the possibility of the long road endemic to a positive life may contribute to the working through of splitting and even, the possibility of forgiveness.

A common denominator of these shootings is that many of these assailants have been bullied. Switching gears to potential strategies to interrupt and prevent bullying is the understanding of the psychoanalytic intersubjective "third" (Kerzner, 2013). Bullies intimidate and coerce as well as abuse victims. They may also influence both victims and bystanders to actively and/or passively encourage them. Psychoanalysts are familiar with unconscious sadomasochistic dynamics that may interfere with the psychoanalytic dyad. The psychoanalytic concept of the "symbolic third" offers clinicians a way to step back from reenactments to monitor coercive power dynamics. Ogden (1994) expands the concept to the "intersubjective third" to emphasize the potential benefits of the complex, shared unconscious space created by the therapeutic dyad. Benjamin (2004) introduced the idea of the "moral third" which adds essential dimensions of uncertainty, humility, and compassion to the third. The moral third parallels the vital role of the helpful bystander who has the moral courage to disrupt the power imbalance in the bully/victim/bystander triad that perpetuates bullying.

Among cases where schizophrenia was not diagnosed, including where we could not gather sufficient diagnostic data, we made the diagnosis of paranoid personality disorder in one case. By way of example, the third mass shooter, which is case 518 from Table 9.1, concerns a perpetrator who met many but not all of the criteria for schizophrenia and suffered from chronic paranoid delusions; we diagnosed paranoid personality disorder based on the available information we had.

After being fired from his job, this black 43-year-old male assailant shot and killed four white coworkers. At trial, the assailant refused a mental state defense and requested a death sentence. According to his forensic psychologist, whom I was able to interview, his childhood victimization was reenacted as he suffered from chronic paranoid delusions and would often misinterpret benign statements and feel denigrated. His abusive childhood trauma contributed to his difficulty developing emotionally stable, interpersonal relationships. By the time he was 13 years of age, he was homeless and grew up a loner. Characteristic of the plight of the deracinated, by the time he was 16 years of age he had traveled to 15 states with a band of gypsies.

Tragically, he waived his appeal for a defense, prevented family members from testifying, and again expressed the wish to be executed. He understood why he was being prosecuted and had no known history of hallucinations. The assailant quoted Acts 25:11 of the Bible, "If, however, I am guilty of doing anything deserving death, I do not refuse to die."

In the cases where we made the diagnosis of schizophrenia, typical psychotic symptoms included command auditory hallucinations to "kill, burn, or destroy," messages from God or demons, paranoid delusions that "the government and CIA were trying to kill them," the delusion that "black men were raping white women to start a race war," and that immigrants "had invaded and taken over the world and had to be killed." Similarly, negative symptoms and poor functioning were prevalent; many of the assailants were unable to maintain employment, housing, or social relationships.

Of the 20 cases in which the assailant died, in five cases there was insufficient information to render a diagnosis. Of the remaining 15 cases, 8 (53%) had schizophrenia, while 7 (47%) did not have schizophrenia. In one of these seven cases where an autopsy report was available and which we reviewed, our best clinical judgment based on the neuropathology report of his brain and other clinical information was to identify a combination of diagnoses including: temporal lobe epilepsy, paranoid personality disorder, neurocognitive disorder secondary to neuropathological changes including corpora amylacea, and an alcohol substance-related disorder.

Many of these shooters experienced estrangement not only from others but most importantly from themselves. Being interpersonally shunned rendered these assailants less able to understand their true sense of self; they became more vulnerable to their untreated psychosis and radicalization online that fostered their violence. Their frequent history of childhood abuse and uprootedness contributed to their sense of worthlessness; they felt that they had no place in the world and nothing to give to the world.

The novelty of our study was in having a standardized process of board-certified psychiatrists who assessed the weight and quality of clinical evidence. Rather than accepting diagnoses from forensic psychiatrists and/or court records, our team independently reviewed the clinical data gathered from multiple sources to apply the DSM-5 criteria to diagnose mental illness. Our determination of clinical diagnosis was in combination with, among others, examining psychosocial history, previous psychiatric illness and treatment, suicidal ideation and/or attempts, history of being bullied, abuse, neglect, significant trauma, criminal history, military service, and radicalization.

Of paramount importance in the psychotherapy of those who suffer from psychiatric illness is the establishment of a solid therapeutic alliance. Similar to the shooting in the first two cases—where warning signs of impending violence were missed—many of the mass shooters had a psychiatric history with recommended outpatient treatments. However, these psychiatric treatments were either not provided or not followed through. Again, perhaps if these shooters had received appropriate psychiatric treatment and support, they may have felt less alienated and less likely to engage in violence.

The therapeutic alliance is an essential factor in the successful treatment of psychiatric illnesses and a vital tool for improving both pharmacological and psychological interventions (Arieti, 1974; Schatzberg, 2019). In the treatment of schizophrenia, direct evidence of the alliance–outcome relation is scarce, but it is consistently positive for psychotherapy (Priebe, 2011; Huddy, 2012), and medication compliance (Lacro, 2002). On a micro level, in my psychoanalytic work with patients, I have been continually amazed to witness the transcendent power of the therapeutic alliance, to not only promote adherence with medication, but to encourage healing and transformation from profound trauma, deprivation, and loss.

Isolation, such as that experienced by these assailants, is the enemy of solitude. When we cannot see our genuine reflection in the eyes and ideas of others, our true self begins to disappear and the potential healing experience of solitude turns into anxious loneliness, which is the distressing feeling of a lack of emotional support. Loneliness can be experienced whether an individual is alone or with others. In Arendt's *The Origins of Totalitarianism*, she described loneliness as the common ground of terror; she maintained that when people lose contact and are isolated from their fellow men, as well as the reality around them, their capacity for rational thought and maturing with experience is diminished. Isolation is the inability to act together with others, which is the source of a person's political and personal power. Isolation can render a sense of psychological impotence.

Because of their perceived grievances and sense of humiliation, many assailants in our study felt they had been betrayed and their violence appeared to be an act of revenge. The feeling of absolute loneliness may have rendered them more vulnerable to becoming radicalized online in order to experience a distorted sense of belonging. Through their radicalization online, these assailants may have seen a chance to not only lessen their intrapsychic sense of impotence, but to create a sense of significance and belonging to a cause greater than themselves (Cerfolio, 2020). Through their hatred, these assailants were able to achieve a false sense of self-organization and stability, providing a sense of equilibrium for their ephemeral, unsettled life.

Many of these traumatized perpetrators, who often suffered from psychosis and untreated psychiatric illness, experienced severe childhood trauma, which was largely ignored. These assailants felt that they were "psychically" murdered and discarded by society during childhood. In committing these violent acts, the assailants often reenacted the abuse and violence they suffered as children. Though some might label these terrorized perpetrators as monstrous, what was done to them as children is as tragic as the violence they committed. We as psychiatrists have a responsibility to our community to better educate parents and society concerning the responsibility involved in raising a child and the importance of identifying fragile young people who suffer and may need psychiatric help.

The dogmatic argument that we should eliminate discussion of the association between mass shootings and mental health because we lack as a society the nuance to examine this association without stigmatizing the extraordinary dimensional range encased in the mental health field prevents us from creating possible solutions (Cerfolio, 2022). It seems to me that our society's refusal to more deeply understand, and preference for turning a blind eye to the uncompromising importance of child development and the vicissitudes endemic to that vital development, causes symptomatology even for us so-called "normal" folks. Yet the disruption of that process including noticeably reluctant parenting—abandonment, neglect, loss, and abuse—is capable of catastrophic distortions of human character. Witness our adolescent shooters.

Our finding of the high prevalence of undiagnosed psychiatric illness in perpetrators of mass shootings is *not* meant to stigmatize those who suffer from mental illness. Rather, it is intended to bring more awareness of the possibility of the under-diagnosis of mental disorders in perpetrators of violence so they can be accurately psychiatrically diagnosed and treated. In fact, most individuals who suffer from schizophrenia and are appropriately treated with antipsychotic medication are *not* more violent and *do not* commit violent crimes more frequently than the rest of the population (Buchanan et al., 2019; Appelbaum, 2020).

Nevertheless, we found that most perpetrators of mass shootings suffered from misdiagnosed or undiagnosed and unmedicated schizophrenia. Without losing sight of the larger perspective that most who are violent are not mentally ill, and most of the mentally ill are not violent, our message is that the public must be made aware that *some* untreated or mistreated psychiatric patients do pose an increased risk of violence (Friedman, 2006).

Many factors account for the under-diagnosis of psychiatric illness among perpetrators of mass shootings. Most of the perpetrators we studied did not have contact with a psychiatrist and shared characteristics with those least likely to visit a physician: young, male, and/or struggling financially (O'Hara & Caswell, 2012; Lankford, 2014). Many of our perpetrators did not seek psychiatric care due to the stigma against mental illness. Prior to their violence, even the few times our perpetrators with mental illness did engage with a healthcare provider, they were misdiagnosed. Many of our perpetrators who claimed to be supported by radical ideologies may have even been more likely to be silenced by stigma against receiving psychiatric care (Maris et al., 2000; Lankford, 2016). Post-crime, they often refused psychiatric evaluation as they wanted their grievance to be brought to public attention and felt that being psychiatrically diagnosed would diminish their "message" from being heard.

It is vital to clarify that we are *not* stating that psychiatric illness causes mass shootings. Rather, our findings suggest that there is a complex interaction between biological, psychological, and sociological factors and an association—not a causal relationship—between mass shootings and *undiagnosed*, *untreated* psychiatric illness.

More in-depth, scientifically sound analysis based on comparative studies of mass shootings using standardized testing and clinical interviews is needed. While there are complex reasons that a person is not diagnosed, becoming aware of the possibility of under-diagnosis of mental disorders in these vulnerable perpetrators is crucial. This awareness of under-diagnosis could help these individuals get the needed psychiatric treatment and support that they deserve and potentially prevent lethal attacks. There remains a vital need to decrease the stigma of mental illness to enable those with severe mental disorders to be more respected and less marginalized in order to receive effective treatment.

NOTE

1 Parts of this chapter appeared in an earlier version in Cerfolio (2022) and are gratefully reprinted with permission from The Guilford Press.

REFERENCES

Alathari, L., Blair, A., Carlock, A., Driscoll, S., Drysdale, D., & McGarry, J. (2019). *Mass attacks in public spaces - 2018*. U.S. Department of Homeland Security, United States

Secret Service, National Threat Assessment Center. https://www.secretservice.gov/sites/default/files/2020-04/USSS_FY2019_MAPS.pdf

Appelbaum, P. S. (2020). Violent acts and being the target of violence among people with mental illness — The data and their limits. *JAMA Psychiatry*, 77(4), 345–346.

Arendt, H. (1968). *The origins of totalitarianism.* Harcourt, Brace, Jovanovich.

Arieti, S. (1974). *Interpretation of schizophrenia.* New York: Basic Books.

Atran, S. (2003). Genesis of suicide terrorism. *Science*, 299(5612), 1534–1539. http://doi.org/10.1126/science.1078854

Benjamin, J. (2004). Beyond doer and done to: An intersubjective view of thirdness. *The Psychoanalytic Quarterly*, 72(1), 5–46.

Bensinger, K., & Haberman, M. (2023, January 28). Trump's evolution in social-media exile: More QAnon, more extremes. *The New York Times.* https://www.nytimes.com/2023/01/28/us/politics/trump-social-media-extremism.html

Buchanan, A., Sint, K., Swanson, J., & Rosenheck, R. (2019). Correlates of future violence in people being treated for schizophrenia. *The American Journal of Psychiatry*, 176(9), 694–701. http://doi.org/10.1176/appi.ajp.2019.18080909

Cartwright, D. (2013). A catastrophic solution: Psychoanalytic perspectives on a samurai school attack in South Africa. In N. Böckler, T. Seeger, P. Sitzer, & W. Heitmeyer (Eds.), *School shootings: international research, case studies, and concepts for prevention* (pp. 217–243). http://doi.org/10.1007/978-1-4614-5526-4_10

Cerfolio, N. (2020). Terrorism and the psychoanalytic origins. *The Journal of Psychohistory*, 47(4), 256–274.

Cerfolio, N. (2021). The origins of terrorism: The obliteration of a sense of belonging. In R. C. Curtis (Ed.), *Belonging through a psychoanalytic lens* (pp. 45–57). Routledge.

Cerfolio, N. (2022). The Parkland gunman, a horrific crime, and mental illness. *The New York Times.*

Cerfolio, N., Glick, I., Kamis, D., & Laurence, M. (2022). A retrospective observational study of psychosocial determinants and psychiatric diagnoses of mass shooters in the United States. *Psychodynamic Psychiatry*, 50(3), 1–16.

Corner, E., & Gill, P. (2015). A false dichotomy? Mental illness and lone-actor terrorism. *Law and Human Behavior*, 39(1), 23–34. http://doi.org/10.1037/lhb0000102

Corner, E., Gill, P., & Mason, O. (2016). Mental health disorders and the terrorist: A research note probing selection effects and disorder prevalence. *Studies in Conflicts & Terrorism*, 39(6), 560–568. http://doi.org/10.1080/1057610X.2015.1120099

Dvoskin, J. (2016, April 11). *"Don't believe the hype": 4 reasons to doubt that most mass shooters are mentally ill.* Psychology Benefits Society. https://psychologybenefits.org/2016/04/11/dont-believe-the-hype-4-reasons-to-doubt-that-most-mass-shooters-are-mentally-ill/

Ferenczi, S. (1988). Confusion of tongues between adults and the child. *Contemporary Psychoanalysis*, 24(2), 196–206. https://doi.org/10.1080/00107530.1988.10746234

Follman, M., Aronsen, G., & Pan, D. (2023, April 10). US mass shootings, 1982–2023: Data from Mother Jones' investigation. *Mother Jones.* https://www.motherjones.com/politics/2012/12/mass-shootings-mother-jones-full-data/2020

Friedman, R. (2006). Violence and mental illness — How strong is the link? *The New England Journal of Medicine*, 355(20), 2064–2066. http://doi.org/10.1056/NEJMp068229

Gill, P., & Corner, E. (2017). There and back again: The study of mental disorder and terrorist involvement. *American Psychologist*, 72(3), 231–241. http://doi.org/10.1037/amp0000090

Gill, P., Horgan, J., & Deckert, P. (2014). Bombing alone: Tracing the motivations and antecedent behaviors of lone-actor terrorists. *Journal of Forensic Sciences*, 59(2), 425–435. http://doi.org/10.1111/1556-4029.12312

Glick, I. D., Cerfolio, N., Kamis, D., & Laurence, M. (2021). Domestic mass shooters: The association with unmedicated and untreated psychiatric illness. *Journal of Clinical Psychopharmacology*, 41(4), 366–369. http://doi.org/10.1097/JCP.0000000000001417

Gruenewald, J., Chermak, S., & Freilich, J. D. (2013). Distinguishing "loner" attacks from other domestic extremist violence. *Criminology and Public Policy, 12*(1), 65–91. http://doi .org/10.1111/1745-9133.12008

Horgan, J. G. (2017). Psychology of terrorism: Introduction to the special issue. *American Psychologist, 72*(3), 199–204. http://doi.org/10.1037/amp0000148

Huddy, V., Reeder, C., Kontis, D., Wykes, T., & Stahl, D. (2012). The effect of working alliance on adherence and outcome in cognitive remediation therapy. *Journal of Nervous and Mental Disease, 200*(7), 614–619. https://doi.org/10.1097/ NMD.0b013e31825bfc31.

Kerzner, S. (2013). The crucial role of the "Third" in bully/ victim dynamics. *Psychoanalytic Inquiry, 33*(2), 116–123. http://doi.org/10.1080/07351690.2013.764700

Lacro, J. P., Dunn, L. B., Dolder, C., Leckband, S. G., & Jeste, D. V. (2002). Prevalence of and risk factors for medication nonadherence in patients with schizophrenia: A comprehensive review of recent literature. *Journal of Clinical Psychiatry, 63*(10), 892–909.

Lankford, A. (2014). Evidence that suicide terrorists are suicidal: Challenges and empirical predictions. *Behavioral and Brain Sciences, 37*(4), 380–393. http://doi.org/10.1017/ S0140525X13003609

Lankford, A. (2016). Detecting mental health problems and suicidal motives among terrorists and mass shooters. *Criminal Behaviour and Mental Health, 26*(5), 315–321. http://doi.org/10.1002/cbm.2020

Lansky, M. R. (2007). Unbearable shame, splitting, and forgiveness in the resolution of vengefulness. *Journal of the American Psychoanalytic Association, 55*(2), 571–593. http://doi .org/10.1177/00030651070550020901

Marazziti, D., & Stahl, S. M. (2018). Evil, terrorism, and psychiatry. *CNS Spectrums, 23*(2), 117–118. http://doi.org/10.1017/S1092852917000517

Maris, R. W., Berman, A. L., & Silverman, M. M. (2000). *Comprehensive textbook of suicidality.* The Guilford Press.

Gun Violence Archive. (2023). *Mass Shootings.* https://www.gunviolencearchive.org/mass -shooting

McCauley, C. (2002). Understanding the 9/11 perpetrators: Crazy, lost in hate or martyred? In M. Matuszak (Ed.), *History behind the headlines: the origins of ethnic conflicts worldwide* (Vol. 5, pp. 274–286). Gale Publishing Group.

Moskalenko, S. (2021). QAnon followers more likely to report being mentally ill, experience trauma. *Newshub.* https://www.newshub.co.nz/home/world/2021/03 /qanon-followers-more-likely-to-report-being-mentally-ill-experience-trauma .html

National Research Council (2003). *Deadly lessons: Understanding lethal school violence.* National Academies Press. https://doi.org/10.17226/10370

Newman, K. S., & Fox, C. (2009). Repeat tragedy: Rampage shootings in American high school and college settings, 2002–2008. *American Behavioral Scientist, 52*(9), 1286–1308. http://doi.org/10.1177/0002764209332546

Newman, K. S., Fox, C., Harding, D. J., Mehta, J., & Roth, W. (2004). *Rampage: The social roots of school shootings.* Basic Books.

O'Hara, B., & Caswell, K. (2012, October 1). *Health status, health insurance, and medical services utilization: 2010.* U.S. Census Bureau. http://www.census.gov/prod/2012pubs /p70-133.pdf

Ogden, T. (1994). The analytic third: working with intersubjective clinical facts. *International Journal of Psychoanalysis, 75*(1), 3–20.

Olmos, S. (2022, March 5). 'Key to white survival': How Putin has morphed into a far-right savior. *The Guardian.* https://www.theguardian.com/us-news/2022/mar/05/ putin-ukraine-invasion-white-nationalists-far-right

Pape, R. A. (2005). *Dying to win: The strategic logic of suicide terrorism.* Random House.

Pivnick, B. A. (2021). Recollecting the vanishing forms of 9/11: Twenty years of ruptures, ripples, and reflections. *Psychoanalytic Perspectives, 18*(3), 279–295. http://doi.org/10 .1080/1551806X.2021.1953874

Priebe, S., Richardson, M., Cooney, M., Adedeji, O., & McCabe, R. (2011). Does the therapeutic relationship predict outcomes of psychiatric treatment in patients with psychosis? A systematic review. *Psychotherapy and Psychosomatics, 80*(2), 70–77.

Rudden, M. G. (2021). Insurrection in the U.S. capitol: Understanding psychotic, projective and introjective group processes. *International Journal of Applied Psychoanalytic Studies, 18*(4), 372–384. https://doi.org/10.1002/aps.1733

Schatzberg, A., & DeBattista, C. (2019). *Manual of clinical psychopharmacology* (9th ed., pp. 17–41). American Psychiatric Association Publishing.

Sheehan, D. V. (2016). *Mini international neuropsychiatric interview (English version 7.0.2) for DSM-5.*

Sheehan, I. S. (2014). Are suicide terrorists suicidal? A critical assessment of the evidence. *Innovations in Clinical Neuroscience, 11*(9–10), 81–92.

Silke, A. (Ed.). (2003). *Terrorists, victims, and society: Psychological perspectives on terrorism and its consequences.* Wiley. http;//doi.org/10.1002/9780470713600

Silver, J., Simons, A., & Craun, S. (2018). *A study of pre-attack behaviors of active shooters in the United States between 2000 and 2013.* U.S. Department of Justice, Federal Bureau of Investigation.

Snyder, T. (2017). *On tyranny: Twenty lessons from the twentieth century.* Tim Duggan Books.

Stone, M. H. (with Kernberg, O. F.). (2017). *The anatomy of evil.* Prometheus Books.

Teitelbaum, B. R. (2020). *War for eternity: The return of traditionalism and the rise of the populist right.* Allen Lane.

Tong, S., & McMahon, S. (2022, January 3). *White, employed and mainstream: What we know about the Jan. 6 rioters one year later.* WBUR Here & Now. https://www.wbur.org/hereandnow/2022/01/03/jan-6-rioters-white-older

Vad, E. (2018). How to fight terrorism? Political and strategic aspects. *CNS Spectrums, 23*(2), 158–162. http://doi.org/10.1017/S1092852917000724

Victoroff, J. (2005). The mind of the terrorist: A review and critique of psychological approaches. *Journal of Conflict Resolution, 49*(1), 3–42. https://doi.org/10.1177/0022002704272040

Vossekuil, B., Fein, R. A., Reddy, M., Borum, R., & Modzeleski, W. (2004). *The final report and findings of the Safe School Initiative: Implications for the prevention of school attacks in the United States.* U.S. Secret Service and U.S. Department of Education. https://www2.ed.gov/admins/lead/safety/preventingattacksreport.pdf

Index

Page numbers in *italics* indicate figures, while page numbers in **bold** indicate tables.